3+1 Stadia for Brazil

jovis

Falk Jaeger
(Ed./Hg.)

3+1 Stadia for Brazil

Belo Horizonte
Manaus
Brasília
+ Rio de Janeiro

jovis

Contents **Inhalt**

Knut Göppert

Creating Stimuli for Brazil

Impulse für Brasilien

Will the World Cup in Brazil herald a fairytale summer in the same way as it did in Germany in 2006, and how will the football championships change the country? These are two of the questions we have asked ourselves since we first began planning the stadia in Brasília, Belo Horizonte, Manaus, and Rio de Janeiro, and especially during the protests that accompanied the Confederation Cup last year. While in Germany it seems we are content not to upset the balance with huge-scale projects—in November 2014, the residents of Munich voted against hosting the Olympic Games for a second time in their city—, many Brazilians need little encouragement to embrace the collective joy of a four-week-long mega-event. Public celebration is as much part of the Brazilian mentality as the public display of emotions, something we see every year during the carnival, and every evening in the samba bars of the cities.

But Brazil itself is in need of stimuli. Stimuli that will help develop political culture and harness the potential of the emerging middle classes. Stimuli to help Brazil find new openings and directions out of its economic isolation. Stimuli to modernize the public infrastructure, much of which stems from the middle of the last century. One need not be a staunch supporter of organizations such as the oft-criticized FIFA to see that the World Cup in 2014 will create such stimuli, and indeed that it already has.

The attention that the World Cup will generate around the world represents a potential platform for the peaceful young Brazilians who want to change things in their country and has the potential to strengthen political awareness in society. The Brazilian construction industry and its architecture and engineering offices work mostly on projects within Brazil and its neighboring countries. The construction projects for the football championships have helped many firms in the industry, whether architects or building contractors, acquire an international outlook. International requirements, interna-

Werden wir auch in Brasilien ein Sommermärchen erleben oder wie wird die Fußballweltmeisterschaft das Land verändern? Das sind Fragen, die wir uns seit Beginn der Planungen für die Stadien in Brasília, Belo Horizonte, Manaus und Rio de Janeiro und verstärkt durch die Proteste während des Confederation Cup im letzten Jahr stellen. Doch während wir Deutschen inzwischen das Glück im Kleinen suchen und sich deshalb die Bewohner Münchens im November 2014 auch gegen erneute Olympische Spiele in der Stadt ausgesprochen haben, brauchen viele Brasilianer keine Impulse, um für vier Wochen einmal die kollektive Freude eines Megaevents zu erleben. Die brasilianische Identität beinhaltet das öffentliche Feiern wie auch die Öffentlichkeit der Emotion. Das kann man jährlich beim Karneval und jeden Abend in den Sambabars beobachten.

Allerdings braucht Brasilien trotzdem Impulse. Impulse, um die politische Kultur und die Einbeziehung der aufstrebenden Mittelschicht weiterzuentwickeln. Impulse, um sich aus einer wirtschaftlichen Isolation in alle Richtungen zu öffnen. Impulse, um die öffentliche Infrastruktur, die vielfach aus der Mitte des letzten Jahrhunderts stammt, auf Vordermann zu bringen. Nun muss man kein Befürworter von Organisationen wie der häufig zu Recht kritisierten FIFA sein, um zu erkennen, dass die kommende Fußballweltmeisterschaft die aufgezeigten Impulse auslösen wird und auch schon ausgelöst hat.

Die weltweite Öffentlichkeit wird den Anliegen der friedlichen, jungen Menschen, die das Land verändern wollen, eine Plattform bieten, die ein Ausgangspunkt für das Erstarken politischen Bewusstseins in der Gesellschaft sein kann. Die brasilianische Bauindustrie und auch die Planungsbüros in Brasilien leben hauptsächlich von Projekten im Inland und in den Nachbarstaaten. Die Bauprojekte für die Fußballweltmeisterschaft haben vielen Bauschaffenden, von Architekten bis zu Bauunternehmern, zu ei-

tional products, international reference projects and, above all, international collaboration have broadened the horizons of our Brazilian colleagues just as they have our own.

The new stadia for the football championships have also heralded a long overdue and much needed general renewal of public infrastructure in Brazil—clear evidence that large-scale events still have the capacity to provide not only the necessary stimuli but also an opportunity to put such plans into action.

And with that we come full circle to the recent cancellation of Munich's bid to host the Olympic Games: the people of Munich have forgotten the fundamental contribution that the Games made in the nineteen-seventies to the development of the now flourishing city. Brazil, however, has remembered, and grasped this chance for 2014. The modern sports facilities have given the face and soul of football in Brazil a new identity, and likewise revived the Brazilian architecture scene. It has awoken from its years of slumber and embarked confidently on the post-Niemeyer era—but without throwing its legacy overboard. In Rio de Janeiro and in Belo Horizonte, the existing stadia represent a first step towards creating new sports complexes. Using the ideas, methods and standards of the twenty-first century, the temples of football tradition in Brazil have been modernized without overwriting their former identity.

We, the architects from gmp and the engineers from schlaich bergermann und partner, have accompanied our Brazilian colleagues on this path and invite our readers to see for themselves how the projects have turned out—with the help of this book, or even better by taking a trip to Brazil to experience them in real life.

ner internationalen Sichtweise verholfen. Internationale Anforderungen, internationale Produkte, internationale Beispielprojekte und vor allem die internationale Zusammenarbeit haben unseren brasilianischen Freunden genauso wie uns selbst den Horizont erweitert.

Die neuen Stadien für die Fußballweltmeisterschaft haben in Brasilien eine längst erforderliche flächendeckende Erneuerung der unbestritten notwendigen öffentlichen Infrastruktur eingeleitet. Hier wird deutlich, dass auch heute noch durch Großereignisse Impulse und zielgerichtetes Handeln ausgelöst werden können.

Und so schließt sich auch der Kreis zur jüngsten Absage der Münchner Bevölkerung an Olympia. Was in den Siebzigerjahren mit den damaligen Sommerspielen als Grundsteinlegung für die Entwicklung einer prosperierenden Stadt zu sehen war, ist in Vergessenheit geraten. Brasilien hat sich dessen erinnert und hat nun 2014 gerade diese Chance genutzt. Die modernen Sportstätten bilden nun eine neue Identität für die brasilianische Fußballseele genauso wie für die brasilianische Architekturszene. Diese scheint aus ihrem jahrelangen Dämmerschlaf erwacht zu sein und den Aufbruch in die Post-Niemeyer-Ära geschafft zu haben – und dies, ohne die Substanz über Bord zu werfen. In Rio de Janeiro und Belo Horizonte wurden die bestehenden Stadien zum Ausgangspunkt für die neuen Sportstätten. Mit Ideen, Methoden und Standards des 21. Jahrhunderts wurden die traditionsreichen Fußballtempel modernisiert, ohne ihre frühere Identität zu zerstören.

Wir, die Architekten von gmp und die Ingenieure von schlaich bergermann und partner, haben unsere brasilianischen Berufskollegen auf diesem Weg begleitet und laden unsere Leser ein, sich selbst ein Bild von den Ergebnissen zu machen – mithilfe des Buches, aber noch viel besser bei einem Besuch vor Ort.

Jens Glüsing

Tomorrow is a Beautiful Promise

Brazil: Hard and Demonic, Soft and Sensual

Das Morgen ist ein schönes Versprechen

Brasilien: hart und dämonisch, weich und sinnlich

"Brazil is not for beginners," as the famous bossa nova composer and musician Antonio Carlos Jobim once said. But even those who think they know Brazil, who have lived here for over 20 years, are surprised time and again by the number of studies that fail to grasp the contradictory reality of this country. Like a capricious lover, Brazil is notoriously hard to pin down. Just as you think you have finally understood what makes it what it is, it surprises you with precisely the opposite.

Not long ago, Brazil was the land of the future, its B proudly heading the list of emerging BRICS economies, a defiantly optimistic colossus. The giant has awoken, rejoiced the investors, and in 2010 *The Economist* ran the headline "Brazil takes off" illustrated by an image of Rio's statue of Christ in the shape of a rocket on the cover. When Rio de Janeiro was selected to host the Olympic Games in 2016, people celebrated on the beach at Copacabana. And when Brazil was chosen to host the 2014 World Cup in 2007, the then President Luiz Inácio Lula da Silva broke down in tears while making the announcement, having done his utmost to bring the World Cup back to Brazil 64 years after the "Maracanazo", the shameful defeat in the 1950 cup final against Uruguay in Rio de Janeiro. His aim was to host the "greatest party in the world" to celebrate Brazil joining the circle of great economic powers. One of Brazil's largest banks ran advertising proclaiming: "We're bringing home the World Cup!" As a five-times winner of the World Cup, Brazil was in the limelight, the sun-blessed child of the nations. The combination of sun, samba, and football seemed unbeatable. The Brazilians as a

Brasilien ist kein Land für Anfänger, hat der große Bossanova-Komponist und Musiker Antonio Carlos Jobim einmal über seine Heimat gesagt. Aber auch wer Brasilien zu kennen meint, wer seit über 20 Jahren hier lebt, staunt immer wieder, wie viele Analysen an der widersprüchlichen Realität dieses Landes scheitern. Brasilien entzieht sich der Annäherung wie eine kapriziöse Geliebte. Wenn man glaubt, sie endlich verstanden zu haben, macht sie garantiert das Gegenteil dessen, was man erwartet.

Gerade noch war Brasilien das Land der Zukunft, das stolze B unter den Schwellenländern BRICS, ein aufstrebender, vor Optimismus strotzender Gigant. Der Riese sei erwacht, jubelten die Investoren. »Brazil takes off«, titelte die angesehene Zeitschrift *The Economist* im Jahr 2010 und zeigte auf ihrem Cover Rios Christusstatue als abhebende Rakete. Am Strand der Copacabana jubelten die Menschen, als Rio de Janeiro für die Olympischen Spiele im Jahr 2016 auserkoren wurde. Bereits 2007 hatte Brasilien den Zuschlag für die Fußball-WM 2014 erhalten, der damalige Präsident Luiz Inácio Lula da Silva brach bei der Verkündung in Tränen aus. Er hatte sich mit aller Kraft dafür eingesetzt, dass die WM 64 Jahre nach dem »Maracanaço«, der schmählichen Niederlage im Endspiel gegen Uruguay in Rio de Janeiro, wieder nach Brasilien kommt. Mit der »größten Party der Welt« wollte er den Aufstieg der Nation in den Kreis der großen Wirtschaftsmächte feiern. »Wir holen die WM nach Hause«, jubelte eine große Bank in Werbeanzeigen – der fünffache Weltmeister fühlte sich als Sonnenkind unter den Nationen. Die Kombination von Sonne, Samba und Fußball galt als

Football is omnipresent in Brazil.
Fußball ist in Brasilien allgegenwärtig.

Cristo Redentor looks down from Corcovado onto Flamengo (left), Botafogo (right), and Niterói in the distance.
Cristo Redentor blickt vom Corcovado hinab auf Flamengo (links), Botafogo (rechts) und Niterói im Hintergrund.

party-loving people were held to be a sure-fire guarantee for a successful football celebration.

But even then, there were critical voices: Brazil is unprepared organizationally, the political class is not ready for the challenge, and the World Cup risks becoming a festival of corruption warned Juca Kfouri, one of Brazil's most respected sports journalists, and was promptly labeled as a spoilsport.

Then, in June 2013, the bubble burst: in São Paolo tens of thousands of young people took to the streets to protest against the rising cost of public transport. The police put down the demonstrators with brutal force and within days the protests had spread like wildfire. The unrest followed the Confederation Cup fixtures from city to city. Tear gas billowed into the stadia and the World Cup buildings suddenly became symbols of the arrogance of a political class that did not see fit to consult its citizens over the hosting of the spectacle. Millions of inhabitants took to the street demanding that hospitals and schools be built instead of football stadia. At the same time, the economy was foundering, growth was slowing and inflation increasing. The sun-blessed child of the BRICS was turning into a problem child. And then Brazil's age-old demons—violence, corruption, inequality—began to bare their ugly faces. The cost of hosting the World Cup exploded, and many of the facilities may not be completed in time. The football championship is fraught with uncertainty.

The mass protests in June 2013 marked a turning point and have turned over many of the old prejudices: that Brazilians are not interested in politics and would rather celebrate than demonstrate; that they are masters of improvisation that somehow muddle through; that they are a likeable but still somewhat immature tropical people. Charles de Gaulle is credited with having said that Brazil is not a serious country. Today he would have to revise his opinion—as would many experts on Brazil who have become blinded by the festival years of rule under President Lula.

I know of no journalist, politician or sociologist who foresaw the upheavals of 2013. After June 2013, numerous optimistic books on Brazil had to be hastily rewritten, and countless political and economic studies were rendered obsolete overnight. The mass demonstrations swept over the land as something of a catharsis, taking pundits from all political camps by surprise. Maybe, this is because Brazil has always been a country onto which we project our own desires. China is too far away and cold, but Brazil is nearby and as a land of immigrants shares our cultural background, and is warm and sensual. We want it to be successful, and when this dream is dreamt by a charismatic leader and man of the people such as President Lula, and moreover in a democracy, we gladly allow ourselves to be seduced.

It is therefore all the more disappointing when things don't transpire as envisaged. Among journalists this is known as "Brazil Blues": at some point or other it befalls each and every one of us who has grown to love this country. For some it is intolerable and they leave. More hard-nosed fans of Brazil stay on: they know that the "Brazil Blues" is like malaria—it comes in waves, but also subsides again.

unschlagbar. Wer, wenn nicht die feierfreudigen Brasilianer, könnte ein schöneres Fußballfest garantieren?

Warner gab es schon damals: Brasilien sei organisatorisch überfordert, die politische Klasse sei nicht reif für diese Herausforderung, die WM werde ein Fest der Korruption, kritisierte Brasiliens angesehenster Sportjournalist Juca Kfouri. Er wurde als Spielverderber beschimpft.

Dann kam der Juni 2013, und der Traum platzte. In São Paulo gingen zehntausende junger Leute gegen Fahrpreiserhöhungen der öffentlichen Verkehrsmittel auf die Straße. Die Polizei knüppelte die Demonstranten brutal zusammen, innerhalb weniger Tage wuchs sich die Protestwelle zu einem Flächenbrand aus. Parallel zum Confederations Cup sprangen die Unruhen von Stadt zu Stadt. Das Tränengas waberte bis in die Stadien, die WM-Bauten wurden zum Symbol für die Arroganz der politischen Klasse, die es nicht für nötig befunden hatte, das Volk über die Ausrichtung des Spektakels zu befragen. Millionen Menschen zogen durch die Straßen, sie forderten Krankenhäuser und Schulen statt Fußballstadien. Gleichzeitig strauchelte die Wirtschaft, das Wachstum schrumpfte, die Inflation nahm an Fahrt auf. Aus dem Sonnenkind wurde das Sorgenkind der BRICS. Und plötzlich zeigen Brasiliens alte Dämonen wieder ihre Fratze: Gewalt, Korruption, Ungleichheit. Die Kosten für die Ausrichtung der WM explodieren, vieles wird nicht rechtzeitig fertig. Das Fußballfest wird zur Zitterpartie.

Die Massendemonstrationen vom Juni 2013 markierten eine Zeitenwende. Sie haben mit alten Vorurteilen aufgeräumt: Dass die Brasilianer unpolitisch seien, dass sie lieber feiern als demonstrieren. Dass sie Improvisationskünstler sind, die alles irgendwie hinkriegen; ein sympathisches, aber irgendwie infantil veranlagtes Tropenvolk. Charles de Gaulle wird der Spruch zugeschrieben, dass Brasilien kein ernsthaftes Land sei. Heute müsste er sein Urteil revidieren – ebenso wie viele Brasilienexperten, die sich von dem Fest der Lula-Jahre blenden ließen.

Ich kenne keinen Journalisten, Politiker oder Soziologen, der den Umbruch vorhergesehen hat. Wie viele optimistische Brasilienbücher mussten nach dem Juni 2013 hastig umgeschrieben werden, wie viele politische und wirtschaftliche Analysen wurden über Nacht hinfällig? Die Massendemonstrationen, die wie eine Katharsis über das Land kamen, haben Brasilienkenner jeder politischen Couleur kalt erwischt. Vielleicht liegt es daran, dass Brasilien immer noch ein Projektionsraum unserer eigenen Sehnsüchte ist. China ist fern und kalt, Brasilien erscheint uns nahe. Es zählt zu unserem Kulturkreis, es ist ein Einwandererland, es ist warm und sinnlich. Wir wünschen uns, dass es Erfolg hat; und wenn dieser Traum unter demokratischen Verhältnissen und mit einem so charismatischen Arbeiterpräsidenten wie Lula geträumt wird, lassen wir uns gern verführen.

Umso enttäuschter sind wir, wenn es nicht so läuft, wie wir es uns vorstellen. Brazil Blues nennen Journalistenkollegen diese Krankheit; sie befällt jeden irgendwann, der dieses Land liebt. Manche halten es nicht aus und gehen weg. Hartgesottene Brasilienfans bleiben. Sie wissen, der Brazil Blues ist wie die Malaria. Er kommt in Schüben, aber er geht auch wieder.

Not everything we love about Brazil has disappeared overnight. Brazil is still warm and sensual. Compared with South Africa or the USA, white and black people live together remarkably happily. It is a vibrant mass democracy and a melting pot, an example of how people of different races and religions can live together.

Few other countries are so mixed. In São Paolo, one finds Japanese and Italian quarters. In the Saara, the largest market in the center of Rio, Arabs and Jews ply their wares next to each other. The descendants of African slaves live alongside indigenous Indians, Bolivians share quarters with immigrants from Paraguay and Peru, and ever more economic refugees from Haiti are settling in the Amazonas.

The south of the land has been shaped by immigrants from Germany, Poland, and Italy, while the north east was once ruled by the Dutch, and in Rio the influence of the French can be seen throughout the city. In the heartlands of Espírito Santo, one can still hear Pomeranian dialect being spoken, and the descendants of southerners from the USA who had fled the American Civil War populate an enclave in the federal state of São Paolo. Near the border with Paraguay, many women wear a veil, immigrants from Syria or the Lebanon. Alongside Catholic and Protestant churches one finds Sunni and Shiite mosques, all religions coexisting peacefully. And, of course, the traces of the Portuguese, Spanish, and Italians can be seen throughout the land.

Twenty million Brazilians have joined the middle classes in recent past, at least when one defines the middle class-

Denn alles, was wir an Brasilien so schätzen, ist ja nicht über Nacht verschwunden. Brasilien ist weiterhin warm und sinnlich. Im Vergleich mit Südafrika oder den USA kommen Weiße und Schwarze erstaunlich gut miteinander aus. Es ist eine pulsierende Massendemokratie und ein Schmelztiegel, ein Vorbild für das Zusammenleben von Rassen und Religionen.

Wohl kein anderes Land ist so bunt gemischt. In São Paulo gibt es japanische und italienische Viertel. In der Saara, dem großen Markt im Zentrum von Rio, betreiben Araber und Juden ihre Stände friedlich nebeneinander. Nachkommen afrikanischer Sklaven wohnen neben indianischen Ureinwohnern, Bolivianer teilen sich die Zimmer mit Zuwanderern aus Paraguay und Peru. Im Amazonasgebiet lassen sich immer mehr Armutsflüchtlinge aus Haiti nieder.

Der Süden wurde von Einwanderern aus Deutschland, Polen und Italien geprägt, im Nordosten herrschten einst die Holländer, in Rio spürt man an vielen Ecken den Einfluss der Franzosen. Im Landesinneren von Espírito Santo spricht man Pommern-Platt, im Bundesstaat Sao Päulo gibt es eine Enklave von Nachkommen US-amerikanischer Südstaatler, die einst vor dem Sezessionskrieg nach Brasilien flohen. An der Grenze zu Paraguay tragen viele Frauen Schleier, hier ist die Hochburg syrischer und libanesischer Einwanderer. Neben katholischen und evangelischen Kirchen erheben sich sunnitische und schiitische Moscheen, alle Religionen existieren friedlich nebeneinander. Portugiesen, Spanier und Italiener haben überall im Land ihre Spuren hinterlassen.

Street market in Rio
Marktszene in Rio

es by their purchasing power. Lula, who managed to bring about this wonder, is admired around the world as a result, and Brazil is seen as a model for many poorer states in Africa and Asia. Few other passports are as welcome around the world as the Brazilian. The much-cited sensuality of the Brazilian people is likewise not just a cliché: Brazil is a musical nation through and through. Music unites the country, as does the Portuguese language, which sounds even softer and more sensual than it does back in Europe.

But for every assertion, one can argue the contrary—which is what makes Brazil so complicated. Racism against blacks and indigenous Indians is widespread and the Protestant church derides the Afro-Brazilian religions as the work of the devil. Football is in decline. In the Brazilian heartlands, rodeo is displacing football as the most popular sport, Brazil being, after all, a land of cowboys. Bossa nova and samba are a minority phenomenon: in the interior of the country the schmaltzy songs of the Música Sertaneja—Brazil's equivalent of country music—are more popular. And the much-vaunted racial mix is likewise not the product of free will: during Portuguese rule, the colonizers, lacking womenfolk of their own, raped their black slaves.

In no other country does Ernst Bloch's principle of the simultaneity of the non-simultaneous apply as well as it does in Brazil. Feudal and modern structures exist alongside one another. Brazil is simultaneously the land of the future and of the past. It brings together Africa and Europe, and aristocracy and democracy exist together. The ideals of the French Revolution and principle of equality that underlie modern

20 Millionen Brasilianer sind in den vergangenen Jahren in die Mittelschicht aufgestiegen, auch das ist wahr, wenn man die Mittelschicht allein über den Konsum definiert. Lula, der dieses Wunder bewerkstelligt hat, wird dafür weltweit geachtet, Brasilien gilt für viele arme Staaten in Afrika und Asien als Vorbild. Mit kaum einem anderen Pass wird man in der Welt so gern gesehen wie mit dem brasilianischen. Auch die viel beschworene Sinnlichkeit der Brasilianer ist nicht nur Klischee: Brasilien ist durch und durch musikalisch. Musik hält das Land zusammen wie die portugiesische Sprache, die in Brasilien so viel weicher und sinnlicher klingt als im alten Europa.

Doch lässt sich zu jeder Aussage auch das Gegenteil behaupten, das macht Brasilien so kompliziert. Rassismus gegenüber Schwarzen und Indianern ist weit verbreitet, evangelische Kirchen bekämpfen afrobrasilianische Religionen als Werk des Teufels. Der Fußball ist auf dem Rückzug. Im Landesinneren verdrängt Rodeo den Fußball als beliebtesten Massensport, denn Brasilien ist ein Land der Cowboys. Bossa nova und Samba sind Minderheitsveranstaltungen, im Landesinneren hört man am liebsten die Schnulzen der Música sertaneja, der brasilianischen Countrymusik. Auch die Rassenmischung erfolgte keineswegs freiwillig: Weil unter den portugiesischen Kolonisatoren Frauenmangel herrschte, vergewaltigten sie ihre schwarzen Sklavinnen.

Auf kein anderes Land trifft Ernst Blochs Wort von der Gleichzeitigkeit des Ungleichzeitigen so zu wie auf Brasilien. Feudale und moderne Strukturen existieren nebeneinander. Brasilien ist gleichzeitig das Land der Zukunft und der Ver-

Fish from the Amazon, served in Manaus
Amazonasfisch, serviert in Manaus

In front of Gustav Eiffel's market hall in Manaus
Vor Gustav Eiffels Markthallen in Manaus

Manaus is a city of small and micro businesses.
Manaus ist eine Stadt des Klein- und Mikrogewerbes.

democracies around the world are rarely more than lip service in Brazil.

"If we want things to stay as they are, things will have to change," said the Sicilian nobleman Prince Salina in the novel *Il Gattopardo* by Giuseppe Tommasi de Lampedusa. For the aristocracy to survive, it had to take on the guise of a bourgeois democracy. The same applies for Brazil. Despite all its social and political transformations, large parts of it remain a class society. Deep in their hearts, the Brazilian elite despises the ideal of equality. They abuse democratic institutions to maintain their own privileges. Political representatives and senators behave like feudal lords. It is these corrupt structures that the demonstrators are up in arms about.

Up until the mid-nineteen-fifties, Brazil was primarily an agricultural land and the society of slave labor has never been totally eradicated from the mentality of the locals: those born into the right circles will live well. The poor have also internalized the aristocratic patterns. Class conflicts are not worked out openly but rather worked around. Brazilians are not friends of public conflict, but at some point even a master of improvisation has nothing more to work with causing tension to build up until it discharges in an explosion. Just as it did in June 2013.

Brazil is a country of continental dimensions, and it is as large as it is contradictory. Brazilians are unafraid to openly show their feelings, but they are also generous forgivers and forgetters. Like in the USA, there is a culture of excess. Portions in restaurants are often large enough for two. The land is fertile, and no one need truly go hungry. But in the north-

gangenheit. Es vereint Afrika und Europa, Aristokratie und Demokratie überlagern sich. Die Ideale der Französischen Revolution, das Streben nach Gleichheit, das jeder Demokratie innewohnt, sind in Brasilien ein Lippenbekenntnis.

»Alles muss anders werden, damit es bleibt, wie es ist«, sagt der sizilianische Fürst Salinas in dem Roman *Il Gattopardo* von Giuseppe Tommasi de Lampedusa. Damit die Aristokratie überleben kann, muss sie sich ein bürgerlich-demokratisches Mäntelchen überstreifen. Das gilt auch für Brasilien. Es ist trotz aller sozialen und politischen Umwälzungen in weiten Teilen noch immer eine Standesgesellschaft. Im tiefsten Inneren verachtet die brasilianische Elite das Ideal der Gleichheit. Sie missbraucht die demokratischen Institutionen zur Wahrung ihrer Privilegien. Abgeordnete und Senatoren gebärden sich wie Feudalherren. Gegen diese korrupten Strukturen rennen die Demonstranten an.

Bis Mitte der Fünfzigerjahre war Brasilien von ländlichen Strukturen geprägt. Die Sklavengesellschaft wirkt bis heute nach. Nirgends lebt es sich so gut, wenn man auf der richtigen Seite geboren ist. Auch die Armen haben das aristokratische Denken verinnerlicht. Klassenkonflikte werden nicht ausgetragen, sondern umdribbelt. Brasilianer mögen keinen offenen Streit. Doch irgendwann scheitern die Improvisationskünstler an den Verhältnissen, dann entlädt sich der Konflikt in einer Explosion. So wie im Juni 2013.

Brasilien ist ein Land von kontinentalen Ausmaßen, und groß ist es auch in seinen Widersprüchen. Brasilianer zeigen ihre Gefühle, sie sind aber auch großzügig im Verzeihen und Vergessen. Wie in den USA herrscht eine Kultur

east of the country one can still see emaciated people and children begging for food. Many of them head southwards in search of work.

Everything in Brazil is super-sized: the cities, the green empty spaces between them, the jungle, the rivers, the sea, the extent of the sky. If one were to project Brazil onto Europe, it would extend from the north of Norway to the south of Algeria. It spans several different climatic and time zones: the journey by plane from Porto Alegre in the south to Manaus in the Amazonas takes six hours, and as soon as one disembarks from the plane, one is floored by the heat. But nevertheless, the similarities outweigh the differences: in the Amazonas one drinks the same ice-cold beer as in the Pampas in the south, and Manaus has the same monotonous high-rise buildings in its Condominios—its guarded residential areas—as there are in Porto Alegre. The country is united by its language, music, and by football.

In Manaus as in Porto Alegre, the young people took to the streets for the same reasons. As if focused by a lens, conflicts have built up, conflicts that Europeans and Americans are no strangers to: many people no longer believe in the parties and parliament as conveyors of the will of the people. The protests in Brazil may be a foreboding of a crisis of legitimacy in Brazil's parliamentary democracy.

So, were all the optimistic prognoses for the future wrong? Will we have to relinquish ourselves to the idea that the giant is tied down for good?

Let us forget for a moment what Antonio Carlos Jobim said of his homeland, and cast ourselves in the role of a Bra-

des Überflusses. Die Portionen in den Restaurants reichen meistens für zwei. Das Land ist fruchtbar, eigentlich müsste niemand Hunger leiden. Doch im trockenen Nordosten sieht man noch immer Kinder um Essen betteln, die Menschen sind ausgemergelt, viele wandern ab in den Süden.

Alles in Brasilien ist überdimensioniert, die Städte und die grüne Leere dazwischen, der Dschungel, die Ströme, das Meer, die Weite des Himmels. Würde man Brasilien auf Europa projizieren, so würde es vom Norden Norwegens bis in den Süden Algeriens reichen. Es umfasst mehrere Klima- und Zeitzonen. Von Porto Alegre im Süden bis nach Manaus im Amazonasgebiet sitzt man sechs Stunden im Flugzeug. Wenn man aussteigt, erschlägt einen die Hitze. Dennoch sind die Gemeinsamkeiten stärker als die Unterschiede: Am Amazonas trinkt man das gleiche eiskalte Bier wie in den Pampas des Südens, in Manaus stehen die gleichen monotonen Hochhäuser in den Condominios, den bewachten Wohnanlagen, wie in Porto Alegre. Die Sprache, die Musik und der Fußball einen das Land.

In Manaus wie in Porto Alegre protestieren die jungen Leute aus den gleichen Gründen. Wie unter einem Brennglas bündeln sich in Brasilien Konflikte, die auch in Europa und den USA wohlbekannt sind: Viele Menschen glauben nicht mehr an Parteien und Parlament als Transmissionsriemen für den Willen des Volkes. Die Proteste von Brasilien sind Vorboten einer Legitimationskrise der parlamentarischen Demokratie. War nun alles falsch an den optimistischen Zukunftsprognosen? Müssen wir uns damit abfinden, dass der Riese dauerhaft gefesselt bleibt?

Belo Horizonte
Belo Horizonte

The Juscelino Kubitschek Bridge in Brasília, designed by Alexandre Chan
Die Juscelino-Kubitschek-Brücke in Brasília, gestaltet von Alexandre Chan

zil-beginner. I came to Brazil for the first time as a backpacker some thirty years ago. I didn't speak Portuguese and hadn't read Stefan Zweig. On my very first evening, a thief stole my wallet, wrenching it from my hand. Rio appeared decadent to my eyes: the few colonial palaces that had not been subjected to the modernization plans of megalomaniacal mayors, were falling apart. The apartment towers of Copacabana and Ipanema were exceptionally ugly, and had Rio not been so spectacularly embedded between green hills, forest, and sea, it would have been little more than a grey and ugly moloch. Two weeks later, I was glad to cross the border into Uruguay where I could at least speak the language and felt almost like a European.

But Brazil did give me a second chance. Six years after my first visit, I found myself back in Rio, this time as a correspondent. To my eyes, Brazil was still decadent and dangerous, and I would rather have travelled on to Buenos Aires. I had no particular expectations, and Rio was regarded among journalists as a distant outpost. But today, I know that that was the best possible starting point. Those who do not harbor great expectations, who do not believe they will be in paradise as soon as they step out of the airplane, will be positively surprised. At some point, he or she will suddenly be surprised to find themselves walking along the sambodrome, decorated with plumage, singing their heart out. After a few months, I belonged to a clique at Ipanema beach, was a regular at my local bar and had a huge circle of friends. And suddenly I knew I never wanted to leave.

Vergessen wir das Zitat von Antonio Carlos Jobim, versetzen wir uns in die Rolle des Brasilienneulings. Ich kam vor fast 30 Jahren zum ersten Mal als Rucksacktourist nach Brasilien. Ich sprach kein Portugiesisch und hatte nicht Stefan Zweig gelesen. Am ersten Abend in Rio wurde ich überfallen, ein Dieb riss mir die Geldbörse aus der Hand. Rio fand ich dekadent: Die wenigen Kolonialpaläste, die nicht dem Modernisierungswahn größenwahnsinniger Bürgermeister zum Opfer gefallen waren, verkamen. Die Apartmentburgen von Copacabana und Ipanema waren von ausnehmender Hässlichkeit. Läge Rio nicht so spektakulär eingebettet zwischen grünen Hügeln, Urwald und Meer – es wäre ein hässlicher, grauer Moloch. Ich war froh, als ich nach zwei Wochen Brasilien die Grenze nach Uruguay überschritt. Dort konnte ich die Sprache, dort fühlte ich mich fast wie in Europa.

Doch Brasilien hat mir eine zweite Chance gegeben. Sechs Jahre nach meinem ersten Besuch stand ich wieder in Rio, diesmal als Korrespondent. Brasilien erschien mir immer noch dekadent und gefährlich, am liebsten wäre ich nach Buenos Aires weitergezogen. Meine Erwartungen waren gering, unter Auslandskorrespondenten galt Rio als Urwaldposten. Heute weiß ich: Das waren die besten Voraussetzungen. Wer keine großen Erwartungen hegt, wer sich nicht im Paradies wähnt, sobald er in Brasilien aus dem Flugzeug steigt, wird positiv überrascht. Der ertappt sich, wie er plötzlich, mit Federbüschen geschmückt, im Karnevalsumzug durch das Sambódromo läuft und sich die Seele aus dem Leib singt. Nach wenigen Monaten gehörte ich zu

The view from Ponta de Copacabana
Am Ponta de Copacabana

Perhaps it is because in Brazil we are aware every day anew of the fragility of our existence. Beneath the thin veil of civilization lies barbarity. We experience feelings more intensely, and with all the senses. Brazil is more colorful, louder, more tender and brutal than old Europe. Happiness shines brighter, pain that much darker. The Brazilian people are not ashamed of their feelings: they cry in joy and in sadness, and it doesn't matter if they're on camera. President Lula let tears run down his face at the slightest opportunity.

In Brazil, not everything is weighed in gold. Personal relationships are not trivialized. Every Brazilian feels like a king, even the poorest. Meu Rei—My King—is how people address each other in Bahia to the present day, just like they did 200 years ago. Tomorrow is a beautiful promise, but it cannot be trusted. Brazil is the land of now. One can rely on one's family and one's friends. Everything else is a deceptive illusion.

So, where is the journey headed in the fateful year 2014? Not even the Brazilians themselves can say, mistrustful as they are of all plans and prognoses. They are not sure of their country any more, can only rub their eyes in wonder. The great Tom Jobin was wrong. One has to see this country in a new light, unencumbered by the ballast of fantasies of the future. Brazil *is* a country for beginners.

einer Clique am Strand von Ipanema, hatte meine Stammkneipe und einen riesigen Freundeskreis. Und plötzlich wollte ich nicht mehr weg.

Vielleicht liegt es daran, dass wir uns in Brasilien jeden Tag neu der Zerbrechlichkeit unserer Existenz bewusst werden. Unter der dünnen Oberfläche der Zivilisation lauert die Barbarei; Gefühle empfinden wir intensiver, alle Sinne werden gefordert. Brasilien ist bunter, lauter, zärtlicher und brutaler als das alte Europa. Das Glück leuchtet heller, das Elend ist dunkler. Brasilianer schämen sich nicht für Gefühle, sie weinen vor Freude oder vor Trauer, gern auch vor der Kamera. Präsident Lula ließ seinen Tränen bei jeder Gelegenheit freien Lauf.

In Brasilien wird nicht alles in Geld aufgerechnet, menschliche Beziehungen werden nicht banalisiert. Jeder Brasilianer fühlt sich wie ein König, auch die ärmsten. »Meu Rei«, »mein König«, spricht man in Bahia sein Gegenüber an, so wie vor 200 Jahren. Das Morgen ist ein schönes Versprechen, man kann ihm nicht trauen, Brasilien ist das Land des Jetzt. Nur auf die Familie und die Freunde ist Verlass, alles andere ist trügerischer Schein.

Wohin geht die Reise jetzt, im Schicksalsjahr 2014? Das wissen nicht einmal die Brasilianer, aus leidvoller Erfahrung misstrauen sie allen Plänen und Prognosen. Sie verstehen ihr eigenes Land nicht mehr, sie reiben sich die Augen und staunen. Der große Tom Jobim hatte unrecht. Man muss dieses Land mit neuen Augen sehen, unbelastet vom Ballast der Zukunftsphantasien. Brasilien ist ein Land für Anfänger.

Knut Göppert,
Thomas Moschner

Conversion or Renewal—a Matter of Principle?

New Building and Construction Techniques for Adapting Existing Sports Facilities to Meet Modern Standards

Umbau oder Neubau – eine Glaubensfrage?

Neueste Bau- und Konstruktionstechniken eröffnen Möglichkeiten, traditionsreiche Sportstätten modernen Standards anzupassen.

The Maracanã in Rio de Janeiro during construction of the roof

Das Maracanã in Rio de Janeiro während des Dachneubaus.

Why do we continue to build new stadia, or to convert and renovate existing stadia? Is it because we want to provide excellent sports facilities or is it to satisfy the demands of global organizations such as FIFA or IOC, which do not always coincide with the needs of athletes or of spectators? Are these vast new sports venues merely a vehicle for satisfying the commercial interests of associations and operators, or are today's new stadia still fascinating new landmark buildings that capture the imagination of sports fans in all sections of society?

Today's large sports arenas must fulfill many functions. In addition to the specifically sports-related aspects, they need to address the needs of spectators and their respective comfort expectations. Many of the new sports venues, particularly those that are conversions of former stadia, must also fulfill a role as a landmark in the urban fabric of their respective cities. The stadia in Kiev, Rio de Janeiro and Vancouver, all of which were comprehensively modernized in the last three years, are three prominent examples.

In all of these cases, the existing stadia no longer satisfied modern-day requirements. Although the game itself has changed little in the decades since the original stadia were built, the requirements that modern sports venues are expected to fulfill have risen significantly. Most initiatives to rebuild or convert a stadium are motivated by a desire to improve the spectators' view of the playing field and viewing comfort. In Rio de Janeiro, Belo Horizonte, and Kiev, for example, the World Championships and the

Warum werden heute neue Stadien gebaut oder bestehende Stadien renoviert und umgebaut? Geht es um den Bau optimaler Sportstätten oder darum, den globalen Organisationen wie FIFA oder IOC Wünsche zu erfüllen, die mit den Bedürfnissen der Sportler und Zuschauer nicht viel zu tun haben? Sollen mit neuen Großsportstätten schnöde kommerzielle Interessen der Verbände und der Betreiber befriedigt werden oder sind die Stadien von heute immer noch die faszinierenden Identifikationsobjekte für Sportbegeisterte quer durch die Bevölkerung?

Die heutigen großen Arenen des Sports übernehmen eine Vielzahl von Funktionen. Neben den sportspezifischen Aspekten werden auch die Bedürfnisse der Zuschauer aller Komfortklassen befriedigt. In vielen Fällen sind vor allem die neuen Sportstätten, die als Umbauten bestehender Stadien entstanden, nach wie vor Wahrzeichen und wichtige Bausteine des städtischen Gefüges. Markante Beispiele dafür sind die Stadien in Kiew, Rio de Janeiro und Vancouver, die in den letzten drei Jahren umfassend modernisiert wurden.

In allen Fällen waren die bestehenden Stadien den heutigen Ansprüchen nicht mehr gewachsen. Denn obwohl sich die Form des Spiels seit Jahrzehnten kaum verändert hat, sind die Anforderungen an eine moderne Sportstätte extrem gestiegen. Die Wünsche nach perfekter Sicht auf das Geschehen und hohe Komfortbedürfnisse sind die Auslöser für die Diskussionen um Um- oder Neubau. In Rio de Janeiro, Belo Horizonte und Kiew waren die Welt- bzw. Europameisterschaften nur der letzte Anstoß

For the European Championships in 2012, the original stadium bowl in Kiev from 1967 was enclosed by a new façade and roof construction.
In Kiew wurde die Stadionschüssel von 1967 für die Europameisterschaft 2012 mit einer Fassaden- und Dachkonstruktion umbaut.

The completely renovated Olympic Stadium in Kiev
Das runderneuerte Olympiastadion in Kiew

European Championships provided the final impetus to put long overdue modernization plans into effect. In Vancouver, on the other hand, the transformation was motivated by economic concerns, and the stadium was converted to serve multiple functions as a venue for American football, soccer, concerts, and trade fairs.

In most cases, the existing stadia are already regarded as being in the right place. Systems for running the stadia have been in place for many years and the surrounding neighborhood has usually developed a synergetic relationship with its respective sports venue. The residents of the cities identify with "their" stadium and perceive it as an important landmark in the urban context. Likewise, adequate public transport facilities are usually already present and used by visitors on a daily basis. The stadia that are located in the inner city are also very often significant historically, both for the sport as well as in their architecture. They constitute part of the urban townscape and have become a symbol for historic matches won and lost.

But while there would seem to be many good reasons for opting for a conversion, the task itself is unbelievably complex and technically challenging. To realize such conversion projects, planners as well as contractors have to come up with creative solutions.

To begin with, the requirements need to be defined and categorized according to importance. As compromises are inevitable and unavoidable, the requirements are classed as either "absolutely necessary and non-negotiable" on the one hand and "nice to have" on the other.

für eine überfällige und lange geplante Transformation. In Vancouver dagegen sollte durch die multifunktionale Nutzung für American Football, Fußball, Konzerte und Messen eine höhere Wirtschaftlichkeit erreicht werden.

Häufig ist unstrittig, dass die existierenden Stadien bereits richtig platziert sind. Jahrelange Erfahrungen mit dem Betrieb liegen vor und die Nachbarschaft hat sich meist synergetisch mit dem Betrieb der Großsportstätte arrangiert. Die Bewohner der Stadt identifizieren sich mit »ihrem« Stadion und sehen es im stadträumlichen Kontext als bedeutende und signifikante Wegmarke. Öffentliche Verkehrsmittel stehen oft in ausreichender Kapazität zur Verfügung und sind den Besuchern aus dem Alltag vertraut. Und sehr häufig sind diese innerstädtischen Stadien auch von hohem baukulturellem und sporthistorischem Wert. Sie gehören zum Stadtbild und stehen symbolhaft für historische Siege und Niederlagen.

So sprechen eigentlich viele Argumente für einen Umbau und ziehen doch eine unglaublich komplexe technische Aufgabenstellung nach sich. Dabei sind die Planer und die ausführenden Baufirmen gefragt, mit kreativen Lösungen einen solchen Umbau zu ermöglichen.

Zunächst gilt es, die Anforderungen zu definieren und diese verschiedenen Kategorien zuzuordnen. Da unweigerlich auch Kompromisse eingegangen werden müssen, werden die Anforderungen in »absolut notwendig und nicht verhandelbar« auf der einen Seite und »nice to have« auf der anderen gruppiert.

Zu den wesentlichen Punkten der ersten Kategorie ge-

The BC Stadium in Vancouver: erection of the new roof supports on top of the existing stadium bowl
Das BC Stadium Vancouver. Montage der neuen Dachstützen auf der bestehenden Stadionschüssel

In 2011, the BC Stadium in Vancouver was given a new façade and new cable-net roof structure with retractable membrane roof covering.
Das BC Stadium in Vancouver erhielt 2011 ein vollständig schließbares, seilgestütztes Membrandach und eine neue Fassade.

In the former category, the most essential minimum requirements include ensuring adequate sight lines of the playing field for all spectators, a roof that ideally covers the entire spectator seating, and, of course, all safety-relevant requirements. Likewise, spectators must be able to hear the sound system, the playing field must be evenly floodlit and every spectator should be able to see a video screen.

The Estádio Maracanã in Rio de Janeiro is a good example of how a stadium bowl can be remodeled in its geometry and construction, and how very large roof surfaces can be incorporated into historical buildings. Not only did the long footballing heritage of the stadium need to be respected, along with its position in the heart of the city and role as the bearer of memories of historic victories and defeats, but the building was also a historically listed monument. Consequently, any new extension to the roof was not permitted to alter the silhouette of the stadium when seen from the streets in the vicinity. A further condition was the need to retain as much as possible of the façade of the building along with its significant ramp constructions.

An analysis of the geometry of the existing stadium revealed that with its capacity of 86,000 spectators, only thirty percent of the seats had a good view of the playing field, 45 percent were open to the sky, the first row of seats was more than twenty meters from the pitch and it would take forty-five minutes to fully evacuate the stadium. As current standards require full evacuation within eight minutes, the venerable Maracanã needed renovating for safety reasons alone.

hören die Mindestforderungen an die Sichtlinien der Zuschauer auf das Geschehen, eine möglichst vollständige Überdachung aller Plätze und selbstverständlich auch alle sicherheitsrelevanten Anforderungen. Bei der Beschallung der Zuschauer und der Beleuchtung des Spielfeldes können ebensowenig Abstriche gemacht werden wie bei der Forderung, dass von jedem Platz aus eine Videotafel zu sehen sein soll.

Wie eine Stadionschüssel geometrisch und konstruktiv neu modelliert werden kann und wie es möglich ist, sehr große Dachflächen sinnvoll in einen historischen Bestand zu integrieren, zeigt beispielhaft das Estádio do Maracanã in Rio de Janeiro. Bei dem sportgeschichtsträchtigen Fußballtempel, der in der Mitte der Stadt liegt, waren nicht nur die Erinnerungen an historische Siege und Niederlagen zu erhalten, sondern auch die Anforderungen des Denkmalschutzes zu berücksichtigen. So sollte vom Niveau der umliegenden Straßen aus keine durch die Dacherweiterung verursachte Änderung der Stadionsilhouette erkennbar sein. Zusätzlich wurde zur Auflage gemacht, dass die Ansicht der Fassade mit ihren signifikanten Rampenbauwerken möglichst vollständig erhalten bleiben sollte.

Die Überprüfung der Bestandsgeometrie ergab, dass bei einer Kapazität von 86.000 Zuschauern nur 30 Prozent der Plätze über ausreichende Sicht auf das Spielfeld verfügten, nur 45 Prozent überdacht waren, die erste Reihe bis zu 20 Meter vom Spielfeld entfernt lag und es 45 Minuten dauerte, bis das Stadion vollständig entleert war. Da der heutige Standard für die Evakuierungszeit bei acht Mi-

At the Maracanã in Rio de Janeiro, the existing concrete roof, which provided only partial cover, and the lower seating tiers with poor sight lines were demolished.
Beim Maracanã in Rio de Janeiro wurden das zu kurze Betondach und die Unterränge mit den ungünstigen Sichtverhältnissen abgerissen.

This made it necessary to provide additional, and much wider, points of entry and exit. The escape stairs in the spectators' area needed widening and the distance between the rows of seats were much too narrow.

A survey of the building structures revealed that the existing concrete roof, built in 1950, was in dire need of repair and that the cantilever arms and their fixtures were not able to sustain additional loads. Despite the disastrous findings of the survey, the project leaders elected to employ all the modern building technology at their disposal to retain as much as possible of the structure of the temple to football.

The designers set about remodeling a new "stadium bowl" between the existing geometric boundaries of the football pitch and the eaves at the perimeter as the lower and upper bounds of the new terraces. While the lower tier of seating was completed replaced, large parts of the curving sections of the upper tier could be retained. The upper stands to the west and east were placed as new elements atop the existing steps of the stands and the existing foundations, columns, and supporting elements around the perimeter were largely re-used, although the raker beams together with the bleachers that rest on them were replaced. To reduce weight and shorten construction times, the sub-construction for the lower tier was made mostly of steel.

This approach made it possible to save almost half of the "grey energy"—the energy required for the manufacture, transport and disposal of the structure—that would have been required to build a completely new stadium bowl.

nuten liegt, musste das ehrwürdige Maracanã schon allein aus Sicherheitsgründen grundlegend renoviert werden.

Dazu waren zusätzliche Zugangsmöglichkeiten sowie wesentlich verbreiterte Ein- und Umgänge zu schaffen. Die Fluchttreppen im Zuschauerbereich waren zu verbreitern und die Sitzreihen erwiesen sich als wesentlich zu schmal bemessen.

Die Überprüfungen ergaben weiterhin, dass das im Jahr 1950 erbaute Betondach extrem sanierungsbedürftig war und die Kragarme und ihre Verankerung keine weiteren Lastkapazitäten aufwiesen. Obwohl die Bestandsaufnahme zunächst ein desaströses Bild ergab, entschlossen sich die Verantwortlichen, alle Möglichkeiten der modernen Bautechnik auszuschöpfen, um die Erhaltung des Fußballtempels zu gewährleisten.

Dazu wurde innerhalb der gegebenen geometrischen Grenzen zwischen Fußballfeld und Traufkante als untere Oberkante der neuen Tribüne eine neue Stadionschüssel modelliert. Während ein komplett neuer Unterrang entstand, konnten in den Kurven große Teile des Oberranges erhalten werden. Auf den West- und Osttribünen wurde der Oberrang neu über den bestehenden Tribünenstufen platziert. Die vorhandenen Fundamente, Stützen und umlaufend angeordneten Tragelemente wurden im Wesentlichen wiederverwendet, während die Zahnbalken und die Sitzstufen neu zu erstellen waren. Um Gewicht zu sparen und die Baustellenmontagezeit zu verkürzen, besteht die Unterkonstruktion für den Unterrang überwiegend aus Stahl.

Durch dieses Vorgehen wurde circa die Hälfte der für

The new construction of the lower tiers at the Maracanã has a steel structural frame with precast concrete elements for the bleachers.
Neuaufbau der Unterränge des Maracanã als Stahlkonstruktion mit aufgesetzten Betonfertigteilelementen

The Maracanã after demolition of the concrete roof cantilever and during the reconstruction of the lower tiers of seating
Das Maracanã in Rio de Janeiro nach Abbruch der Betondachkonstruktion und während des Neubaus der Unterränge

The wish to roof over every seat in the stadium could not be realized by adding a new cantilevering section to the roof. The doubling of the span distance would have led to a quadrupling of the stresses acting on the point of fixture. Even replacing the concrete roof with a steel construction to reduce the self-weight of the roof would, taking into account wind, hail, and self-weight loads, have resulted in approximately twice the bending moment at the point of fixation.

A very efficient solution for such situations is a roof structure with a spoke-wheel construction principle similar to that of a bicycle wheel. This principle makes it possible to develop lightweight constructions that only need supporting vertically at their outer edge, obviating the need for complex anchoring in the existing structure or additional foundations. For the roof of the Estádio Maracanã we employed a twin spoke-wheel construction for the first time which has an especially flat profile making it possible to satisfy conservation concerns. The new roof of the stadium is only visible from afar from one of the many viewing points in the hills around Rio and cannot be seen from street level.

die Errichtung einer vergleichbaren vollständig neuen Tribüne erforderlichen grauen Energie eingespart. »Graue Energie« bezeichnet hier die Energie, die für Herstellung, Transport und Entsorgung des Tragwerkes benötigt wird.

Die Forderung nach vollständiger Überdachung aller Sitzplätze konnte durch ein neues Kragdach nicht erfüllt werden. Eine Verdopplung der Spannweite führt zur Vervierfachung der Beanspruchung an der Einspannstelle. Auch bei einem Ersatz des Betondaches durch eine Stahlkonstruktion und der damit verbundenen Reduktion des Eigengewichts muss unter Berücksichtigung der Belastung aus Wind, Hagel und Eigenlast immer noch ungefähr das doppelte Einspannmoment verankert werden.

Als sehr effiziente Lösung bietet sich in einem solchen Fall eine Dachkonstruktion an, die sich konstruktiv am Prinzip des Speichenrades anlehnt, wie wir es vom Fahrrad kennen. Damit lassen sich gewichtsminimierte Konstruktionen entwickeln, die an ihrem Außenrand nur vertikal gestützt werden müssen und dadurch keine großen Verankerungen im Bestand oder gar zusätzliche Fundamente erfordern. Für das neue Dach des Estádio do Maracanã wurde zum ersten Mal eine doppelte Speichenradkonstruktion gewählt, die ein sehr flaches Profil aufweist und damit auch die Belange des Denkmalschutzes ausreichend berücksichtigt. Das neue Dach ist somit von außen nur von einem der hochgelegenen Aussichtspunkte Rios zu sehen, nicht aber vom Straßenraum aus.

Die überlegene Effizienz einer solchen Konstruktion beruht auf drei wesentlichen Aspekten. Zum Ersten

The particular efficiency of this construction can be attributed to three key aspects. Firstly, all of the internal forces within the pre-stressed system are taken up by the rim, which in engineering terms is a compression ring. This elegantly obviates the need for elaborate foundation anchors, a common problem with cable-stayed structures. Secondly, all construction elements can be unequivocally defined as structural members under tension or compression. This makes it possible to optimize their cross-section and material. For example, the elements under tension are made of high-strength steel cables that are three times as strong for the same mass compared to typical structural steel constructions. And thirdly, the combination of the textile membrane covering made of Teflon-coated fiberglass fabric and the cable-net is better in terms of weight and durability than any other combination. A one-meter-wide strip of the membrane material used in Rio has a tensile strength of almost 140 kN (kilo-newtons).. A single strip of this membrane would be able to sustain the weight of seven Mercedes S class cars were one to conduct a test. The entire roof construction of the Estádio Maracanã weighs a total of just 3,900 tons despite having an area of 46,000 square meters. The self-weight of the structure and the additional external loads are light enough to be sustained by the existing roof bearings of the former cantilever arms.

A further aspect that increasingly needs to be considered in the design of stadia is sustainability, which in construction terms is mostly dictated by energy consumption and achieving the best-possible CO_2 balance. Constructions that

werden in dem vorgespannten System alle inneren Kräfte in der Felge, die von den Ingenieuren Druckring genannt wird, kurzgeschlossen. Damit löst man elegant das bei Seiltragwerken häufig auftretende Problem des großen Aufwandes für die Fundamentverankerungen. Zum Zweiten werden die Bauteile konsequent als zug- oder druckbeanspruchte Tragelemente definiert. Damit werden diesen Elementen jeweils auch die optimalen Querschnitte und Materialien zugeordnet. So bestehen beispielsweise die Zugelemente aus hochfesten Stahlseilen, die bei gleicher Masse die dreifach höhere Festigkeit aufweisen. Und drittens zeigt sich die Kombination von Membraneindeckung aus teflonbeschichteten Glasfasergeweben und Seiltragwerk jeder anderen Kombination in puncto Gewicht und Dauerhaftigkeit überlegen. Ein ein Meter breiter Streifen des in Rio eingesetzten Membranmaterials hat eine Zugfestigkeit von nahezu 140 Kilonewton. In einem Zugversuch könnte man sieben Mercedes-S-Klasse-Fahrzeuge an einem solchen Membranstreifen aufhängen. So wurde für die Dachkonstruktion des neuen Maracanã bei einer Größe von 46.000 Quadratmetern ein Gesamtgewicht von lediglich 3900 Tonnen erreicht. Dieses Eigengewicht und die zusätzlichen äußeren Lasten waren die bestehenden Dachauflager des Kragdaches in der Lage aufzunehmen.

Ein weiterer Aspekt, der bei der Planung von Stadien immer stärker Berücksichtigung findet, ist die Nachhaltigkeit, die im konstruktiven Bereich besonders durch den Energieverbrauch und die bestmögliche CO_2-Bilanz defi-

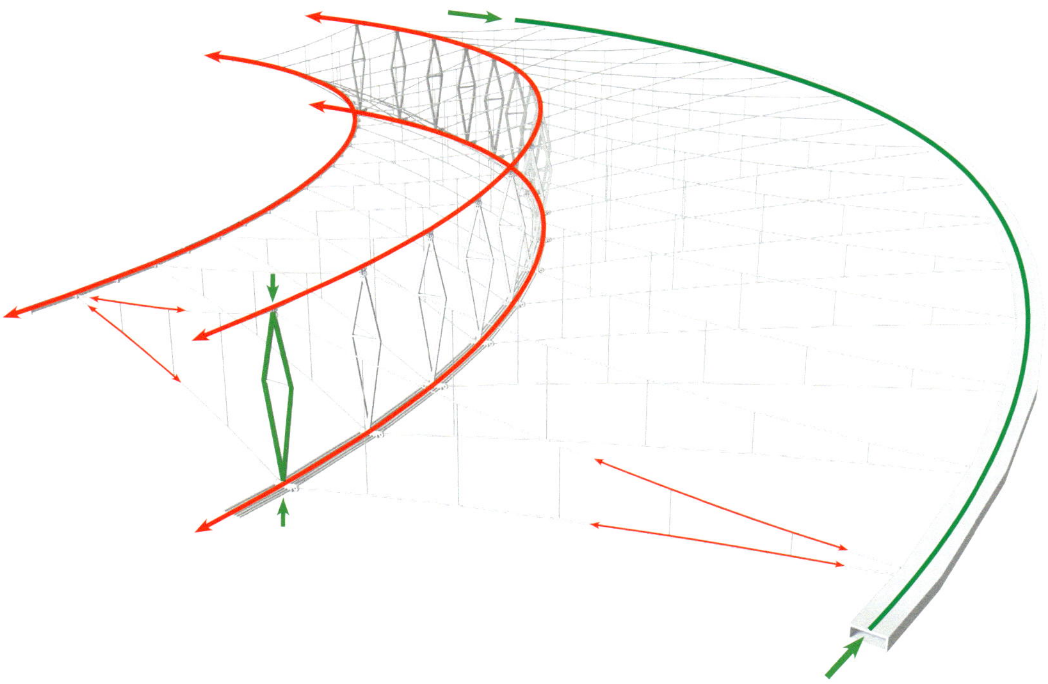

Functional principle of the cable-net structure showing the tension forces (red) in the three tension rings and radial cables and the compression forces (green) in the perimeter compression ring and flying struts

Funktionsprinzip des Seiltragwerks mit Zugkräften (rot) in den drei Zugringen und in den Radialseilen sowie Druckkräften (grün) im äußeren Druckring und in den Luftstützen

Erection of the cable-net structure
Aufziehen des Seiltragwerks

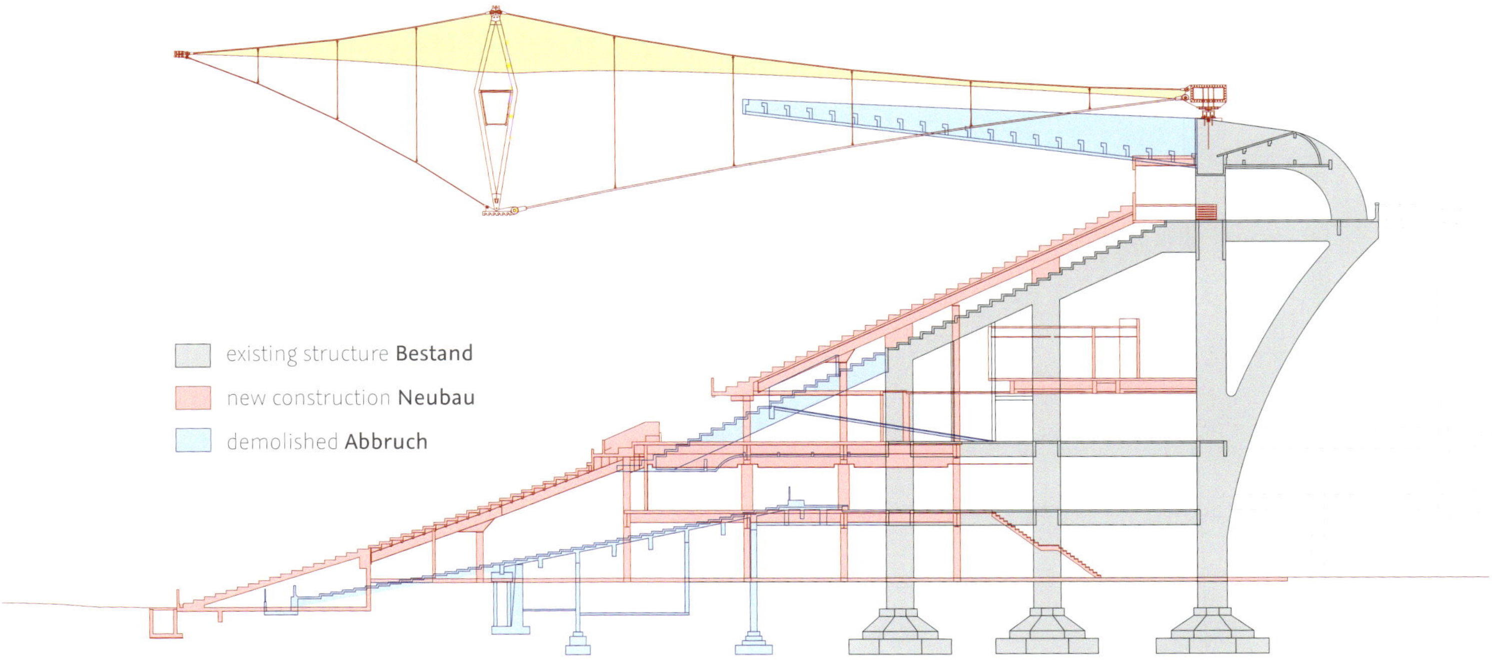

The conversion of the Maracanã showing the existing structure (grey), the demolished former structure (blue) and the new construction (red)

Der Umbau des Maracanã mit übernommenem Bestand (grau), Abbruch von originaler Substanz (blau) und Neubau (rot)

are easy to dismantle and can be separated into their constituent parts for later recycling are, of course, particularly advantageous. All of this applies to ring cable roofs. Compared with a "normal" stadium roof, such as the new stadium for the Corinthians football club in São Paolo, the difference is very apparent. While the cantilevered structure of the construction in São Paolo has a CO_2-equivalent value of 2,900 tons, the primary construction of the Estádio Maracanã has a CO_2-equivalent of just half this value. The CO_2-equivalent is a measure of the construction's contribution to the greenhouse effect. In addition, the spoke-wheel construction is a visually attractive construction with a legible structural principle that provides a lightweight roof and light-filled interior space ideal for sporting events.

Another aspect of particular relevance for conversion projects is the logistics of construction when the stadium still needs to be used during the construction phase. Here too cable-based roofs offer considerable benefits: they can be largely prefabricated and erected comparatively quickly without the need for temporary constructions that can be disruptive in the often cramped conditions of existing buildings. More than once, we have been able to erect a complete cable-net roof within a ten-week period during the summer break between fixtures.

The above advantages explain why this new ring cable roof construction method has been used in the conversion of numerous stadium conversion projects in the last ten years. In addition to the aforementioned Estádio Maracanã in Rio, a similar solution was proposed for the Estádio

niert wird. Vorteilhaft sind selbstverständlich auch Konstruktionen, die leicht demontierbar sind und deren Bauteile am Ende der Nutzungszeit wiederverwendet werden können.

All dies trifft auf die Ringseildächer zu. Ein Vergleich mit einem »normalen« Stadiondach wie zum Beispiel dem des neuen Stadions für den brasilianischen Klub Corinthians in São Paulo zeigt diese Unterschiede deutlich auf. Während sich für die Kragkonstruktion in São Paulo ein CO_2-Äquivalent von 2900 Tonnen errechnet, muss für die Primärkonstruktion des Estadio do Maracana in Rio nur der halbe Wert aufgewendet werden. Das CO_2-Äquivalent ist eine Einheit, mit der beschrieben wird, welchen Beitrag eine Konstruktion zum Treibhauseffekt liefert. Dazu kommt, dass die Speichenradkonstruktionen auch visuell sehr ansprechend sind, der Betrachter ein Verständnis für das Tragverhalten entwickelt und der leichte, lichtdurchflutete Innenraum perfekt zum Sportereignis passt.

Von großer Bedeutung bei der Umsetzung eines Stadionumbaus ist auch die Baulogistik im Zusammenwirken mit der Nutzung des Stadions während der Umbauphase. Auch in dieser Beziehung haben die seilgestützten Dächer große Vorzüge. Insbesondere der hohe Vorfertigungsgrad und die schnelle Montage nahezu ohne störende Hilfskonstruktionen sind auf Großbaustellen mit meist beengten Verhältnissen von großem Vorteil. Bereits mehrfach konnte unter Beweis gestellt werden, dass es möglich ist, ein komplettes Seiltragwerk in einer zehn Wochen langen spielfreien Sommerpause zu montieren.

Bearing point where the compression ring rests on the renovated original concrete supports of the former roof
Auflager des neuen Druckrings auf dem sanierten Kopf einer Betonstütze

Workmen assembling the cables for the new tension ring
Arbeiter bei der Montage der Seile für den Zugring

The Maracanã in Rio de Janeiro after completion of the new roof
Das Maracanã in Rio de Janeiro nach Fertigstellung der neuen Überdachung

Minerão in Belo Horizonte, although the method was never employed due to a lack of experience and excessive respect for this method among those involved. Similarly ingenious systems in combination with high-performance materials have, however, been employed for the stadia in Stuttgart (Mercedes Benz Arena), Kiev (Olympic Stadium), and Vancouver (New BC Place), as well as for both of the large stadium conversions in Madrid (for Real and Atlético).

Diese Vorzüge machen erklärlich, warum in den letzten Jahren eine Vielzahl von Stadionumbauten mit neuen Ringseil-Dachkonstruktionen verwirklicht wurde. Neben besagtem Estadio do Maracana in Rio war auch für das Estádio Minerão in Belo Horizonte eine solche Lösung geplant. Der allzu große Respekt vor einer neuen, für die Beteiligten unbekannten Lösung hat die Verwirklichung leider verhindert. Unter anderem in Stuttgart (Mercedes-Benz-Arena), Kiew (Olympiastadion), Vancouver (New BC Place) und auch bei den beiden großen Stadionumbauten in Madrid (für Real und Athletico) haben sich clevere Systeme in Kombination mit neuen Hochleistungsmaterialien jedoch durchgesetzt.

Crowds and Market Power

The Architects Volkwin Marg and Hubert Nienhoff in Conversation with Falk Jaeger

Masse und Marktmacht

Die Architekten Volkwin Marg und Hubert Nienhoff im Gespräch mit Falk Jaeger

BMG

Falk Jaeger
The process of urbanization is accelerating around the world. As part of this, are we seeing a return to building stadia in cities? Although the Arena in Munich was built on the outskirts of the city next to a motorway junction with parking for 10,000 cars, what we have seen in Italy, Spain, and Brazil would seem to indicate a trend towards favoring traditional inner-city locations that can be reached with public transport?

Volkwin Marg
The impression is deceptive. Town planners do all they can to avoid causing the kind of traffic congestion associated with such huge events in the heart of cities. Since Roman times, stadia have always been located at the edge of cities.

Barcelona's famous "Camp Nou" stadium, for example, holds this clue in its name, which means "new field". The fact that it no longer lies outside the city is simply because Barcelona has expanded to such a degree that it now encompasses the stadium. The intention is to modernize and urbanize the stadium at its present location, and we took part in the competition for that project.

Hubert Nienhoff
In Madrid, however, the opposite has happened. The Estadio Santiago Berabéu, used by Real Madrid, was previously situated on a traffic artery on the outskirts of the city and here too the city has grown to surround it. In this case, however, the decision was taken to make a virtue of necessity and to embark on a two-year-long architecture competition to find an optimal solution for its conversion that exploits the multi-functional possibilities offered by an inner-city location. We recently won this competition together with our Spanish partners L35 and Ribas & Ribas.

Falk Jaeger
So, by retaining its location within the city, the intention is to use it for a broader and more complex range of functions than beforehand. What is the reasoning behind this?

Volkwin Marg
The cost of building sports stadia has traditionally been supported by the state. Sporting events and physical training were seen as being important for public health and were state-subsidized. Club sports are regarded as a service to the community and are exempt from taxes.

But football arenas are now increasingly used for all manner of large-scale entertainment events put on and organized by market enterprises with profit-oriented motives. For reasons of political prestige, the cost of building stadia is still largely borne by the state, province or city but the number of privately funded stadia is increasing steadily, as is the case with the Arena in Munich, although here too the state provided extensive transportation infrastructure at a cost approaching that of the stadium itself.

The increasing commercialization and privatization of stadium building is, of course, accompanied by a desire to

Falk Jaeger
Die Urbanisierung beschleunigt sich weltweit. Gibt es Zeichen für die Rückkehr des Stadions in die Stadt? Münchens Arena wurde zwar noch weit draußen am Autobahnkreuz für Autofahrer mit 10.000 Parkplätzen gebaut, aber in Italien, Spanien oder Brasilien gewinnt man den Eindruck, als ob es einen Trend zurück zu traditionellen Innenstadtlagen mit der Erschließung durch öffentliche Verkehrsmittel gäbe.

Volkwin Marg
Der Eindruck täuscht. Kein Stadtplaner will das Verkehrsgewühl solcher Massenveranstaltungen mitten in der Stadt. Schon seit Römerzeiten und bis heute verlagert man Stadien nach draußen an den Stadtrand. In Barcelona heißt das berühmte Stadion deswegen »Camp Nou«, das heißt »Neues Feld«. Dass es inzwischen nicht mehr draußen, sondern drinnen liegt, hat den simplen Grund, dass Barcelona rasch gewachsen ist und inzwischen das Stadion umgibt. Man will den Standort erhalten und das »Camp Nou« modernisieren und urbanisieren. Dafür hatten wir einen Wettbewerbsbeitrag geliefert.

Hubert Nienhoff
In Madrid läuft es allerdings anders. Das Estadio Santiago Bernabéu des Vereins Real Madrid liegt auch am ehemaligen Stadtrand an einer Ausfallstraße und ist inzwischen auch urban eingewachsen. Aber hier hat man sich entschlossen, aus der Not eine Tugend zu machen und in einem zweijährigen Wettbewerbsverfahren unter Architekten nach einer optimalen Lösung für einen Umbau zu suchen, der die Möglichkeiten einer sich aufdrängenden innerstädtischen Mehrfachnutzung eröffnet. Diesen Wettbewerb haben wir gerade mit unseren spanischen Freunden von L35 und Ribas & Ribas gewonnen.

Falk Jaeger
Mit dem Verbleib innerhalb der Stadt wird also aus gegebenem Anlass eine komplexere Nutzung als vorher angestrebt. Was ist die eigentliche Ursache hierfür?

Volkwin Marg
Bislang werden die Kosten für den Stadionbau sozialisiert. Das entspricht der überkommenen Tradition, Sportveranstaltungen als Teil der Volksgesundheit und Körperertüchtigung öffentlich zu subventionieren. Der Vereinssport gilt ja als gemeinnützig und ist steuerbefreit.

Inzwischen sind Fußballarenen aber für unterhaltende Massenevents da, die von merkantilen Unternehmen profitorientiert organisiert und veranstaltet werden. Es wird zwar aus Gründen des politischen Prestigewettkampfes der Städte, Provinzen oder Nationen der Aufwand für den Stadionbau immer noch weitgehend sozialisiert, aber die Zahl der privat finanzierten Stadien nimmt zu, wie zum Beispiel die Arena in München, wobei aber auch dort die aufwändige Erschließungsstruktur mit etwa gleich hohem Kostenaufwand vom Staat geliefert wurde.

minimize costs and maximize income. And that is most effectively achieved by designing stadia to accommodate a variety of uses so that they can also be used between sporting fixtures.

Hubert Nienhoff
The stadia of the large football clubs usually contain a shop for memorabilia, a "hall of fame", restaurants and cafés, facilities for guided tours, a museum, and, where stadia are used for multiple uses, a closable roof. In Madrid, however, we've taken this a step further: we've planned a hotel with a view into the stadium, conference facilities, and a flagship store for product presentations and shopping. The intention is to make the stadium usable round the clock, instead of just for fortnightly events, so that it becomes a focal point in the local urban quarter with the capacity to attract visitors from beyond the immediate vicinity.

Falk Jaeger
Over time, society has gradually dispensed with the rigid regulation of trade and commerce: for example, there are now drugstores in petrol stations, shopping centers in railway stations, and shopping plazas between airport security and flight gates. Are we going to see a similar development in stadia to exploit the market potential of the masses?

Mit der Kommerzialisierung und Privatisierung des Stadionbaus verbindet sich natürlich das Streben der Stadionbetreiber nach Minderung der Kosten und Steigerung der Einnahmen. Das gelingt am besten durch die Mehrfachnutzung der Arena und Zusatznutzungen ergänzend zum periodischen Veranstaltungsbetrieb.

Hubert Nienhoff
Bislang üblich ist bei den Stadien bedeutender Vereine Devotionalienhandel, eine »Hall of Fame«, Gastronomie, Besucherrundgang und ein Museum sowie für die Mehrfachnutzung der Arena oft ein schließbares Dach. Aber in Madrid gehen wir weit darüber hinaus. Dort planen wir zusätzlich ein Hotel mit Stadioneinblick, Kongresseinrichtungen sowie ein Flagship-Store-Zentrum für Produktpräsentationen und Einzelhandel. Es geht darum, anstelle der zweiwöchigen Großveranstaltungen einen alltäglichen Betrieb rund um die Uhr als urbanen Gravitationspunkt des Quartiers mit überregionaler Anziehungskraft zu schaffen.

Falk Jaeger
Unser Gesellschaftssystem hat die früheren Reglementierungen für den Einzelhandel weitgehend aufgehoben, man denke an die Tankstellen-Drugstores, die Bahnhofseinkaufszentren oder die Wegelagerer zwischen Sicherheitskontrolle und Gates in den Flughäfen. Bahnt sich das auch für Stadien an, weil dort Massen für den Umsatz animiert werden können?

The architects Volkwin Marg and Hubert Nienhoff in conversation with Falk Jaeger
Die Architekten Volkwin Marg und Hubert Nienhoff im Gespräch mit Falk Jaeger

Volkwin Marg
Yes, market liberalization is spreading rapidly, but traditional retail shopping can only function properly in stadia when there is a constant stream of potential consumers—as is the case with petrol stations, railway stations and airports. And this is only likely to succeed in specific inner-city locations.

Hubert Nienhoff
What is possible, however—and that applies to all kinds of large-scale events in stadia and arenas—is to extend the duration that people spend at the venue.

In Europe, a visit to the theatre, a concert, an opera or museum has traditionally been dominated by the actual event or content and is correspondingly short. The same goes for large-scale events in stadia. If these visits can be extended by providing attractions so that people stay on longer, that would be good both commercially as well as socially.

Falk Jaeger
In publications and exhibitions on stadium building, you have talked extensively about "the choreography of the masses". Ever since the paramilitary Olympic Games in Ancient Greece and the "panem et circenses" (bread and games) policy of the Romans, stadia and arena have always been a mirror of the respective social power structures. The same can be said of sporting events during the Nazi era and the competing social systems in thenineteenth and twentieth century. How is this reflected at the beginning of the twenty-first century?

Volkwin Marg
Today, unrestricted market forces are gaining ground. The architecture for such global choreographed mass events—whether for the Olympic Games, Commonwealth Games, Asian Games, World Cup, or American, European, African, or Asian Championships—remains a way for nations to present themselves. In addition to perfectly fulfilling the designated function with an appropriate construction, such buildings must also serve as landmarks that communicate the political self-representation of a country, province, or a city: they have to be a unique architectural icon. Class divisions are also successively influencing the design of what were once egalitarian stadia for the people: there are now special areas for VIPs, for business guests, and their respective consumer preferences.

Hubert Nienhoff
That also applies to the stadia for the World Cup in Brazil. We were fortunate that in Brazil—a veritable Eldorado of Latin American football—the stadia were already well known or even legendary, and their architecture had acquired a corresponding iconic status in their respective cities, for example the Maracanã in Rio de Janeiro, the Morumbi in São Paolo, and the Mineiro in Belo Horizonte.

For these stadia, our friends from schlaich, bergermann und partner consulting engineers and ourselves were tasked with adapting these monuments, built during the heroic period of Brazilian expansion under socialist rule in the nineteen-seventies, to fulfill modern-day requirements as stipu-

Volkwin Marg
Ja, der liberalisierte Markt ist überall auf dem Vormarsch, aber hinsichtlich des klassischen Einzelhandels kann das bei Stadien nur unter der Voraussetzung gelingen, dass wie bei Tankstelle, Bahnhof und Flughafen ein wirklich permanenter Massenverkehr existiert. Dies dürfte aber auf ganz spezielle Innenstadtlagen beschränkt bleiben.

Hubert Nienhoff
Was sich aber grundsätzlich bei allen Großveranstaltungen in Stadien und Arenen ausdehnen ließe, wäre die Verweildauer der Besucher. Die europäische Tradition des Konzert,- Theater,- Opern- und Museumsbesuchs war bislang dominant inhaltsorientiert und dementsprechend kurz, gleichermaßen auch der Aufenthalt bei Massenveranstaltungen im Stadion. Wenn solcherlei Besuche durch attraktive Angebote zum Verweilen zeitlich ausgedehnt würden, wäre das nicht nur ein kommerzieller, sondern auch gesellschaftlicher Gewinn.

Falk Jaeger
Sie haben sich intensiv in Publikationen und Ausstellungen mit der »Choreografie der Massen« im Zusammenhang mit dem Stadionbau beschäftigt. Seit den paramilitärischen Olympischen Spielen der antiken Griechen und »panem et circenses« bei den Römern war der Bau der Stadien immer auch Spiegel der jeweiligen gesellschaftlichen Machtverhältnisse, auch während des Nationalismus und der konkurrierenden Gesellschaftssysteme im 19. und 20. Jahrhundert. Wie sieht das zu Beginn des 21. Jahrhundert aus?

Volkwin Marg
Der uneingeschränkte Markt gewinnt an Macht. Zwar präsentieren sich die Staaten nach wie vor bei den globalisierten Events durch die Architektur für die choreografierten Massenveranstaltungen, seien es Olympische Spiele, Commonwealth Games, Asian Games, Fußballweltmeisterschaften, Amerika-, Europa-, Afrika- oder Asienmeisterschaften. Es wird über die perfekte Funktionserfüllung und dafür angemessene Konstruktion hinaus immer auch eine Landmarke für die politische Deutung eines Landes, einer Provinz oder einer Stadt in Gestalt einer unverwechselbaren architektonischen Ikone erwartet. Aber aus den egalitären Volksstadien werden schrittweise Klassenstadien, zugeschnitten auf das Konsumverhalten von VIPs, Business-Gästen und Fans.

Hubert Nienhoff
Das war auch in Brasilien für die WM-Stadien nicht anders. Allerdings hatte dieses Eldorado des lateinamerikanischen Fußballspiels schon allgemein bekannte und legendäre Stadien vorzuweisen, die bereits als architektonische Inkunabeln unverwechselbar für ihre Städte standen, zum Beispiel Maracanã für Rio de Janeiro, Morumbi für São Paulo und Mineiro für Belo Horizonte.

Bei diesen Stadien hatten wir und unsere Ingenieurfreunde von schlaich, bergermann und partner die Aufga-

lated by FIFA, for example to ensure spectator stands conform to modern safety and comfort standards and to roof over the majority of the stadium.

In Brasília and Manaus, we had the opportunity to construct new iconic buildings that each respond to the specific *genius loci* of their respective location.

FALK JAEGER
How can we expect things to develop in the future in Brazil?

HUBERT NIENHOFF
Brazil has its own enduring football tradition and its historical stadia have long epitomized the notion of stadia for the people. The conversion measures aimed at improving safety and comfort will, hopefully, change none of this. After the World Cup, football will continue to be played as before where it has enjoyed a long tradition, and perhaps with renewed vigor in the new venues in the modern city of Brasília or the isolated rainforest city of Manaus.

Despite the influence of market forces, where the masses are ideally segmented into consumer groups and citizens are seen as manipulable consumers, Brazil's World Cup stadia will in the future continue to be arenas for enthusiasm, team spirit, discipline, and fair play and as such will hopefully uphold the tradition of football as a national sport that transcends all the classes.

be, die Baudenkmale aus der heroischen Zeit des brasilianischen Aufbruchs in den sozialistischen siebziger Jahren an die modernen Betriebserfordernisse der FIFA anzupassen, die Tribünen nach neuen Sicherheits- und Komfortrichtlinien umzubauen und für eine möglichst vollständige Überdachung zu sorgen. Für die Neubauten für Brasília und Manaus konnten wir aber neue Zeichen setzen, die den Genius loci reflektieren.

FALK JAEGER
Was ist für die weitere Entwicklung in Brasilien zu erwarten?

HUBERT NIENHOFF
Brasilien hat eine eigene und unverwüstliche Fußballtradition. Seine traditionsreichen älteren Stadien stehen für den Begriff des Volksstadions. Daran wird sich hoffentlich auch durch Sicherheitsumbauten und mehr Zuschauerkomfort nichts ändern. Nach der Weltmeisterschaft wird das Kicken weitergehen wie früher, an den Traditionsplätzen sowieso. An neuen Standorten wie dem jungen Brasília oder der entlegenen Urwaldinsel Manaus wird es wahrscheinlich erst richtig losgehen.

Trotz der vordringenden Marktmacht, die am liebsten die Massen nach Verbrauchergruppen sortieren und aus Bürgern manipulierte Verbraucher machen möchte, werden in Brasiliens WM-Stadien auch in Zukunft begeisterte Massen mit Teamgeist, Disziplin und fairem Verhalten zusammentreffen, und diese Tradition wird hoffentlich den Fußball als klassenlosen brasilianischen Volkssport erhalten.

Rio de Janeiro

Michaela Metz

Rio de Janeiro—Living the Myth

An Eccentric Metropolis: Cultural Center, Tourist Destination and Social Flashpoint

Rio de Janeiro lebt den Mythos

Die exzentrische Metropole ist Kultort, Traumziel für Touristen und sozialer Brennpunkt.

"In Rio de Janeiro, nature in an exceptional mood of extravagance has concentrated into a small space all the elements of scenic beauty which elsewhere are distributed over whole countries," wrote Stefan Zweig in 1941 in his book *Brazil—Land of the Future* while in exile in the tropical country. "Something is happening everywhere; there is color, light, and movement everywhere. Nothing is repeated, nothing goes together and yet it all fits together." Above all, the writer was overwhelmed by the warmth and hospitality of the locals in Rio de Janeiro.

Rio's reputation as an eccentric metropolis reaches as far back as the 19th century, when it was the capital of Brazil. King João VI of Portugal, who in 1808 fled to Brazil along with his entire Royal Court to escape Napoleon, described the city as a "tropical Versailles". Later, his son Pedro of Portugal would be instrumental in liberating the colony from imperial rule with his famous "Cry of Ipiranga" in 1822, in which he cried "Independence or death!" on the banks of the red river.

For years, Rio de Janeiro modeled itself after Paris, and only much later did the city—and the rest of Brazil—emancipate itself from the European ideals that originated from the period of colonial rule. During this period, intellectuals and the literati frequented the many illustrious cafés in the center, among them the famous Café Papagaio, where guests were greeted by a torrent of abuse from a parrot called Bocage. This parrot would later become a symbol of the *malandro*, the suave but wily dandies of the burgeoning urban metropolis, immortalised in Walt Disney's figure *Zé Carioca*, a dapper parrot who becomes a compadre to Donald Duck. Today, one can still catch a glimpse of times past in the Con-

»In Rio de Janeiro hat die Natur in einer einmaligen Laune von Verschwendung von den Elementen der landschaftlichen Schönheit alles in einen engen Raum zusammengerückt, was sie sonst sparsam auf ganze Länder verteilt«, schrieb Stefan Zweig 1941 in seinem Buch *Brasilien – Land der Zukunft* über sein tropisches Exil. »Überall geschieht etwas, überall ist Farbe, Licht und Bewegung, nichts wiederholt sich, nichts passt zusammen, und doch passt alles zusammen.« Der Schriftsteller war überwältigt von dem herzlichen Empfang, den ihm die Brasilianer in Rio de Janeiro bereiteten.

Schon im 19. Jahrhundert genoss Rio, damals Brasiliens Hauptstadt, den Ruf einer exzentrischen Metropole. Der portugiesische König Joao VI., der 1808 mit seinem gesamten Hofstaat vor Napoleon nach Brasilien floh, nannte die Stadt sein »Versailles in den Tropen«. 1822 löste sich die Kolonie mit dem berühmten »Schrei von Ipiranga« seines Sohnes Pedro von Portugal. »Unabhängigkeit oder Tod!«, rief er am Ufer des rot gefärbten Stromes.

Rio de Janeiros großes Vorbild war Paris, und erst viel später sollte sich die Stadt – und ganz Brasilien – von den europäischen Idealen emanzipieren, die noch aus der Kolonialzeit stammten. In den illustren Cafés im Zentrum trafen sich Literaten und Intellektuelle. Besonders berühmt war das Café Papagaio. Dort wurden die Gäste von einem Papagei namens Bocage mit wüsten Schimpfwörtern empfangen. Der Papagei wurde zum Symbol für den gerissenen Gecken der Großstadt, den Malandro. Später setzte ihm Walt Disney mit »Zé« Carioca als Freund von Donald Duck

Year-round holiday atmosphere on Rio's famous Copacabana beach

Am berühmten Strand von Copacabana ist allzeit Urlaub.

Copacabana and Sugarloaf Mountain seen from Ponta de Copacabana

Copacabana und der Zuckerhut vom Ponta de Copacabana aus

feitaria Colombo, with its cut-glass chandeliers and bombastic cakes.

The world-famous beach in the Copacabana district was not originally part of the city as a large rock separated from the city making it hard to reach. At that time, the potential of the beach as an arena for social interaction had not been discovered and the sea was used mostly for medicinal bathing. But in 1892, a tunnel provided a first means of passage for a tram that linked the city center to Copacabana—and with it came the vibrant townsfolk and high society.

Music, football, and body culture are part of life in Brazil and there are few better places to parade one's physicality than the beaches of Rio de Janeiro. With the development of the Copacabana, beach culture rapidly became the new avant-garde, and with it beach fashion: woolen body-length robes gave way to high-neck one-piece swimsuits (a sensation at the time) and finally to lycra thongs. A particularly memorable fashion highlight was the miniature knitted triangles covering one's privates, as debuted by Gaetano Veloso on the beach at Ipanema in the seventies. An anti-bikini association was founded in 1947 but it could do little to hold back the sun worshippers. Rio de Janeiro is a city in which curves trump straight lines, a *cidade maravilhosa* ("marvelous city") with its own very special way of life, and its own illustrious residents, its artists and musicians, prostitutes (of all three genders), and, of course, the *Cariocas*, as the veteran locals like to call themselves.

Since the 1920s, the Avenida Atlântica and its beach promenade have been the epitome of fashionable seaside

ein filmisches Denkmal. Die Confeitaria Colombo mit ihren Kristalllüstern und bombastischen Torten vermittelt heute noch einen Eindruck aus dieser Zeit.

Der weltberühmte Strand des Stadtteils Copacabana lag anfangs noch fast unerreichbar außerhalb der Stadt, denn ein großer Felsen trennte ihn vom Zentrum. Der Strand als Bühne des gesellschaftlichen Lebens musste da erst noch erfunden werden; das Meer diente höchstens als Ort für medizinische Tauchbäder. Doch 1892 öffnete ein Tunnel den Weg für die erste Straßenbahn von Rios Zentrum nach Copacabana. Und mit der Tram kamen das quirlige Volk und die High Society.

Musik, Fußball und der Körperkult gehören zu Brasilien. Und die erste Bühne dieser identitätsstiftenden Körperlichkeit sind die Strände von Rio de Janeiro. Schnell wurde die Strandkultur zum avantgardistischen Prinzip erhoben, die Mode entwickelte sich rasant. Vom wollenen Ganzkörperanzug über den (damals skandalösen) hochgeschlossenen Einteiler bis zum Tanga aus Lycra. Ein modisches Highlight war das gehäkelte Mini-Körbchen fürs Gemächt, das Gaetano Veloso am Strand von Ipanema in den Siebzigerjahren ausführte. 1947 wurde ein Anti-Bikini-Verein gegründet. Aufhalten ließen sich die Sonnenanbeter davon nicht. Rio de Janeiro, das ist der Sieg der Kurven über die Linie. Die »wunderbare Stadt« – *a cidade maravilhosa* – steht für ein ganz spezielles Lebensgefühl. Mit all seinen illustren Bewohnern, den Künstlern und Musikern, Prostituierten und den alteingesessenen Cariocas, wie sich die Einheimischen selbst nennen.

life. Its boulevard, replete with iconic wave-pattern paving, has existed since 1919. Its most recent incarnation dates back to a design from the 1970s by the landscape architect Burle Marx who considerably widened the pavement and changed the orientation of the waves to run parallel to the boulevard rather than across it.

The Avenida Atlântica is also home to the Edificio Ipiranga, known locally as "Mae West" due to its feminine curves. The top floor contained Oscar Niemeyer's office until the architect's death in 2012, although, contrary to popular opinion, he was not responsible for its design. Even at the age of 104, he could be found there nearly every day.

In the 1920s, the Copacabana Palace luxury hotel was built as a replica of the Carlton in Cannes and remains a landmark of the city to this day. Over the years, everyone from Stefan Zweig, Marlene Dietrich, Jeanne Moreau, Walt Disney, Jean-Paul Sartre and Simone de Beauvoir to Henry Fonda, Mick Jagger, Princess Diana, Nelson Mandela, Michael Schumacher and Helmut Kohl have stayed there.

But the city has also not been afraid to implement unpopular plans. In 1937, Getulio Vargas established the Estado Novo ("the New State") and declared himself the nation's dictator. In the early 1940s he proceeded to build the "greatest boulevard in the world", cutting through the heart of historic Rio. Rather than a grand boulevard in the manner of the Champs-Elysées in Paris, it was to be a parading ground more akin to those of Stalin. The cosmopolitan Praça Onze, once a vibrant central square with a multitude of bars and shops populated by mulattos from Bahia as well as Portu-

Die Avenida Atlântica mit der Strandpromenade ist seit den Zwanzigerjahren Schauplatz mondänen Badelebens. Seit 1919 kennt man den Boulevard mit der charakteristischen Pflasterung des Bürgersteigs in wellenförmigem Dekor. Die aktuelle Version stammt aus den Siebzigerjahren, entworfen vom Landschaftsarchitekten Burle Marx, der den Bürgersteig wesentlich verbreitern und die zuvor quer verlaufenden Wellen in Längsrichtung legen ließ.

An der Avenida Atlântica steht auch das Edificio Ipiranga, das wegen der weiblichen Rundungen den Beinamen »Mae West« erhielt. Oscar Niemeyer unterhielt im obersten Geschoss des Gebäudes bis zu seinem Tod 2012 sein Büro, wenngleich er es entgegen landläufiger Meinung nicht selbst entworfen hat. Selbst im Alter von 104 Jahren ging er noch fast jeden Tag dorthin.

In den Zwanzigerjahren entstand das Luxushotel Copacabana Palace, ein Abbild des Carlton in Cannes und bis heute ein Wahrzeichen der Stadt. Stefan Zweig, Marlene Dietrich, Jeanne Moreau, Walt Disney, Jean-Paul Sartre und Simone de Beauvoir, Henry Fonda, Mick Jagger, Prinzessin Diana, Nelson Mandela, Michael Schumacher und Helmut Kohl haben hier schon übernachtet.

Doch auch unpopuläre Pläne hat die Stadt nie gescheut. Getulio Vargas hatte 1937 den Estado Novo – den »Neuen Staat« – ausgerufen und herrschte als Diktator. Anfang der Vierzigerjahre schlug er eine Schneise ins historische Rio, um den »größten Boulevard der Welt« zu bauen. Keine Prachtstraße wie die Champs-Élysées in Paris, sondern einen Aufmarschplatz nach stalinistischem Vorbild.

Built in 1923 and modeled after the Carlton in Cannes, the Copacabana Palace Hotel is the most famous hotel in South America.
Das nach dem Vorbild des Carlton in Cannes 1923 erbaute Hotel Copacabana Palace ist das bekannteste Hotel Südamerikas.

On the Avenida Atlântica, the waves of the Atlantic Ocean are echoed in the paving of the beach promenade.
An der Avenida Atlântica verwandeln sich die Wellen des Atlantischen Ozeans in Pflasterdekor.

guese, Spaniards, Italians, and Jews, was knocked down to make way. Now all that remains of the square is its name on the Metrô station. The square and its history are now buried beneath the traffic jams that congest the many lanes of the Avenida Presidente Vargas and it is now one of the ugliest parts of Rio. Stefan Zweig also voiced his misgivings, remarking that: "Rio shoots forth new avenues again and again from within, brushing away entire blocks of buildings the way a racing locomotive deflects a sheet of paper." In 1960, however, the spotlight of politics swung away from Rio de Janeiro with the inauguration of Brasília as the new capital city by President Juscelino Kubitschek.

Bossa Nova also has its origins in Rio. Bossa Nova—meaning "new trend" or "new wave"—was a musical revolution that arose among the young intellectual middle classes: a form of samba with cool sensibilities, mixed with the jazz influences spilling over from the USA. It began with João Gilberto's recording of "Chega de Saudade" (No more blues). Gilberto quickly became the leading representative of the bossa nova, with Tom Jobim, Carlos Lyra, Roberto Menescal, Milton Banana, Sérgio Mendes, and Luiz Bonfá following in his footsteps. The new sound of the bossa nova, with its smooth progression of guitar chords and the bossa beat of the snare drum, captivated the Carioca. They frequented the clubs in the "Beco das Garrafas", which derived its name—Bottle Lane—from the bottles thrown down by irate residents onto the noisy throng below. While the musicians were renowned for their flamboyant playing, their remuneration was meager. Sérgio Mendes, then 20 years old,

Die kosmopolitische Praça Onze, ein lebendiger, zentraler Platz mit vielen Bars und Läden, musste weichen. Hier hatten sich Mulatten aus Bahia niedergelassen, Portugiesen, Spanier, Italiener und Juden. Heute erinnert nur noch der Name einer Metrostation an die Praça Onze. Der Platz und seine Geschichten ruhen irgendwo unter dem Stau auf der vielspurigen Avenida Presidente Vargas. Eine der hässlichsten Gegenden Rios. Das kritisierte auch schon Stefan Zweig: »Rechts und links stößt sich Rio immer neue Avenuen frei, ganze Häuserblöcke wegfegend, wie eine vorwärtsrasende Lokomotive ein papierenes Blatt.« 1960 rückte Rio de Janeiro als politische Bühne aus dem Fokus. Staatspräsident Juscelino Kubitschek weihte die neue Hauptstadt Brasília ein.

Auch die Wiege des Bossa nova stand in Rio. Bossa nova, wörtlich das »neue Ding« im Sinne von »neuer Trend«, »neue Welle«, war eine musikalische Revolution, die die junge intellektuelle Mittelschicht in ihren Bann zog. Eine Art gezähmter Samba vermischt mit dem Jazz, der von den USA herüberschwappte. João Gilbertos Aufnahme von *Chega de Saudade* (*Schluss mit dem sehnsüchtigen Verlangen*) machte den Anfang. Gilberto galt bald als die führende Figur des Bossa nova. Und mit ihm Tom Jobim, Carlos Lyra, Roberto Menescal, Milton Banana, Sérgio Mendes und Luiz Bonfá. Der Bossa nova, dessen Charme die durchgängig gespielten Akkorde der Gitarre mit dem Bossa-Schlag der Snare Drum ausmachten, faszinierte die Menschen. Man traf sich in einem der Clubs im »Beco das Garrafas«, der »Flaschengasse«. Die fielen von oben aus den Fenstern

Early morning visitors and late night guests on Copacabana beach
Frühe Besucher und späte Gäste am Strand von Copacabana

counted himself lucky to earn a glass of whiskey for a performance. Years later, a rap version of his hit "Mas que nada", recorded together with the Black Eyed Peas, would become a hit around the world.

Cultural and musical hubs like these still exist to this day in Rio de Janeiro. The Bip-Bip, for example, is a small bar tucked away behind the beach promenade in Copacabana. Although at first glance just a narrow, neon-lit room with a single long table, its walls testify to its cult status. Framed photographs and newspaper articles show stars from the samba scene and prominent politicians in the company of Alfredinho, the owner of the bar. Aside from the flamboyant eroticism that engulfs the city during the carnival, it is in places like these that samba brings together black and white, and rich and poor. Originally brought to Brazil by African slaves, the fast-paced two-four beat from the black communities of Salvador spread throughout Brazil and to this day remains *the* aesthetic expression of its Afro-Brazilian identity. Rio's innumerable samba schools also provide an opportunity for the poor to don a lavish costume and take part in the carnival and the samba parade in the 700-meter-long arena of the Sambódromo, which holds up to 60,000 spectators. Also designed by Oscar Niemeyer, this palace for the carnival parade has hosted the annual competition of the samba schools since 1984, with sometimes up to 6,000 dancers, flagbearers and drummers in each school parading their elaborately decorated and allegorical floats. The Sambódromo will also host the opening ceremony and parade of the athletes for the Olympic Games in 2016.

auf die lärmenden Gäste. Die Musiker traten mit grandioser Geste auf, doch reich wurden sie mit ihrer Kunst nicht. Der damals 20-jährige Sérgio Mendes bekam höchstens ein Glas Whisky für einen Auftritt, wie Dawid D. Bartelt in seinem schönen Buch *Copacabana* beschreibt. Viel später wurde die Rap-Version seines Hits *Mas que nada*, die er mit den Black Eyed Peas aufnahm, ein Welterfolg.

Solche Kultorte der Musik gibt es bis heute in Rio de Janeiro. Etwa das Bip-Bip. Die kleine Bar liegt versteckt hinter der Strandpromenade in Copacabana. Ein schmaler, neonbeleuchteter Raum, in dem ein einziger langer Tisch steht. Doch die Wände erzählen vom Kult um diesen Ort. Gerahmte Fotografien und Zeitungsartikel, die die Stars der Sambaszene und hochrangige Politiker mit Alfredinho, dem Chef der Bar zeigen. Jenseits der schrillen Erotik, die während des Karnevals die Stadt vereinnahmt, verbindet an Orten wie diesem der Samba Schwarz und Weiß, Arm und Reich. Von den afrikanischen Sklaven importiert, nahm der schnelle Zweivierteltakt vom schwarzen Salvador aus ganz Brasilien für sich ein und ist bis heute ästhetischer Ausdruck seiner afro-brasilianischen Identität. Die zahllosen Sambaschulen Rios verhelfen auch den Armen zu einem der prächtigen Kostüme für die Show im Karneval und zu einem Auftritt in der 700 Meter langen Arena des Sambódromo, wo bis zu 60.000 Zuschauer Platz finden. Auch diesen Palast der Karnevalsparaden hat Oscar Niemeyer entworfen. Seit 1984 findet hier jedes Jahr der Wettstreit der Sambaschulen statt, mit bis zu 6000 Tänzerinnen und Tänzern, Fahnenträgern und Trommlern pro

In the mid-twentieth century, Brazil's cities underwent a process of rapid modernization, industrialization, urbanization and proletarianization. Over a period of just two to three decades, they transformed vastly, in turn creating extreme social divisions that have given rise to recurring public protests, most recently in 2013. Rio has more favela-dwellers than any other city in Brazil: every fifth Carioca lives "in the hills", as the more than 1,000 slum districts are euphemistically known. But since the UPP, the Police Pacification Unit, has started to wrest back control of some of the territories from the hands of drug traffickers, life has become more peaceful. Small hotels, shops and bars have started to appear, such as The Maze, a trendsetting jazz club in the heart of a favela. Club-goers can now safely make their way up the hill via a narrow path and are rewarded by a breathtaking view. Above them, the distinctive peaks of the Dois Irmãos (Two Brothers) surrounded by the tropical rainforest of the Floresta da Tijuca invite them to venture further. Nevertheless, the favelas still lack many public facilities such as medical centers, schools and sewage infrastructure. And it is unlikely that the drug bosses will be so easily defeated—the fear is that they will simply resurface elsewhere.

Schule und ihren kunstvollen allegorischen Festwagen. Bei den Olympischen Spielen 2016 werden im Sambódromo die Athleten einmarschieren.

Brasiliens Städte durchliefen wie im Zeitraffer einen Prozess der Modernisierung, der Industrialisierung, Urbanisierung und Proletarisierung. In zwei, drei Dekaden vollzogen sich enorme Umwälzungen. Die Folge ist eine extrem gespaltene Gesellschaft. Nicht zuletzt deswegen gingen die Bürger 2013 immer wieder auf die Straße. In keiner anderen Stadt Brasiliens leben mehr Menschen in Favelas als in Rio de Janeiro: Jeder fünfte Carioca lebt »auf dem Hügel«, also in einem der mehr als 1000 Armenviertel. Doch seitdem die UPP, die »Befriedungseinheit« der Polizei, einige Viertel besetzt und die Macht der Drogenbosse gebrochen hat, ist das Leben friedlicher geworden. Vielerorts entstanden kleine Hotels, Läden und Bars. Wie das The Maze, ein angesagter Jazzclub mitten in einer Favela. Auf schmalem Pfad pilgern die Gäste furchtlos den Hügel hinauf. Der Weg lohnt sich, denn die Aussicht ist atemberaubend. Weiter oben locken die Gipfel der markanten Felsen Dois Irmãos, umgeben vom tropischen Regenwald, der Floresta da Tijuca. Doch in den Favelas fehlen noch immer Krankenstationen, Schulen und Abwasseranlagen. Man befürchtet, dass sich die gefährlichen Drogenbosse nicht geschlagen geben, sondern nur weiterziehen.

The favelas have spread to cover entire hillside areas of Rio.
Die Favelas breiten sich an den Berghängen Rios immer weiter aus.

Over time the favelas have become more permanent, with more durable houses and the introduction of infrastructure.
Mit der Zeit verfestigen sich die Favelas, solidere Häuser entstehen und Infrastruktur entwickelt sich.

Falk Jaeger

The Legend Lives On!

The Second Flowering of the Estádio Maracanã in Rio de Janeiro

Die Legende lebt!

Das Estádio do Maracanã in Rio de Janeiro erlebt seinen zweiten Frühling.

In the heart of the city lies the Estádio Municipal do Maracanã, although everyone knows it simply as Maracanã despite the fact that since 1966 it officially goes by the name of Estádio Jornalista Mário Filho. Named after the journalist who lobbied for the stadium to be built at Maracanã, it was erected to host the World Cup in 1950 and was the largest stadium in the world with a capacity of 200,000 spectators. This is, however, not the only reason for its fame. Its mythical status can be attributed both to the legendary matches and players that it has hosted—Pelé scored his first goal for the nation here and, years later, his thousandth goal as a professional player—as well as to some of the most traumatic moments in Brazilian football it has witnessed: on July 16, 1950, almost a tenth of Rio's population was in the Maracanã and broke down in tears as Brazil lost the World Cup final 1:2 to Uruguay.

Over the years it has cemented its mythical status hosting legendary rock concerts as well as the two largest masses ever held on the American continent on the occasion of Pope John Paul II's two visits in 1980 and 1997. A year later, the arena was listed as a national monument. Today, it remains one of the largest stadia in the world, even after several adaptations and its eventual conversion to an all-seater stadium for safety reasons successively reduced its capacity to 82,000.

But the concrete structure was showing its age and needed comprehensive renovation in order to be brought up to FIFA standards for the World Cup in 2014. The upper spectator tier was renewed and the lower tier completely rebuilt

Es liegt mitten im Stadtgebiet, das Estádio Municipal do Maracanã, das jedermann in Brasilien nur Maracanã nennt, obwohl es seit 1966 offiziell als Estádio Jornalista Mário Filho firmiert. Benannt wurde es nach einem Journalisten, der sich um seinen Bau verdient gemacht hatte. Für die Fußballweltmeisterschaft 1950 errichtet, hatte es damals ein Fassungsvermögen von mehr als 200.000 Zuschauern und galt als größtes Stadion der Welt. Nicht nur dieser Umstand machte die Arena berühmt, auch zahlreiche legendäre Spiele und Spieler (Pelé schoss hier sein erstes Länderspieltor und, Jahre später, sein tausendstes Tor als Profi) trugen zum Mythos bei, aber vielleicht auch das noch immer nicht überwundene Trauma: Jeder zehnte Einwohner Rios war am 16. Juli 1950 im Maracanã und brach in Tränen aus, als Brasilien das WM-Endspiel gegen Uruguay 1:2 verlor.

Der Mythos lebte weiter, auch durch legendäre Rockkonzerte und die beiden größten Messen auf amerikanischem Boden mit Papst Johannes Paul II. 1980 und 1997. Im Jahr darauf wurde das Bauwerk unter Denkmalschutz gestellt. Eines der weltgrößten Stadien blieb es auch nach einigen Umbauten und sicherheitsbedingten Neuordnungen der Zuschauerränge, die die Abschaffung der Stehplätze und Reduktionen auf zuletzt 82.000 Zuschauer mit sich brachten.

Doch der Betonbau war in die Jahre gekommen und sollte zur WM 2014 grundlegend saniert und auf FIFA-Standard gebracht werden. Der Oberrang wurde erneuert und der Unterrang mit besseren Sichtverhältnissen völlig neu

Testing the assembly of the hollow-section profiles of the compression ring in the workshop

Probemontage der Hohlkastenprofile des Druckrings in der Stahlbauwerkstatt

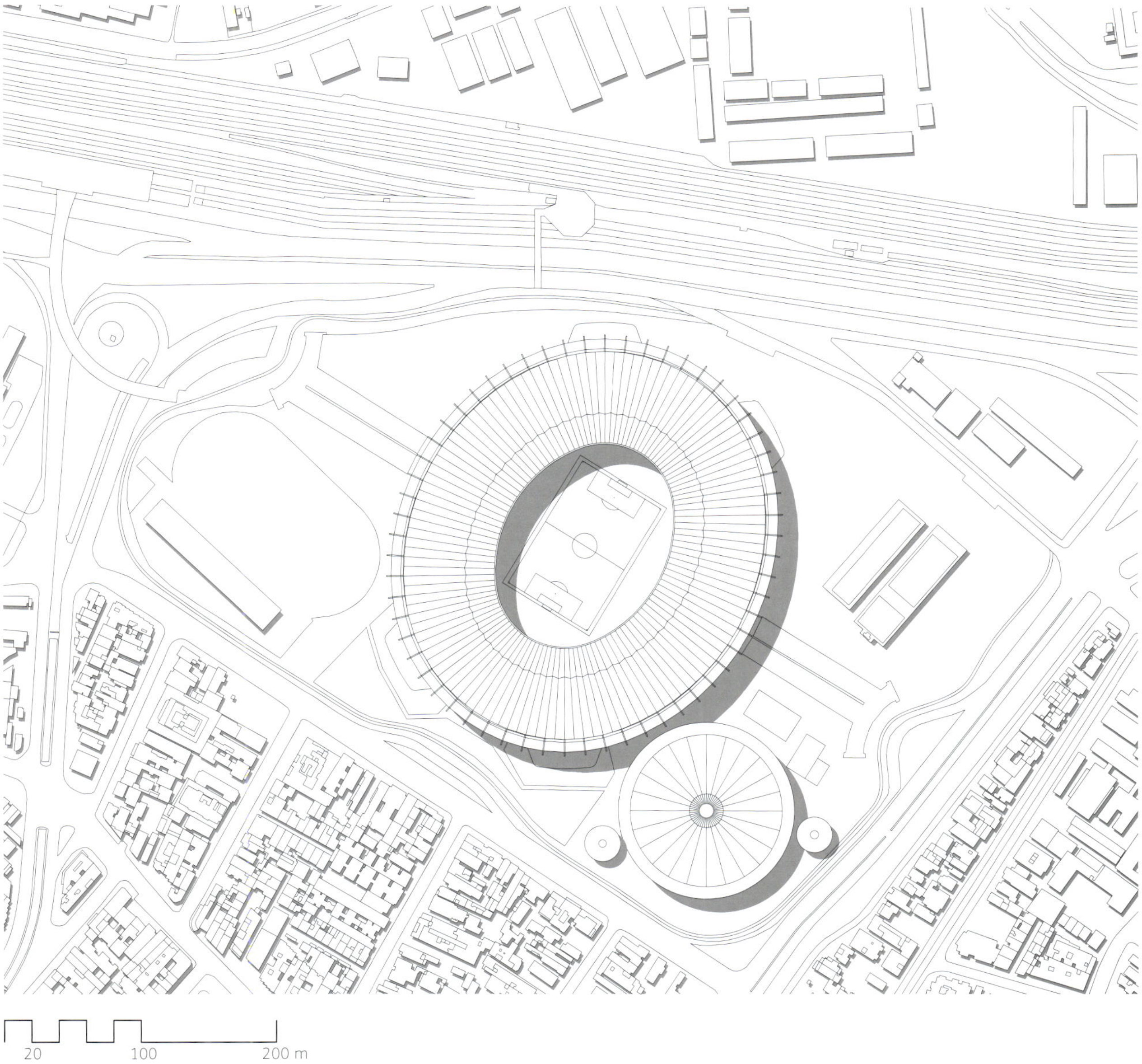

Removal of the former concrete roof construction leaving only the supports standing

Abbau der historischen Betondachkonstruktion bis auf die Stützenköpfe

with improved sight lines. The main problem, however, was the roof: a concrete construction that cantilevered forward just enough to cover 45 percent of the seats.

At first, the planners pursued the strategy used so successfully in Belo Horizonte—namely to preserve the external appearance of the building by extending the existing roof coverage inwards, retaining the existing roof construction. But the existing concrete cantilevers, now more than half a century old, could neither be strengthened nor were they capable of supporting the roof in the existing constellation. It was not possible to add a new roof structure above the existing structure, and it would also not have been a viable option, as it would have altered the stadium's appearance.

The engineers at schlaich bergermann und partner finally developed a roof construction that was so flat that it could be inserted into the historical construction without altering its iconic silhouette. The approach applies a new variant of the spoke-wheel principle that minimizes the overall construction height, employing a compression ring around the perimeter, an inner tension ring and a radial connecting cables as the spokes. And because the majority of the structural members are under tension, the resulting structure is delicate and sparing in its use of materials.

After removal of the cantilever arms, all that remained was the concrete supports of the main building and the façade and a continuous ring beam at eaves level, all of which underwent extensive repair works. The sixty columns of the existing structure correspond to the sixty segments of the roof, while the spoke-wheel roof lies like a rigid lid, the

gebaut. Ein Hauptanliegen dabei: Das Stadiondach, eine Betonkragkonstruktion, hatte eine zu geringe Dachtiefe und überdeckte nur 45 Prozent der Zuschauerplätze.

Was in Belo Horizonte gelang, versuchte man zunächst auch am Maracanã, nämlich die äußere Erscheinung des Bauwerks unverfälscht zu erhalten, indem man die Dachfläche nach innen unter Beibehaltung der bestehenden Dachkonstruktion vergrößert. Doch die mehr als ein halbes Jahrhundert alten Betonkragträger konnten weder ertüchtigt werden noch waren sie in der bestehenden Konfiguration länger tragfähig. Und so schied eine oben aufgesetzte zusätzliche Tragstruktur nicht nur aus, weil sie das Erscheinungsbild des Stadions nachhaltig verändert hätte.

Schließlich entwickelten die Ingenieure von schlaich bergermann und partner eine Dachkonstruktion, die sich in den historischen Bestand so flach einfügt, dass sie die berühmte Silhouette nicht verändert. Sie bedienten sich des mittlerweile erprobten Speichenradprinzips in einer neuen Komposition, die mit wenig Konstruktionshöhe auskommt, mit äußerem Druckring, innerem Zugring und verbindenden »Speichen« in Form von Radialseilen. Und weil die auf Zug belasteten Bauteile des Seiltragwerks überwiegen, fällt es sehr filigran und materialsparend aus.

Nach dem Abschneiden der Kragträger blieben die Gebäude- und Fassadenstützen sowie ein umlaufender Ringbalken in Traufhöhe bestehen und wurden betonsaniert. Diese Gliederung wurde vom neuen Dach übernommen. Den 60 historischen Stützen entsprechen die 60 Dachfel-

one-by-two-meter cross-section hollow beam of the compression ring resting on the tops of the sixty columns, fifty-two of which do not produce transverse forces. Horizontal forces resulting from wind loads are dissipated only via four pairs of diagonally arranged tangential anchor points.

The stability of the cable-net roof and the overall stiffness of the roof system is achieved by employing flying struts to hold apart the array of cables about two-thirds of the way into the roof, creating flattened kite-shaped cable trusses with one compression ring and three tension rings at its corners. The tops of the flying struts are also the highest points of the roof, which is covered by a teflon-coated fiberglass membrane. The snow-white membrane spans between the radial cables and is held down by additional valley-cables between each pair which also lend the roof surface the necessary double curvature that gives the roof its stiffness. Seen from above (for example from the viewing platform at Cristo Redentor), the alternating high and low points of the roof give it the impression of having been neatly folded.

Resting on the six cables of the lower tension ring are 13.5-meter-high flying struts, their hollow steel profiles parting in the middle to form a diamond-shape through which the catwalk passes. This circumferential maintenance gangway serves as a rail from which all the technical installations in the roof are neatly hung and easily reached for maintenance purposes. It holds the floodlights, stand lighting and sound system as well as 14 goal-line control cameras made by the German firm GoalControl Systems. A second ring of floodlights is suspended directly beneath the inner edge of

der. Wie ein in sich stabiler Deckel liegt die Speichenradkonstruktion mit dem im Querschnitt rund 1 mal 2 Meter messenden stählernen Hohlkastenprofil des Druckrings auf den 60 Stützenköpfen, 52 Mal, ohne Querkräfte einzubringen. An viermal zwei ausgewählten, diagonal positionierten tangentialen Festpunkten werden die Horizontalkräfte abgetragen, die sich lediglich bei Windbelastung ergeben.

Die Stabilität des Seildaches und die Steifigkeit des Dachkörpers werden dadurch erreicht, dass die Radialseile nach zwei Dritteln Dachtiefe von Luftstützen auseinandergespreizt werden und dadurch Seilbinder mit drachenförmigem Querschnitt mit einem äußeren Druckring und drei inneren Zugringen an den Eckpunkten entstehen. Die Luftstützen bilden gleichzeitig die Hochpunkte der Bespannung des Dachs mit teflonbeschichtetem Glasfasergewebe. Die schneeweiße Membran wird über die Radialseile gespannt und zur Erreichung der für die Stabilität notwendigen zweiachsigen Krümmung durch Kehlseile in den Zwischenfeldern nach unten gezogen. So ergibt sich zwischen den Hoch- und Tiefpunkten ein auch in der Dachaufsicht (beispielsweise vom Aussichtspunkt Cristo Redentor aus) optisch reizvolles Faltwerk.

Die auf dem unteren, aus sechs Seilen bestehenden Zugband stehenden, 13,5 Meter hohen Luftstützen aus Hohlkastenprofilen sind rautenförmig aufgespreizt und nehmen den Catwalk auf. In dem rings umlaufenden Wartungsgang ist die gesamte Installation des Daches ästhetisch und wartungsfreundlich untergebracht. Der Laufsteg

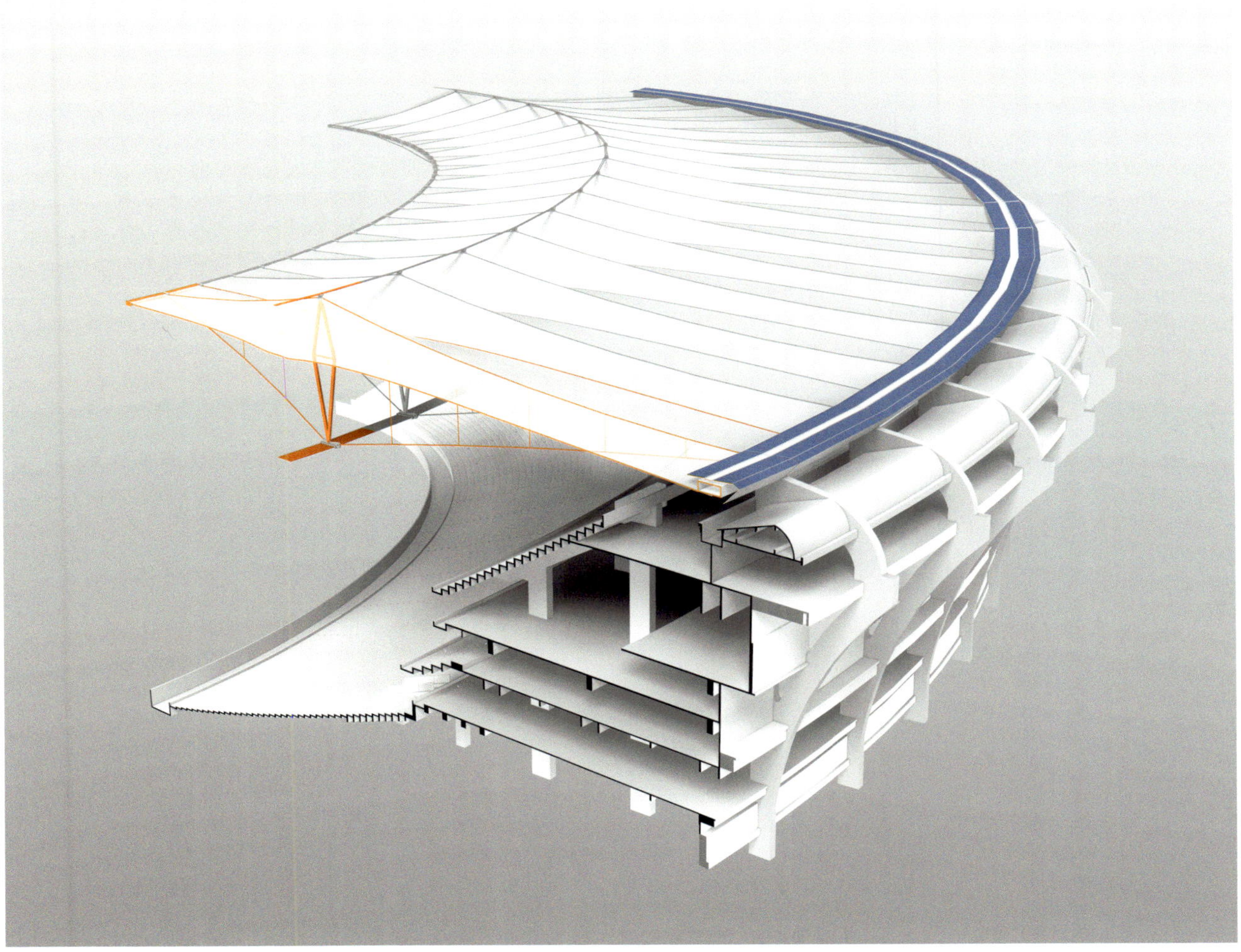

The new seating tiers have been erected on the original supports of the upper tier.
Auf der bestehenden Unterkonstruktion des Oberrangs werden die neuen Tribünenstufen aufgebaut.

Section through the converted seating tiers and the new roof construction
Schnitt durch die umgebaute Tribüne und das neue Dachtragwerk

the roof. The low profile of the roof, which resulted from the need to preserve the silhouette of the existing building, made it necessary to illuminate the pitch from two positions to avoid glare.

The roof extends evenly 68 meters from all sides into the oval of the stadium leaving an opening measuring 160 by 122 meters in the center. Weighing a total of approximately 4,000 tons, equivalent to 90 kilograms per square meter, it is an extremely lightweight and graceful construction that appears to float over the stadium, held just by the points at the perimeter, an impression heightened by its translucent skin during the day and lighting effects at night.

While many a football fan feared that the start of building works on their beloved Maracanã signaled the end of a myth, the final result will appease their concerns: the functional and aesthetic gain of the new snow-white roof of the national monument in no way detracts from its legendary aura. The myth lives on, and if this time around it proves possible to avoid the curse of 1950, then the new Maracanã will be at least as legendary as its previous incarnation.

trägt Ausrüstungen wie Flutlicht, Tribünenbeleuchtung und Lautsprecher, aber auch die 14 Torlinienkameras des deutschen GoalControl-Systems. Ein zweiter Flutlichtring befindet sich direkt über dem inneren Dachrand. Das den Randbedingungen des Bestands geschuldete niedrige Profil des Daches erfordert diese zweite Flutlichtposition, um eine blendfreie Beleuchtung des Spielfeldes zu erreichen.

68 Meter spannt das Dach gleichmäßig über das gesamte Oval des Stadions nach innen und lässt eine Öffnung von 160 mal 122 Meter frei. Mit rund 4000 Tonnen Gesamtgewicht, das heißt 90 Kilogramm pro Quadratmeter Flächengewicht, ist eine extrem leichte Konstruktion entstanden, die luftig und aufgrund der kleinen Auflagepunkte fast schwebend wirkt, ein Eindruck, der durch die Transluzenz am Tag und die Effektbeleuchtung am Abend noch verstärkt wird.

Manch eingefleischter Fußballfan hatte zu Beginn der Bauarbeiten schon dem vergangenen Mythos des vertrauten Maracanã nachgetrauert. Nach der Fertigstellung wird er feststellen können: Der funktionale und ästhetische Zugewinn mit dem schneeweißen Dach hat dem legendären Baudenkmal sicher keinen Abbruch getan. Der Mythos lebt, und wenn nun auch noch der Fluch von 1950 besiegt werden kann, dann wird das neue Maracanã so legendär wie das alte!

The view of the legendary Maracanã as seen from the street has changed very little.
Vom Straßenniveau aus gesehen hat sich das Bild des legendären Maracanã kaum verändert.

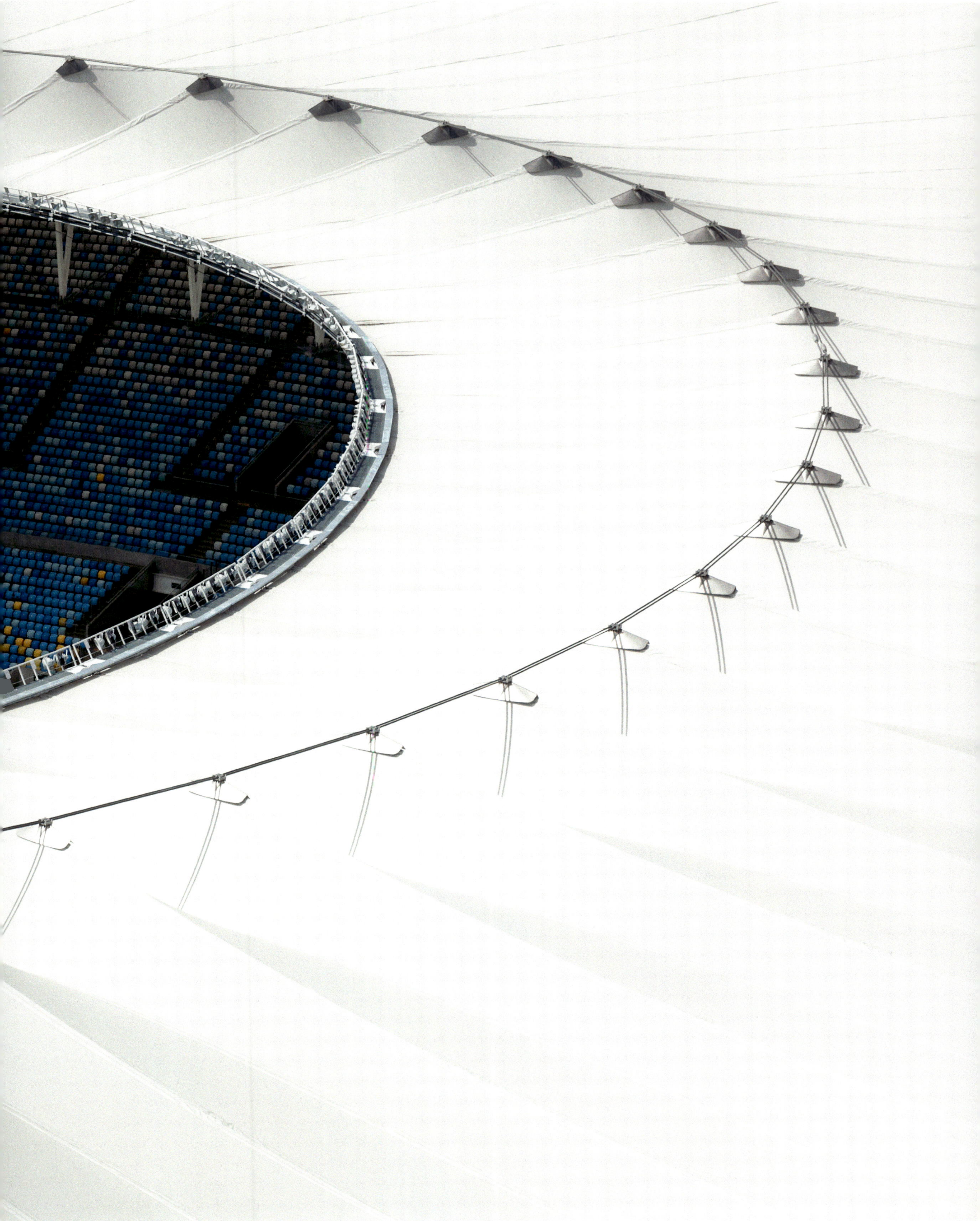

Diamond-shaped flying struts stand on the lower tension ring and hold the upper and lower radial cables apart. The catwalk, from which the loudspeakers and floodlighting are suspended, is threaded through them.
Rautenförmige Luftstützen stehen auf dem unteren Zugring und spreizen untere und obere Radialseile auseinander. Gleichzeitig tragen sie den Catwalk mit den Lautsprechern und Scheinwerfern.

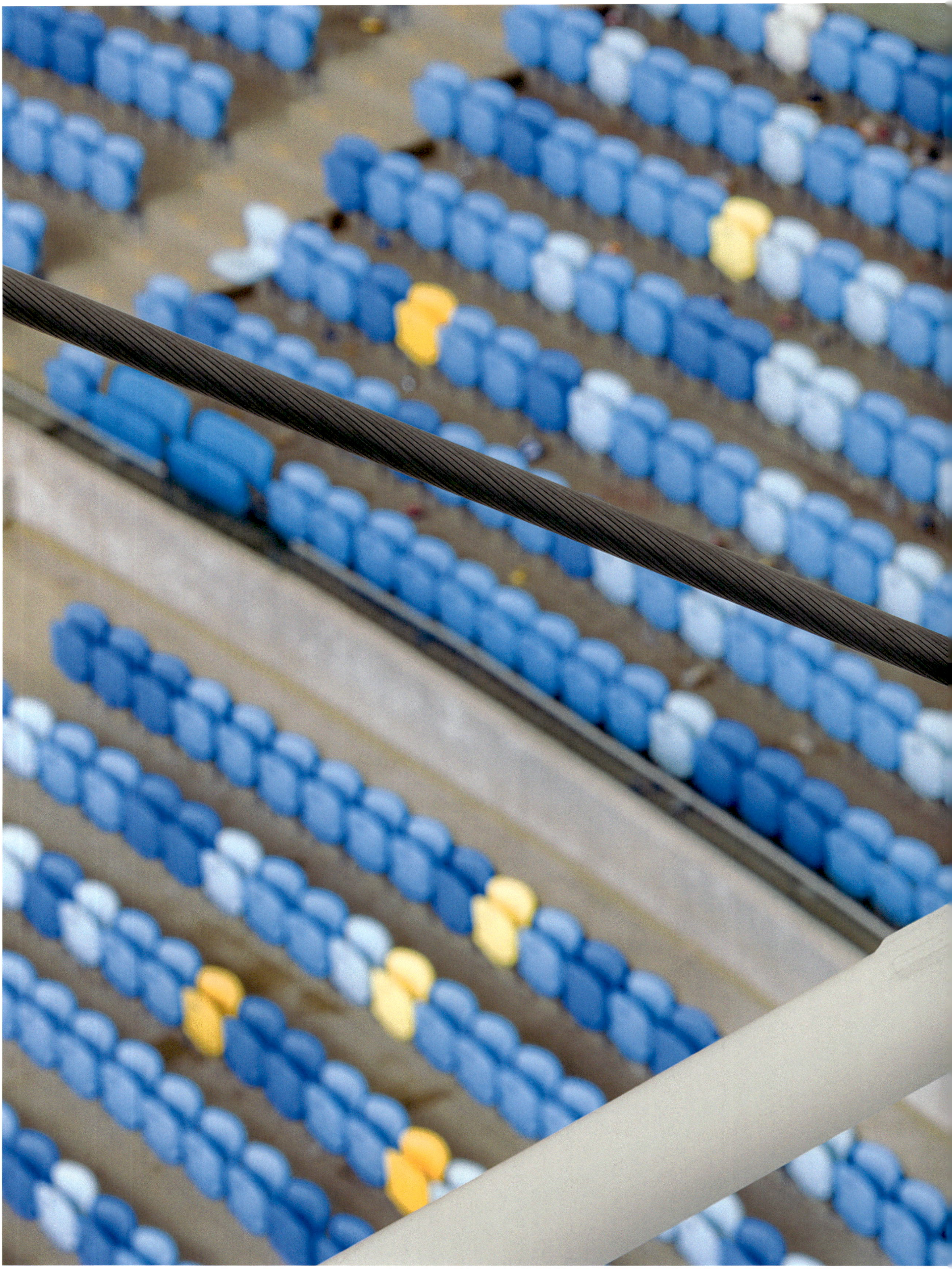

Previous page: The suspension cables and compression members are attached via articulated connections to clamps on the radial cables.
Vorige Seite: Hängeseil und Druckstab sind gelenkig an die Seilklemmen des Radialseils angeschlossen.

The roof membrane is held taught by an alternating series of ridge and valley cables that lend it three-dimensional stability.
Die Dachmembran wird zwischen die im Wechsel angeordneten Grat- und Kahlseile gespannt und erhält dadurch ihre stabile, räumliche Form.

E
E
E
E

E
E

Belo Horizonte

Carl D. Goerdeler

A Heart of Gold and Breast of Iron

Belo Horizonte—City of Mines and Mineiros

Herz aus Gold und Panzer aus Eisen

Belo Horizonte, die Stadt der Minen und der Mineiros

Every city has its own particular smell: in Rio de Janeiro, for example, it is the sweet patchouli scent of ripe fruit; in São Paolo, a stifling fog of nitrogen oxide. In Belo Horizonte, the third-largest metropolis in Brazil with six million inhabitants, one can smell an aroma not unlike that of roasting coffee, although this is often obscured by the smell of smoldering charcoal and the acrid fumes of hot brake discs.

One hundred years ago, the breeze in the mountains of the Serra do Curral bore the scent of country air infused with the stench of cow dung. It was here that herds of cattle stopped to graze and drink before the caravans pushed on towards the coast. And it was here that the stroke of a pen marked the position of a city 850 meters above sea level that was given the name Belo Horizonte ("Beautiful Horizon") because of the then unobstructed view over the hills of Minas Gerais.

Belo Horizonte was the first newly-planned capital city to be built in Brazil and was founded in 1897/98 because the dignitaries of the province of Minas Gerais ("General mines") felt that the then capital of the province, Vila Rica d'Ouro Preto ("Wealthy Village of Black Gold"), had become too constricting. And besides, the time had come to create a new capital worthy of the new state.

In nearby Ouro Preto, every cobblestone is a reminder of the yoke of colonialism, of the slave workers in the gold mines and, of course, of the "tooth puller" ("Tiradentes") Joaquim Jose da Silva Xavier, who in 1789, inspired by the revolutions in France and North America, unsuccessfully attempted to incite a revolt against the rulers in Lisbon.

Städte haben ihre eigene Duftnote: Rio de Janeiro zum Beispiel trägt das süßliche Patschuli vergorener Früchte und São Paulo durchdringt der atemraubende Nebel von Stickoxiden. Belo Horizonte aber, mit rund sechs Millionen Einwohnern die drittgrößte brasilianische Metropole, verströmt ein Aroma, das hin und wieder nach gebranntem Kaffee duftet, was aber meistens vom Schwelbrand der Holzkohle und dem beißenden Dunst heißgelaufener Bremsbeläge überlagert wird.

Vor 100 Jahren wehte dort in den Bergen der Serra de Curral gesunde Landluft, in die sich der strenge Geruch von Kuhdung mischte. Der Flecken war eine Sammelstelle, an der die Rinder zu fressen und zu saufen bekamen, bevor die Karawanen gestärkt zur Küste weiterziehen konnten. An dieser Stelle entstand auf 850 Metern Höhe über dem Meeresspiegel per Federstrich die Stadt, die den Namen Belo Horizonte – Schöne Aussicht – erhielt, denn der weite Blick über das Bergland von Minas Gerais war damals noch nicht verbaut.

Belo Horizonte, die erste Reißbrett-Hauptstadt Brasiliens, wurde 1897/98 errichtet, weil den Honoratioren der Provinz Minas Gerais (»Allgemeine Minen«) die Provinzialhauptstadt Vila Rica d'Ouro Preto (»Reiches Dorf des Schwarzen Goldes«) zu eng geworden war. Und außerdem: War es nicht an der Zeit, der jungen Republik und dem Fortschritt ein Denkmal zu setzen?

Im nahe gelegenen Ouro Preto erinnert bis heute jeder Pflasterstein an die Zeit des kolonialen Jochs, an die Sklaverei in den Goldminen, aber natürlich auch an den

In Belo Horizonte, those buildings that can't claim to be designed by Niemeyer are instead decorated with Niemeyer.
Was in Belo Horizonte nicht von Niemeyer stammt, wird mit Niemeyer geschmückt

Oscar Niemeyer's Casino on the banks of Lagao da Pampulha is now an art gallery.
Oscar Niemeyers Casino am Pampulha-See ist heute Kunstmuseum.

The people of Minas Gerais are to this day proud of their heritage as the birthplace of the rebellion and of freemasonry. But as the Portuguese King's son assumed a leading role in the independence movement, eventually proclaiming himself Emperor of Brazil, the people of Minas remained skeptical. Only after ambitious generals ousted Emperor Pedro II of Brazil from Rio de Janeiro and proclaimed the Republic of the United States of Brazil in 1889 did they feel the time was right to establish a new state capital.

The motto "Order and Progress" is inscribed into the flag of Brazil and derives from the national philosophy of the French Enlightenment which inspired the founding of the republic—and also the planning of Belo Horizonte. The engineer Aarão Reis was entrusted with the task of designing a city for 200,000 inhabitants. Disregarding the hilly topography of the site, he laid out coordinates for the city, driven by the conviction that technology would triumph over nature.

The plan for the city of Belo Horizonte follows the pattern of the British flag—the streets intersect perpendicularly and are twenty meters wide, while the thirty-meter-wide Avenidas run diagonally, meeting at the center where the palace of the state government was located. The arrangement of the curbstones therefore followed the principles of rationalism and centralism, regardless of how impractical this was. The first cars arrived some ten years after the laying of the foundation stone, but by then the straight roads had already demonstrated their unsuitability, regularly turning into torrential streams whenever there were strong rains, which occurs frequently in the Serra.

»Zahnzieher« (»Tiradentes«) Joaquim Jose da Silva Xavier, der 1789, wohl beeinflusst von nordamerikanischen und französischen Revolutionären, vergeblich einen Aufstand gegen die Krone in Lissabon angezettelt hatte.

In Minas Gerais ist man bis auf den heutigen Tag stolz darauf, die Wiege der Rebellion und der Freimaurergeheimbünde gewesen zu sein. Doch als sich der Sohn des portugiesischen Königs an die Spitze der Bewegung zur Unabhängigkeit vom Mutterland setzte und sich schließlich zum Kaiser von Brasilien ausrufen ließ, blieb man in Minas misstrauisch. Erst als ehrgeizige Generäle den Kaiser Pedro II. 1889 aus Rio de Janeiro vertrieben hatten und die Republik, die Vereinigten Staaten von Brasilien, ausriefen, hielt man die Zeit für reif, die heimatliche Provinz mit einer neuen Hauptstadt zu schmücken.

»Ordnung und Fortschritt«, dieser Spruch ist in die Fahne Brasiliens gestickt. Die Staatsphilosophie der französischen Aufklärung stand Pate bei der Geburt der brasilianischen Republik – und ebenso bei der Planung von Belo Horizonte. Dem Ingenieur Aarão Reis wurde die Aufgabe zuteil, eine Hauptstadt für 200.000 Bewohner zu entwerfen. Unbeeindruckt von der hügeligen Topografie des Ortes legte er die Koordinaten fest, schließlich galt es, die Natur durch Technik zu beherrschen.

Der Stadtplan von Belo Horizonte gleicht der britischen Flagge – die Straßen, jede 20 Meter breit, schneiden sich rechtwinklig, die 30 Meter breiten Avenidas aber verlaufen im schrägen Winkel dazu und treffen sich im Brennpunkt, dem Regierungspalast. Rationalismus und Zentra-

In Belo Horizonte, there was enough money to build palaces in the new Parisian style, such as the Palácio de Liberdade, the seat of the local governor, in the center of the city. The money for these buildings did not come from the gold and diamond mines, coffee plantations, or dairy and livestock farming, but from the smelting of iron ore, which was abundantly available just beneath the surface of the hills.

Wilhelm Ludwig von Eschwege, the Prussian geologist and cartographer, had already begun researching the abundance of ore deposits in Minas Gerais in the eighteen-thirties and constructed the first smelteries and forges on behalf of the Brazilian Emperor. Charcoal was not available for smelting, so entire swathes of forests were cut down to produce the necessary fuel. This technique is still used today, except that the jungle no longer exists; in its place, acre after acre of eucalyptus plantations now serve as a raw material for coking.

The smoke produced by the charcoal burners' earthen ovens settled as a veil of acrid fumes over the land, coloring the skin and making the *Mineiros*, as the locals are known, immune to frivolity or overstatement. It has been said of the Mineiros that they have a heart of gold and a breast of iron. The popular stereotype propagated by their contemporaries is that they are tight-fisted and wary: as the saying goes, why else would they have drawers built into their tables if not to hide the food should an unexpected visitor knock at the door? Likewise, the seriously-minded Mineiros are anything but frivolous, and the carnival in Minas Gerais lacks the exuberance and fervor of its counterparts elsewhere in Brazil.

lismus bestimmten den Verlauf der Bordsteinkanten, ob das nun praktisch war oder nicht. Das erste Auto tauchte schließlich erst zehn Jahre nach der Grundsteinlegung auf. Allerdings machten schon damals die Regengüsse zu schaffen, die in der Serra reichlich fallen und die schnurgeraden Straßen regelmäßig in Sturzbäche verwandeln.

In Belo Horizonte konnte man sich Paläste leisten, die den neuesten Pariser Stil kopierten, wie etwa den Palacio da Liberdade, den Sitz des Gouverneurs im Zentrum. Das Geld für solche Bauten stammte nicht mehr aus den Gold- und Diamantenminen, den Kaffeeplantagen oder der Milch- und Fleischwirtschaft, sondern aus der Verhüttung der Eisenerze, die, wenn man nur ein wenig am Boden kratzte, reichlich zutage traten.

Wilhelm Ludwig von Eschwege, der preußische Geologe und Kartograf, hatte bereits in den Dreißigerjahren des 19. Jahrhunderts die Erzlager in Minas Gerais erforscht und im Auftrag des brasilianischen Kaisers die ersten Schmelzen und Schmieden errichtet. Steinkohle zur Verhüttung gab es weit und breit nicht, also schlug man den Wald nieder und verkohlte das Holz. Bei dieser Technik ist es bis heute geblieben – bloß dass der Urwald längst abgeholzt ist und nun monotone Eukalyptusplantagen den Rohstoff zur Verkokung liefern.

Der beißende Qualm, den die Lehmöfen der Köhler ausspucken, legt sich wie ein bitterer Schleier über das Land, er gerbt die Haut und macht die Mineiros (die Bewohner der Provinz) immun gegen Leichtlebigkeit und Prahlerei. Die Mineiros haben ein Herz aus Gold und darü-

Oscar Niemeyer's São Francisco de Assis church also stands on the banks of Lagao da Pampulha.

Oscar Niemeyers Kirche São Francisco de Assis am Pampulha-See

The Governor's Palácio da Liberdade

Der Gouverneurspalast Palácio da Liberdade

As unpretentious as the people in Belo Horizonte are, so too is its traditional fare. Fatty sausages and blood pudding, stewed cabbage, polenta and pork ribs cooked in iron pots and skillets over an open fire are what warm the heart of a Mineiro. To make the heavy meal more palatable, it is washed down with a generous swig of Cachaça, a spirit distilled from sugarcane juice. While many different varieties are on sale—some say as many as 200 different blends—true aficionados care not, as almost everyone knows a farmer who makes their own blend on the side.

Oh Cachaça! In Rio, it is drunk as Caipirinha, watered down with ice and squeezed lemon. Not so in "Belo" as the ever-economical Mineiros call their city. Here they drink it neat and unchilled, the triangle of liquid in the tilted glass echoing Belo's diagonal corners, its surface forming a "beautiful horizon".

During the week, the "beautiful horizon" of the Avenida Afonso Pena, the main boulevard in the city, is little more than a slow-moving stream of metal, but on Sundays it is taken over by traveling salesmen hawking their wares. Those who escape the labyrinth of special offers and super savings inevitably find themselves in the city's park which with its swans, carousels, and pavilions appears to have been transplanted from a provincial town in France. Belo Horizonte, however, no longer houses the 200,000 inhabitants it was originally planned for, but thirty times that number!

As a consequence, the palace from the founding period made way for tenement blocks. Since then, the tenements have in turn made way for skyscrapers. To begin with, the

ber einen Panzer aus Eisen, heißt es. Sie seien die Schwaben Brasiliens, warnen missgünstige Zeitgenossen, denn warum sonst hätten die roh gezimmerten Tische dort Schubladen? Damit darin das Essen schnell verschwindet, wenn ein ungebetener Gast an die Tür klopft. Frivolität ist das Letzte, was man den ernsten Bewohnern der Region nachsagen kann. Der Karneval wird dort so heftig gefeiert wie etwa in Hannover.

Rustikal wie der Menschenschlag ist die Küche in Belo Horizonte. Fette Blut- und Bratwürste, gedünsteter Kohl, Polenta und Schweinerippen, in eisernen Pfannen und Töpfen und auf dem offenen Feuer geschmort, das erfreut das Herz der Mineiros. Erträglich wird die schwere Last erst durch großzügig bemessene Schlucke von Cachaça, dem Schnaps aus Zuckerrohr. Wie viele handelsübliche Sorten es davon gibt – die Schätzungen gehen bis zu zweihundert – ist für den wahren Freund des Klaren unerheblich, denn jeder kennt einen Bauern, der heimlich brennt.

Oh, Cachaça! In Rio de Janeiro trinkt man ihn verdünnt mit Eis und gequetschten Limonen als Caipirinha. Nicht so in »Belo«, wie die maulfaulen Mineiros ihre Hauptstadt nennen. Hier wird er pur und handwarm gekippt. Und siehe da, die schrägen Ecken Belos strecken sich: schöne Aussicht!

Schöne Aussicht auf die Avenida Afonso Pena, den Boulevard der Metropole – wochentags ein Lavastrom aus Blech, am Sonntag aber eine Meile der fliegenden Händler. Wer diesem Labyrinth der Sonderangebote und der Superschnäppchen entflieht, landet unweigerlich im Stadtpark,

center grew skywards before Belo Horizonte started to expand outwards, spilling into the surrounding hills. Belo Horizonte is like a pizza that has started to bubble: the bubbles and crust that have risen out of the mass of concrete are the better districts—for example, Pope Square (Praça Israel Pinheiro)—from which one can still enjoy the view that gives Belo Horizonte its name.

In the modern age, Belo Horizonte did not expand in the linear fashion that its founders had envisaged. What began as a peaceful town with clean air became a smoky industrial metropolis. Heavy industry, steel works and iron foundries sprung up around Belo Horizonte making extruded pipes, originally for Mannesmann, construction steel for Belgo-Mineira, and cars for Fiat. The people in and around Belo Horizonte work hard and spend little, qualities highly prized by the corporate bosses: "the Mineiros are reliable and hard-working." Instead of whiling away their time on beautiful beaches, they invest their energy in professional and vocational advancement. No other city in Brazil has as many educational institutes per inhabitant as Belo Horizonte.

The province of Minas Gerais covers an area of 588,000 square kilometers, an area larger than the whole of France, and despite its population of just 20 million—many of whom have Italian surnames—Belo Horizonte as the provincial capital sees itself as the "Little Paris" of Brazil. It matters not that it has no Eiffel Tower, as it has the mountains; and it matters not that its own version of the Seine, the Rio Arrudas, has been filled in with concrete: it has the Pampulha.

der mit seinen Schwänen, Karussells und Pavillons so tut, als befände er sich in einer französischen Kleinstadt. Belo Horizonte beherbergt aber inzwischen nicht mehr nur, wie einst geplant, 200.000 Bewohner, sondern dreißigmal so viel!

Die Palais der Gründerjahre mussten den Mietskasernen weichen, die Mietskasernen den Wolkenkratzern. Erst wuchs das Zentrum in die Höhe, dann breitete sich Belo Horizonte aus und überschwemmte die Hügel der Umgebung. Belo Horizonte gleicht einer Pizza, die Blasen schlägt. Auf diesen Blasen oder Krusten, die sich aus der Betonmasse erheben, liegen die besseren Viertel, und nur noch von dort oben, etwa vom »Papst-Platz« (Praça Israel Pinheiro), lässt sich der Blick genießen, den Belo Horizonte im Namen führt.

Die Moderne hat sich nicht so linear entwickelt, wie die Gründer geglaubt hatten. Aus der ruhigen Hauptstadt mit der guten Luft wucherte eine rauchende Industriemetropole. Um Belo Horizonte legten sich die Ketten der Schwerindustrie, der Stahlkocher und Eisengießer. Nahtlose Röhren einst von Mannesmann, Baustahl von Belgo-Mineira, Autos von Fiat: in und um Belo Horizonte wird hart gearbeitet und wenig ausgegeben. »Die Mineiros sind zuverlässig, und sie packen an«, loben die Firmenbosse. Den schönen Künsten sind sie wenig zugeneigt, dem beruflichen Fortkommen umso mehr. Keine andere Stadt Brasiliens verfügt über so viele Bildungsstätten pro Bewohner wie Belo Horizonte.

Die Provinz Minas Gerais ist mit 588.000 Quadratkilometern größer als Frankreich, und wenn in ihr auch nur 20

Musical and culinary hospitality in a leafy restaurant in Belo Horizonte
Gastfreundschaft der Mineiros in einem Laubenrestaurant

The Parque Da Pampulha adjoins an artificial lake and is home to São Francisco de Assis Church, the Yachting Club, and the Pampulha Art Museum (formerly the Pampulha Casino), an ensemble of low pavilions and arcing concrete arches, which sixty years ago caused a scandal that is hard to imagine today. The bishop initially refused to hold mass in the "concrete pipe" of the church and local residents poked fun at the naked architecture devoid of all decorations or comfortable corners. The architecture was the creation of Oscar Niemeyer, who enjoyed the protection of the mayor Juscelino Kubitschek, and was also responsible for designing the Edificio Niemeyer with its elegant flowing forms. Situated in the midst of this aesthetic landscape is the new Estadio Gouvernador Magalhães Pinto. Built, as one would expect of the economical Mineiros, on the foundations of the old arena, it was completed on schedule in February 2013 ready to host the match between the regional archrivals Atlético and Cruzeiro.

Who would have guessed at the time that Pampulha would be a test-run for the "capital city of the third millennium"—for the building of Brasília? Juscelino Kubitschek, then mayor of the city, was elected President of the Republic in 1957 and appointed his friend Oscar Niemeyer to design much of Brasília. The new national capital city was erected in the space of just over three years in the middle of the savannah 700 km north of Belo Horizonte, on a territory that formerly belonged to Minas Gerais. It is designed with the functionality of a motorway interchange and is today a monument to a past future.

Millionen Menschen leben – darunter viele mit italienischen Namen –, so versteht sich die Hauptstadt Belo Horizonte doch als Klein-Paris Brasiliens. Einen Eiffelturm braucht man nicht, dazu hat man die Berge, und die hiesige Seine, den Rio Arrudas, hat man lieber zubetoniert. Dafür zeigt man dem Gast Pampulha.

Im Park von Pampulha liegen an einem künstlichen See die Kirche São Francisco de Assis, der Yachtclub und das Museum für moderne Kunst (das ehemalige Kasino), ein Ensemble flacher Pavillons und schwungvoller Bögen aus Beton, denen heute nicht ohne Weiteres mehr anzusehen ist, warum sie vor 60 Jahren einen Skandal auslösten. Der Bischof wollte in den »Betonröhren« der Kirche keine Messe halten und die Bürger der Stadt belustigten sich über die nackte Architektur ohne Schnörkel und gemütliche Ecken, errichtet von Oscar Niemeyer, der die Protektion des Bürgermeister Juscelino Kubitschek genoss. Aus seiner Feder stammt auch das Edifício Niemeyer mit seinen elegant geschwungenen Formen. Und in dieses von Ästhetik geprägte Umfeld passt das Estadio Gouvernador Magalhães Pinto recht gut. Die sparsamen Mineiros haben es auf den Grundmauern der alten Arena errichtet und pünktlich – so wie sie sind – bereits im Februar 2013 mit dem Anstoß der ewigen regionalen Rivalen Atlético gegen Cruzeiro eröffnet.

Aber wer konnte schon damals ahnen, dass Pampulha nur die Fingerübung für die »Hauptstadt des dritten Jahrtausends«, Brasília nämlich, sein sollte? Juscelino Kubitschek, der Bürgermeister, wurde 1957 zum Präsidenten der

Belo Horizonte, once the dream of the nineteenth century, is now a sprawling conurbation. Ever more new roads, a second airport, and a tramline have been unable to resolve the transportation problems. Progress, it seems, is sometimes a roundabout. At the weekends, the traffic arteries are jammed full of residents leaving Belo Horizonte for Ouro Preto or one of the other Baroque towns nearby where they can breathe fresh mountain air and stroll through the narrow lanes. Or they head sixty kilometers to the Centro de Arte Contemporânea Inhotim, a tropical mecca for artists around the world founded by the former mining magnate Bernardo Paz. For those who remain in Belo there is one small consolation: the city reportedly has 14,000 bars, the highest density of bars in Brazil! There's just no samba school worthy of the name.

Republik gewählt, und sein Freund Oscar Niemeyer von ihm auserkoren, Brasília zu errichten. Die neue Hauptstadt der Nation wurde in nur drei Jahren 700 Kilometer weiter nördlich von Belo Horizonte aus der Steppe gestampft (und aus dem Territorium von Minas Gerais geschnitten) und so funktional gebaut wie ein Autobahnkreuz – sie ist heute ein Denkmal der vergangenen Zukunft.

Belo Horizonte, ein Traum aus dem 19. Jahrhundert, ist inzwischen völlig ausgeufert. Immer neue Straßen, ein zweiter Airport und auch eine S-Bahn-Linie vermögen den Transport nicht zu beschleunigen. Der Fortschritt, so scheint es, ist eben manchmal ein Kreisverkehr. Aus Belo Horizonte fährt man am Wochenende auf verstopften Straßen hinaus nach Ouro Preto oder in die anderen Barockstädtchen der Umgebung, frische Bergluft zu schnappen und ein wenig durch die Gassen zu flanieren. Oder man reist 60 Kilometer weit zum Park für Gegenwartskunst in Inhotim, ein tropisches Mekka weltweit bekannter Künstler, das der Stahlmagnat Bernardo Paz gestiftet hat. Wer in Belo zurückbleibt, kann sich trösten: es soll dort 14.000 Kneipen geben. Die höchste Kneipendichte Brasiliens! Aber keine Sambaschule, die diesen Namen verdient.

The Praça Israel Pinheiro was renamed the Praça do Papa (Pope's Square) after Pope John Paul II's visit in 1980.

Die Praça Israel Pinheiro wird seit dem Besuch des Papstes Johannes Paul II. im Jahr 1980 auch Praça do Papa (Papst-Platz) genannt.

The Edifício Niemeyer on Praça da Liberdade (Freedom Square)

Das Edifício Niemeyer an der Praça da Liberdade (Platz der Freiheit)

Retorno

Falk Jaeger

Tradition and Elegance in Pampulha

The Estádio Governador Magalhães Pinto in Belo Horizonte

Tradition und Eleganz in Pampulha

Das Estádio Governador Magalhães Pinto in Belo Horizonte

Situated in pleasant surroundings on an elevated site above the Lagao da Pampulha, the Estádio Governador Magalhães Pinto occupies a commanding position overlooking the landscape. A striking and expressive building unashamedly realized in *béton brut*, it exemplifies the optimism of the sixties and is not without a certain sleek elegance. The locals are proud of their stadium which, as a national cultural monument, is rightfully already a listed building. Football fans, however, have unsurprisingly never warmed to its official statesmanly title and the arena is known colloquially simply as the "Mineirão" (Big Miner), a reference to the "Mineiros" (miners), the people of the federal state of Minas Gerais, of which Belo Horizonte is the capital.

The artificially created Lagao da Pampulha and the stadium are part of a grand urban landscape composition that also encompasses the neighboring multi-purpose hall known as the "Mineirinho" (Little Miner), as well as a series of distinctive early buildings by Oscar Niemeyer, which he situated on the banks of the lake for maximum effect. The most famous of these is a church, the Igreja de São Francisco de Assis (1943), which is often photographed in the foreground of views of the stadium, but he also designed a yachting club, casino, and a residence for the governor of Minas Gerais, at the time Juscelino Kubitschek, who had previously been Mayor of Belo Horizonte and later became President of the Republic.

The Mineirão Stadium itself was built between 1963 and 1965 to plans by the architects Eduardo Mendes Guimarães

In einer freundlichen Umgebung, auf einer leichten Anhöhe über dem Pampulha-See gelegen, tritt das Estádio Governador Magalhães Pinto als erhabene Erscheinung vor Augen. Ein markanter, expressiver Bau in *béton brut*, der den Optimismus der sechziger Jahre veranschaulicht und gleichzeitig eine schnittige Eleganz zur Schau stellt. Die Leute sind stolz auf ihr Stadion, das nicht zu Unrecht bereits als nationales Kulturdenkmal unter Denkmalschutz steht. Natürlich konnten sich die Fußballfans für den staatstragenden Stadiontitel nie erwärmen und nennen die Arena lieber »Mineirão« (großer Mineiro), bezugnehmend auf die Bezeichnung »Mineiros« (Minenarbeiter) für die Menschen in der traditionellen Bergbaumetropole Belo Horizonte, der Hauptstadt des Bundesstaats Minas Gerais.

Zur großartigen stadtlandschaftlichen Komposition des künstlich aufgestauten Pampulha-Sees und des Stadions gehören noch die benachbarte Multifunktionshalle »Mineirinho« (»kleiner Mineiro«). Hinzu kommt eine Reihe von markanten frühen Bauten Oscar Niemeyers. Er hatte sie an malerischen Uferpartien wirkungsvoll platziert, darunter die Kirche Igreja de São Francisco de Assis (1943), die besonders gerne mit dem Stadion im Hintergrund abgelichtet wird. Aber auch einen Yachtclub und ein Kasino sowie das Wohnhaus des Gouverneurs von Minas Gerais, Juscelino Kubitschek, zuvor Bürgermeister von Belo Horizonte, später Staatspräsident Brasiliens, baute Niemeyer ans Ufer des Lagoa da Pampulha.

The Estádio Governador Magalhães Pinto during construction in 1965

Das Estádio Governador Magalhães Pinto während der Bauzeit im Jahr 1965

The Mineirão and the Mineirinho stand on a raised platform overlooking the artificial Lagao da Pampulha

Mineirão und das Mineirinho thronen hoch über dem künstlich aufgestauten Pampulha-See.

Júnior and Caspar Garreto as a track and field stadium. It has since attained legendary status as a venue of momentous events, for example, the memorable cup-winning triumph over Pelé's club FC Santos in 1968. In 1997, it played host to a championship final attended by 132,834 people, a record-breaking number of spectators. However, the safety concerns that ensued led to a drastic reduction in its capacity, and the stadium now hosts a maximum of 75,800 spectators.

The job facing the architects and engineers was to renovate the iconic landmark, which is often photographed together with its reflection in the lake, to upgrade its dilapidated structure and to provide a protective roof to cover all its seats so that the arena is suitable for use as a venue for the FIFA World Cup in 2014.

gmp · von Gerkan, Marg und Partner together with local architects Gustavo Penna and the structural engineers schlaich bergermann und partner were charged with developing a concept for strengthening the listed structure of the arena and reorganizing the functions of the stadium. Gustavo Penna was responsible for the surrounding terraced landscaping while the design of the stadium conversion itself was produced by a team of architects and engineers from gmp and schlaich bergermann und partner along with the Brazilian architectural office BCMF, who oversaw the subsequent construction process.

The primary task facing the structural engineers was to extend the existing short concrete roof of the upper tier inwards to cover the entire spectators' area. The engineers

Das Stadion selbst wurde 1963 bis 1965 nach den Plänen der Architekten Eduardo Mendes Guimarães Júnior und Caspar Garreto als Leichtathletikstadion gebaut und ist schon zum mythischen Ort geworden, über den Geschichten erzählt werden. Beispielsweise von dem triumphalen Pokalerfolg 1968 über den Pelé-Klub FC Santos. 1997 wurde bei einem Meisterschaftsendspiel ein Rekordbesuch von 132.834 Zuschauern registriert. In der Folge führten Sicherheitsbedenken zur drastischen Verringerung der Kapazität auf 75.800 Zuschauer.

Das oft fotografierte Wahrzeichen des sich im Wasser des Pampulha-Sees spiegelnden Mineirão zu erhalten, dabei das in die Jahre gekommene Stadion zu erneuern und es mit einem alle Sitzplätze schützenden Dach zu versehen, war die Aufgabe für die Architekten und Ingenieure, nachdem die Arena als Austragungsort für Spiele der FIFA WM 2014 auserkoren worden war.

gmp · von Gerkan, Marg und Partner standen vor der Herausforderung, gemeinsam mit dem örtlichen Architekturbüro von Gustavo Penna und den Tagwerksplanern schlaich bergermann und partner ein Konzept zu entwickeln, wie die denkmalgeschützte Bausubstanz der Arena zu ertüchtigen und die Funktionen des Stadions neu zu ordnen seien. Dabei übernahm Penna die Planung der terrassierten Umbauung. Für das Stadion selbst entstanden die Entwurfs- und Ausschreibungsplanungen bei gmp im Team mit schlaich bergermann und partner und den lokalen Planungspartnern, woran sich die Ausführungsplanung durch das brasilianische Architekturbüro BCMF anschloss.

recall that they "did not dare apply the additional load of a new cantilevered structure with twice the existing overhang to the existing historical structure," opting instead to design a separate, autonomous cable-net structure inserted just beneath the existing roof. Resting on a series of supports discreetly incorporated into the existing structure are two pairs of concentric compression and tension ring systems that cantilever from the outer rim into the stadium. To avoid obstructing sight lines the new construction was kept as flat as possible.

A particular difficulty was to accommodate the different depths of the cantilevers on the long and narrow sides of the oval stadium, which necessitated supporting trusses of differing length. Nevertheless, the engineers were successfully able to balance out the forces acting on the compression ring to almost totally eradicate the occurrence of bending moments.

A secondary structure made of solid polycarbonate panels would then span between the radial trusses serving as a translucent roof covering. This approach would leave the building's external appearance unchanged.

But things were to turn out differently. After reshuffles in the building consortium and the construction planning, the plans for the roof construction changed fundamentally. The design team's solution for the construction that was eventually built took an entirely different approach. Trusses made of tubular steel members now extend inwards from beneath the existing historical roof structure and are attached to the existing concrete cantilever arms. To accommodate

Die Aufgabe der Tragwerksplaner bestand vor allem darin, das bestehende, zu kurze Betondach des Oberrangs nach innen zu erweitern und somit alle Zuschauerplätze zu überdachen. »Das historische Tragwerk mit der neuen, doppelt so weit ins Stadioninnere auskragenden Konstruktion zu belasten, hätten wir nicht gewagt«, sagten die Ingenieure später. Ihr Entwurf sah ein unter das Bestandsdach geschobenes, autonomes Seilnetztragwerk vor. Auf neuen, unauffällig in den Bestand »gefädelten« Stützen sollten zwei im Tandem angeordnete, konzentrische Druck- und Zugringsysteme vom Außenrand in den Stadionraum kragen. Um die Sichtlinien nicht zu stören, sollte die neue Konstruktion extrem flach ausgebildet werden. Eine Schwierigkeit bestand darin, die unterschiedlichen Kragweiten an Längs- und Schmalseiten des Stadionovals zu berücksichtigen, was in der Länge variierende Fachwerkbinder erforderte. Trotzdem gelang es, die Kräfteverhältnisse im Druckring nahezu biegemomentfrei auszutarieren.

Eine Sekundärstruktur sollte zwischen den radialen Fachwerkträgern spannen und mit soliden Polycarbonatplatten die transluzente Dachfläche bilden. Die Außenansicht wäre durch diese autonome Konstruktion gänzlich unverändert geblieben.

Doch es sollte anders kommen. Auf Revirements im Baukonsortium und bei der Bauausführung folgte eine grundlegende Änderung der Pläne für die Überdachung. Die letztlich von den Autoren der Ausführungsplanung realisierte Konstruktion folgt einem ganz anderen An-

the additional weight, the existing concrete supports needed to be strengthened. For this steel tensioning members were attached to the flanks of the concrete cantilever arms that act as external prestressing elements. These, however, are clearly visible and impact significantly on the building's external appearance.

The measures undertaken within the stadium are more in tune with the original structure. The most significant changes occurred in the lower tier which originally provided only standing room. This was demolished entirely and rebuilt in a new form. The removal of the running track made it possible to extend it closer to the playing field, which was lowered by 2.5 meters.

The characteristic upper tier on the other hand was retained and renovated. Two new stories of boxes are inserted between the lower and upper tiers and provide the necessary VIP seating. The total capacity of the new stadium has been increased to 66,000 seats, all of which have an optimal view of the pitch.

The functional and ancillary areas stipulated by FIFA guidelines are located in the lower sections of the new lower tier. The playing field, the internal access routes, and VIP foyer on level −1 can be reached directly from street level. A platform around the entire stadium covers the entry ramps and car parking and allows spectators to walk up to the building from all directions. Spectators access the stadium from this platform (level 0) with separate entrances for the upper and lower tiers for easier orientation and faster access. Level +1 contains offices, spaces for the media and

satz. Nun schieben sich Fachwerkträger aus Rundrohren unter das historische Dach, werden aber von den existierenden Betonkragträgern getragen. Die in die Jahre gekommenen Träger mussten für diese zusätzliche Aufgabe jedoch verstärkt werden. Seitlich an den Flanken der Kragarme angefügte stählerne Zugstangen zur externen Vorspannung der Betonkragträger treten deutlich in Erscheinung und verändern die Außenansicht des Bauwerks merklich.

Enger am Original blieben die Maßnahmen beim Stadion selbst. Die größte Veränderung ergab sich beim Unterrang mit seinen nicht mehr zeitgemäßen Stehplatzrängen. Er wurde abgerissen und komplett neu gebaut und, bei Wegfall der Laufbahnen, vor allem an den Schmalseiten näher an das um 2,5 Meter abgesenkte Spielfeld herangeführt.

Der charakteristische Oberrang blieb hingegen erhalten und wurde generalsaniert. Zwei neue Logengeschosse zwischen Ober- und Unterrang der Haupttribüne bieten die gewünschten VIP-Bereiche. So wurde das Stadion auf eine Kapazität von 66.000 Sitzplätzen mit optimaler Sichtliniengeometrie gebracht.

Die gemäß den FIFA-Richtlinien erforderlichen Funktions- und Nebenräume fanden im Unterbau des neuen Unterrangs Platz. Das Spielfeld, die internen Zufahrten und das VIP-Foyer auf Ebene −1 werden von der Straße aus niveaugleich erschlossen. Eine Plattform rings um das Stadion überdeckt die Zufahrten und die Parkplätze und führt die Besucher weiträumig an das Stadion heran.

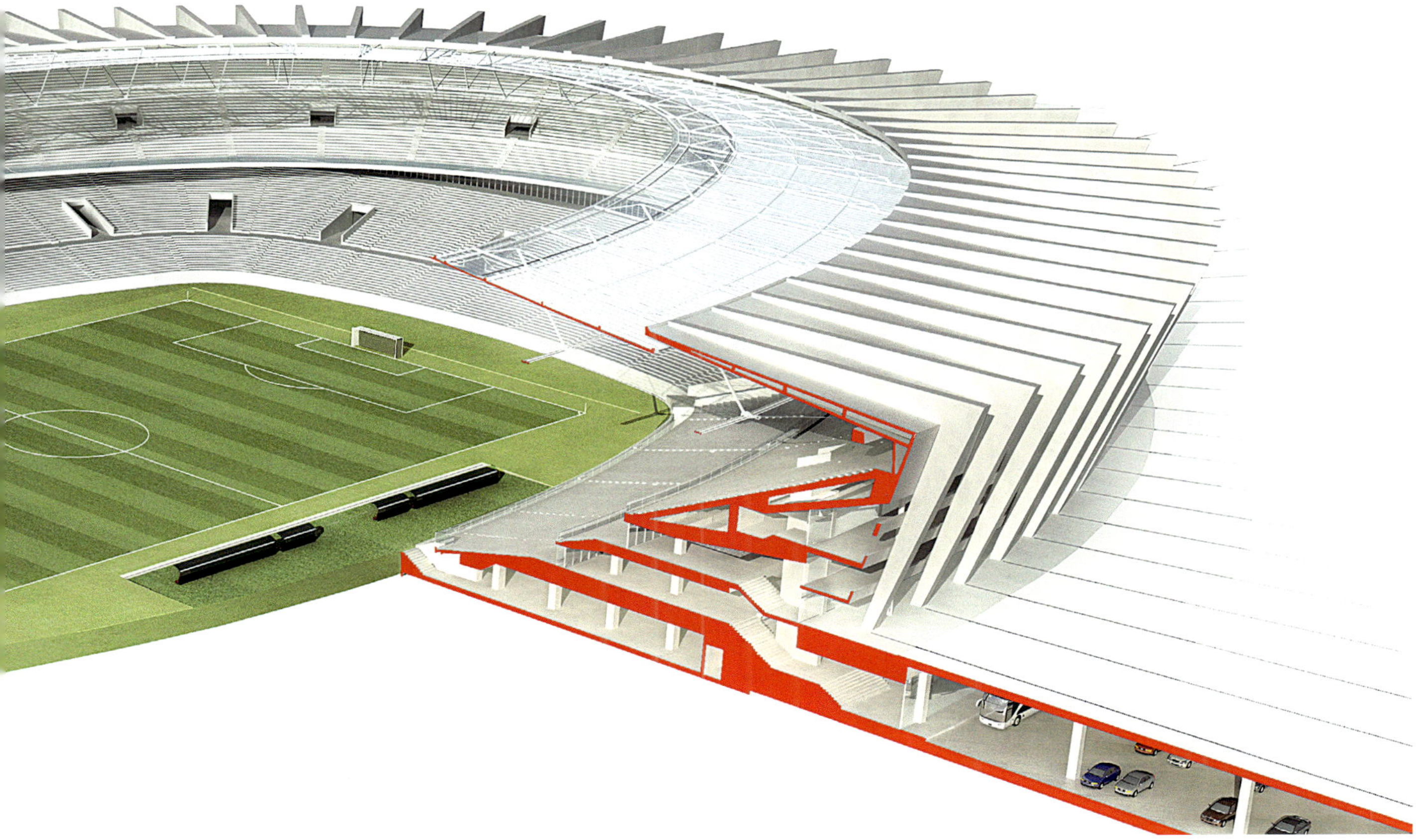

VIP rooms while level +2 contains toilets and kiosks for the spectators above.

A special aspect of the stadium is the split-level zone between the actual seating tiers and the outer skin which facilitates less complicated entry and exit routes and makes it possible to access peripheral areas, the toilets, and waiting areas.

With the exception of the platform and the projecting steel, cage-like structures that house the entrance stairs, von Gerkan, Marg und Partner's design concept has been largely implemented as planned by the local architects. As the investor will also later be the operator of the building, there were none of the usual cost-cutting measures that impact on the usability, solidity, quality, and operational costs. The result is a high-quality and well-appointed building.

Like the other World Cup stadia in Brazil, the Mineirão also has to undergo LEED certification, which presents the designers with a challenge, as the LEED procedure is not expressly designed for sports arenas. During construction, the building site also had to conform to LEED specifications. A photovoltaic solar panel plant on the roof of the stadium and a rainwater retention basin with a capacity of 6,200 cubic meters are two of the stadium's main ecological features. Monitoring data will be captured for a period of three years before LEED certification is awarded.

The Mineirão is home to two top league clubs in Brazil: Atlético Mineiro and Cruzeiro Esporte Clube, and the proud legacy of football in Belo Horizonte will be continued in the

Auf dieser Ebene 0 liegen die Publikumszugänge von der umgebenden Plattform aus, zur besseren Orientierung und für reibungslosen Verkehr jeweils getrennt für die Blocks in Unterrang und Oberrang. Die Ebene +1 ist Büros, Medien und VIP-Räumen vorbehalten, die Ebene +2 im Wesentlichen den Sanitärräumen und Kioskbetrieben für das Publikum.

Eine Besonderheit des Stadions ist die Split-Level-Zone zwischen den eigentlichen Rängen und der äußeren Raumschale, deren Höhenversatz spezielle Lösungen bei der komplikationsfreien Erschließung und Entfluchtung, aber auch bei der Anbindung der peripheren Räume, der Toiletten und Aufenthaltsräume notwendig machte.

Bis auf die Plattform und die dort in stählernen, käfigartigen Vorbauten endenden Zugangstreppen ist die von gmp erarbeitete Konzeption durch die die Ausführung planenden Architekten weitestgehend umgesetzt worden. Die üblichen Einsparungen zulasten der späteren Nutzbarkeit, Solidität, Werthaltigkeit und Betriebskosten waren nicht im Sinn des Investors, der anschließend auch als Betreiber fungiert, was sich in einem merklichen Gewinn an Bau- und Ausstattungsqualität ausdrückt.

Wie alle WM-Stadien in Brasilien wird auch das Mineirão nach LEED zertifiziert werden, eine gewisse Herausforderung an die Planer, denn das LEED-Verfahren ist nicht gerade spezifisch auf Sportarenen zugeschnitten. Schon die Baustelle war dem Verfahren unterworfen. Eine Photovoltaikanlage auf dem Dach und ein Regen-

Floor plan of Level 0 and longitudinal and cross sections. The roof design by schlaich bergermann und partner has not been realised.
Grundriss Level 0, Längsschnitt und Querschnitt mit dem nicht realisierten Dachentwurf von schlaich bergermann und partner

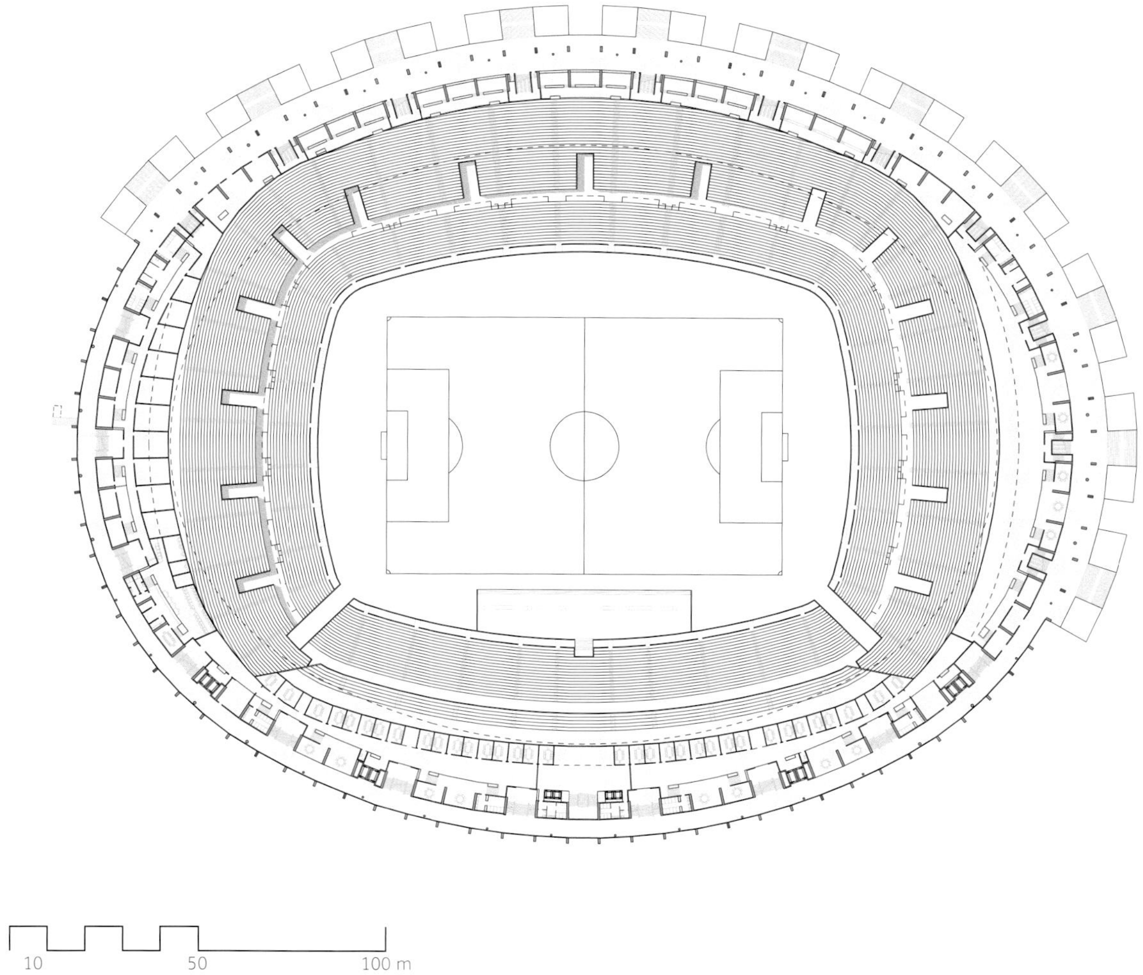
10
50
100 m

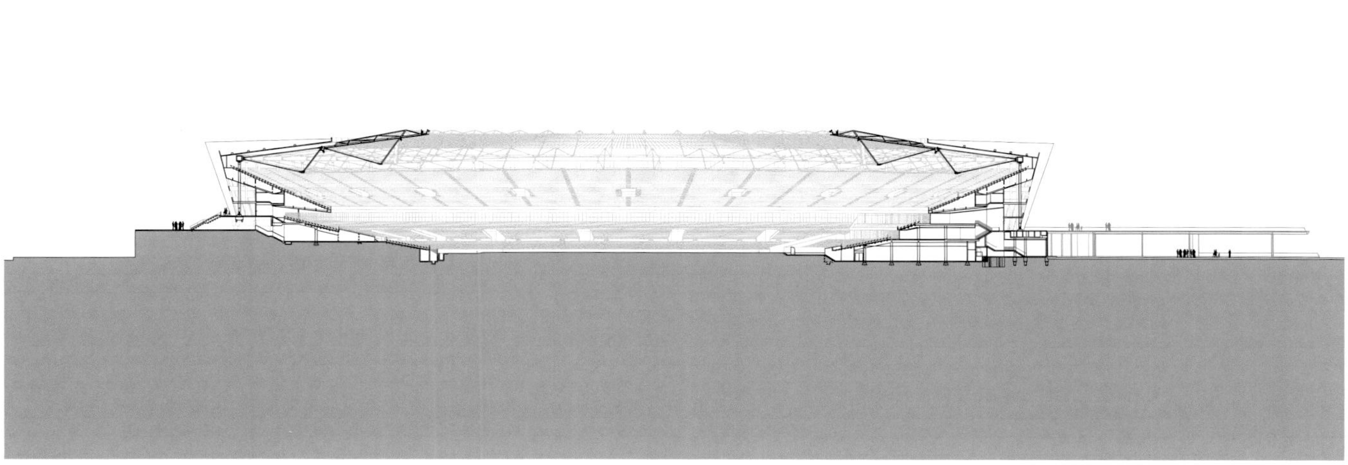

renovated stadium. Football traditions are celebrated in the fan restaurant and in the popular football museum on the lower ground floor, which has been extended and redesigned for the World Cup. Alongside the Maracanã in Rio and the Morumbi in São Paulo, the Mineirão is one of the main traditional venues for Brazilian football. For this reason, it was all the more important that the historic building was maintained in its outward appearance and its essential characteristics. At the same time, the building has been brought up to contemporary technical and ecological standards and will therefore continue to serve Brazilian football and the mineiros of Belo Horizonte as a landmark building for decades to come.

wasserspeicher mit 6200 Kubikmetern Fassungsvermögen gehören zu den ökologischen Maßnahmen. Drei Jahre lang müssen Monitoringdaten geliefert werden, dann kann das Zertifikat erteilt werden.

Mit Atlético Mineiro und Cruzeiro Esporte Clube füllen gleich zwei Erstligaclubs das Stadion Mineirão mit Leben. Die Fußballhistorie, auf die man in Belo Horizonte stolz ist, wird im erneuerten Stadion fortgeschrieben. Die Tradition wird hoch gehalten, im Fanrestaurant und im gut besuchten Fußballmuseum im Sockelgeschoss, das zur WM wesentlich erweitert und neu inszeniert wurde. Neben dem Maracanã in Rio und dem Morumbi in São Paulo ist das Mineirão der Traditionsträger im brasilianischen Fußball. Umso wichtiger, dass es gelungen ist, den historischen Bau in seiner Erscheinung und seinem Wesen weitgehend zu erhalten, auf einen kompromisslos zeitgemäßen technischen und ökologischen Stand zu bringen und auf diese Weise dem brasilianischen Fußball und den Mineiros von Belo Horizonte für weitere Jahrzehnte als Identifikationsobjekt zu bewahren.

TRI CAMPEAO
BRASILEIRO

Espantalho
SOLUÇÕES EM PNEUS
YOKOHAMA
Lírios

Manaus

Carl D. Goerdeler

Manaus—
Between River and Rainforest

From Rubber Boomtown to Free Trade Zone

Manaus zwischen Strom und Regenwald

Von der Kautschuk-Boomtown zur Sonderwirtschaftszone

Manaus is a city of mythical proportions, as is its Teatro Amazonas, a megalomaniacal temple of the muses: planned in 1883 during the rubber boom, it opened on 7 January 1897 with a performance of the opera *La Gioconda*, only to be closed ten years later. Once surrounded by treetops swaying in the breeze, the building now stands in the middle of a sea of buildings. Its dome, covered by 36,000 glazed tiles in the colors of the Brazilian flag, glints under the glare of the tropical sun, while its vast renaissance portal stares blankly like a large eye into the distance. The cobblestones around the building were made of a special composite of sand and rubber so that performances would not be disturbed by horse-drawn carriages rattling past outside. Almost all of the building materials were imported from the "Old World": the tiles for the dome came from Alsace, the chandeliers from Venice, and the mirrors from Flanders. Italian and French painters, having never had to toil in the "green hell", painted gloriously romanticized Amazonian scenes. In their scenes, hardly a mouse seems to squeak—a far cry from contemporary portrayals such as Klaus Kinski's interpretation of the maniacal rubber baron Fitzcarraldo in Werner Herzog's film of the same name, or Christoph Schlingensief's production of the *Flying Dutchman*, performed at the Teatro Amazonas more than one hundred years after its founding.

Since the first Europeans set foot here in the seventeenth century, Manaus has changed its skin several times over. In 1859, the German doctor and naturalist Robert-Christian Avé-Lallemant stopped here and recorded his impression of the village and its 9,000 inhabitants: "Strewn haphazardly in the

Manaus, ein Mythos. So wie sein Teatro Amazonas, der Musentempel des Größenwahns. 1883 im Kautschukboom geplant, am 7. Januar 1897 mit der Oper *La Gioconda* eröffnet, zehn Jahre später schon geschlossen. Wo einst die Baumkronen wogten, ruht es nun inmitten eines Häusermeeres. Die Kuppel aus 36.000 Glasziegeln in den Farben der brasilianischen Flagge gleißt unter der grellen Tropensonne, das Portal im Stil der Renaissance starrt wie ein großes Auge ins Leere. Die Pflastersteine rund um das Gebäude hatte man eigens aus einem Sand-Kautschuk-Gemisch angefertigt, um die Vorführungen nicht durch die vorbeiratternden Pferdefuhrwerke zu stören. Die meisten Baumaterialien wurden aus der Alten Welt importiert, die Kacheln der Kuppel aus dem Elsass, die Lüster aus Venedig, die Spiegel aus Flandern. Italienische und französische Maler hatten ihrer Amazonas-Romantik keine Zügel angelegt; sie brauchten ja nicht in der »grünen Hölle« zu schuften. Wer dächte nicht an Fitzcarraldo alias Klaus Kinski im Film von Werner Herzog, der den wahnsinnigen Kautschukbaron verkörperte, oder an den *Fliegenden Holländer*, den Christoph Schlingensief hier aufführte, nach 100 Jahren, während derer im Teatro Amazonas meistens nur die Mäuse pfiffen?

Manaus hat sich mehrfach gehäutet, seit die ersten Europäer im 17. Jahrhundert dort auftauchten. Hier ging 1859 der deutsche Arzt und Naturforscher Robert Christian Avé-Lallemant an Land; er notiert über das Dorf mit seinen 9000 Bewohnern: »Im grünen Dschungel, der bis an die trägen Flussläufe heranreicht, liegen wild verstreut

The residents of the mangrove forests in the vicinity must cope with water levels that change by up to 14 meters.

Die Bewohner des nahen Mangrovenwaldes müssen mit wechselnden Wasserständen von 14 Metern Unterschied leben.

green jungle that extends right up to the slow moving water are brown huts that the Tapuai inherited from their predecessors, inside each a hammock—a first class item of furniture worthy of the noble seal of the forest—swaying back and forth whispering sweet nothings until slumber sets in."

Six years later, the travel writer Elizabeth Agassiz was more disparaging of Manaus, describing it as, "a small collection of huts, half of which are on the point of collapsing. One has to laugh on hearing the pompous names given to the ramshackle public huts: 'Treasury', 'Parliament', 'Post Office', 'Customs', 'President's Palace'... Its location, however, at the confluence of the Rio Negro and the Amazon or Solimões has been well chosen. Although presently insignificant, Manaus looks certain to become an important harbor and trade center."

Twenty years later, Elizabeth Agassiz's prophecy had already come to pass. Through the invention of vulcanization by the American chemist Charles Goodyear, the milky solution—latex—extracted from the bark of the rubber tree became a highly desirable raw material for all kinds of rubber, not least for making tires.

The new universal material turned the region into an El Dorado. The rubber barons, among them one Brian Sweeney Fitzgerald, who the Peruvians called Fitzcarraldo, led lifestyles befitting of a Baroque opera: they had their dirty clothes shipped to Paris for washing, and champagne brought back on the return journey. For a while latex from the jungle accounted for a third of Brazil's entire income, and Manaus was the capital of rubber.

die braunen Hütten, in deren Innerem eine Hängematte schaukelt, ein ganz erstrangiges Möbel mit dem noblen Siegel des Waldes, die unablässig hin und her schwingt und jenes ›dolce far niente‹ bis zum Schlummer wiegt, das die Tapuai von ihren Ahnen übernommen haben.«

Sechs Jahre später mokiert sich die Reiseschriftstellerin Elizabeth Agassiz über Manaus: »Eine kleine Ansammlung von Hütten, die Hälfte davon schien zu verfallen, und man musste schon wirklich lachen über die pompösen Bezeichnungen der öffentlichen Bruchbuden wie etwa: ›Schatzamt, Stadtparlament, Post, Zoll, Präsidentenpalast‹. Andererseits war der Ort an der Vereinigung von Rio Negro mit dem Amazonas oder Solimões eine glückliche Wahl. Heute noch unbedeutend, wird sich Manaus mit Sicherheit als wichtiger Hafen und als Handelszentrum mausern.«

20 Jahre darauf war die Prophezeiung von Elizabeth Agassiz Realität geworden. Die Erfindung der Kautschukvulkanisierung durch den amerikanischen Chemiker Charles Goodyear hatte die Milch, die aus der Rinde des Parakautschukbaumes gewonnen wurde, den Latex, zum Grundstoff für alle Arten von Gummi gemacht, nicht zuletzt zur Herstellung von Reifen.

Das neue Universalmaterial machte die Region zum Eldorado. Die Kautschukbarone, darunter auch ein gewisser Brian Sweeney Fitzgerald, den die Peruaner Fitzcarraldo nannten, inszenierten ihr Leben als barocke Oper. Die Schmutzwäsche ließen sie in Paris waschen, von wo sie mit dem Champagner zurückkam. Zeitweise beruhte ein Drittel aller Staatseinnahmen Brasiliens auf nichts anderem

The waters of the earth colored Salimões and the dark Rio Negro have still not mixed many kilometers downstream of the confluence of the two rivers in the Amazon.
Viele Kilometer nach dem Zusammenfluss des lehmfarbenen Salimōs und des dunklen Rio Negro zum Amazonas haben sich die Wasser noch nicht vermischt.

Water-borne gas station on the Rio Negro
Schwimmende Tankstelle auf dem Rio Negro

Following the explosion of the rubber market, Manaus transformed overnight into a modern metropolis in the heart of the jungle. At the time, Eduardo Ribeiro, a young military engineer from Maranhão, was half way through his term of office as governor of the state of Amazonas. With plentiful reserves of money to hand and a city in which "everything needed doing", he set about turning the backwater into a "Paris of the rainforest".

Topographically, Manaus lies sandwiched between rivers and the rainforest. The urban environment had to compete against the forces of nature, which made its presence felt forcefully at regular intervals. The *igarapés* (water courses) that wound their way through the city alternatively threatened to flood the city, or dried out entirely depending on the water cycle of the river. Ribeiro laid out an orthogonal plan with parallel and axial paths that extended out into the forest and spanned over the *igarapés* in the form of iron bridges. The envisaged constructions were to be built using technologically advanced modern materials such as iron and glass, stone blocks and bricks. None of these materials were available in the jungle and had to be shipped over from Europe on the ships that had previously transported the rubber over there.

During Ribeiro's period of office and that of his successor, broad Avenidas were created flanked with trees to shade the pavements paved with granite slabs from Portugal. Squares were created with monuments made of bronze, marble and cast iron. An electrical tram was introduced in 1894 along with electric lighting for the streets and squares a year later,

als auf dem Latex aus dem Dschungel. Und Manaus war die Hauptstadt des Kautschuks.

Durch den explosionsartigen Kautschukboom beflügelt, verwandelte sich Manaus über Nacht in eine moderne Metropole mitten im Dschungel. In jenen Jahren hatte der junge Militäringenieur aus Maranhão, Eduardo Ribeiro, gerade die Hälfte seiner ersten Amtszeit als Gouverneur des Staates Amazonas hinter sich. Mit gut gefüllter Kasse, in einer Stadt, in der »einfach alles anzupacken war«, machte er aus dem elenden Nest sein erträumtes »Paris im Urwald«.

Manaus lag topografisch eingezwängt zwischen Strom und Regenwald. Der städtische Raum rivalisierte mit der Natur, die sich immer wieder aggressiv und rücksichtslos bemerkbar machte. Die *igarapés* (Flussläufe), die sich quer durch die Stadt schlängelten, stiegen gefährlich an oder trockneten aus – je nach dem Wasserzyklus des Flusses. Ribeiro plante einen rechtwinkligen Stadtplan mit parallelen und axialen Wegen, die hinaus zum Wald und über die *igarapés* mit eisernen Brücken führen sollten. Die vorgesehenen Konstruktionen sollten besonders modern und technologisch anspruchsvoll sein, aus Eisen und Glas, Steinblöcken und Ziegeln. Dieses Material war vor Ort nicht zu bekommen und musste mit Schiffen aus Europa herangeschafft werden, die zuvor den wertvollen Kautschuk dorthin transportiert hatten.

Während der Regierungszeit von Ribeiro und seinen Nachfolgern wurden breite Avenidas angelegt, die Straßen mit Schatten spendenden Bäumen bepflanzt und die Bürgersteige mit Granitplatten aus Portugal belegt. Plätze

BANCA DE REVISTA
SUPER DDD DDI CHIPS VIVO TIM OI CLARO

followed by canalization in 1906 and eventually also a telegraph network that connected Manaus and Belém with Europe and the United States via an underwater cable.

In 1902, construction began for a floating quay called the Roadway, an exceptionally complex technical facility for ship docking that took until 1909 to complete. Like the customs building completed in 1905, the entire plans and all construction parts were imported from England. Further imposing buildings included the Justice Palace, the governor's office, prison, library, various state-run schools, and the Mercado Municipal whose iron structure was based on a design by Gustav Eiffel in Paris. And, of course, the opera.

A large portion of the rubber market was in the hands of German merchants who lived like kings in palatial residences. Some of these can still be seen today, such as the pretty Palacio Rio Negro commissioned by the rubber baron Waldemar Scholz. Not long after, however, the rubber boom collapsed as quickly as it had appeared, taking the money with it. The reason: British landowners had managed to cultivate rubber tree plantations more cheaply in their protectorate on the Malay Peninsula.

For a while, some one hundred years ago, the jungle once again threatened to encroach on Manaus. During the Second World War there was a brief revival of fortunes when the Japanese occupied the plantations in Malaysia, causing the American military to dispatch rubber tappers into the Amazon rainforest where they saw a potential strategic resource of their own. This gave the Brazilians food for thought: Getúlio Vargas, Brazil's counterpart to Perón, wanted not just

wurden geschaffen mit Denkmälern aus Bronze, Marmor und Gusseisen. Eine elektrische Straßenbahn kam 1894 hinzu, im Jahr darauf die elektrische Beleuchtung der Straßen und Plätze, 1906 ein Kanalnetz und schließlich auch ein lokales Telefonnetz sowie ein Telegrafendienst, der durch ein Unterseekabel Manaus und Belém mit Europa und den Vereinigten Staaten verband.

1902 begann die Konstruktion eines schwimmenden Kais, des genannten Roadway. Erst 1909 wurde die sehr komplexe und aufwendige technische Anlage für den Schiffsverkehr vollendet. Wie das 1905 errichtete Zollgebäude wurde sie samt Plänen und Bauteilen vollständig aus England eingeführt. Dazu kamen dann noch imposante Gebäude wie der Justizpalast, der Sitz des Gouverneurs, das Gefängnis, die Bibliothek, einige öffentliche Schulen sowie der Mercado Municipal, dessen Eisenbausystem von Gustave Eiffel aus Paris stammte. Und, natürlich, die Oper.

Der Kautschukhandel lag zu einem wesentlichen Teil in den Händen deutscher Kaufleute, die in Manaus im Stil kleiner Könige residierten. Davon zeugt noch heute der schmucke Palacio Rio Negro, den sich der Kautschukbaron Waldemar Scholz erbauen ließ – kurz bevor aller Reichtum mit dem Boom so schnell zusammenbrach, wie er ausgebrochen war. Den Briten in ihrem Protektorat auf der malaiischen Halbinsel war es gelungen, Kautschukbäume kostengünstiger in Plantagen zu pflanzen.

Der Dschungel drohte vor 100 Jahren Manaus wieder zu überwuchern. Doch dann gab es ein kurzes Strohfeuer: Die Japaner besetzten im Zweiten Weltkrieg die Plantagen in

to further industrialization but also to make the largely uninhabited interior of the country accessible. His intention was to establish "Brasil Grande"—the great nation of Brazil. But it wasn't until the military came to power in 1964 that this was put into action. A red line was drawn on the map that cut through the green and linked the Atlantic with the Andes: a 5,000-kilometer-long highway—the Transamazônica—that intended to provide "land without people for the people without land".

In the minds of the military, their geostrategic objectives of making the land habitable, of colonization and pushing forward the boundaries, were motivated by a mixture of socio-utopian visions, the need to counter an influx of North American companies and missionaries in Amazonia, and a fear of social revolts in the cities.

Manaus was to play a key role in this geostrategic plan. Like a spider, it sat at the heart of a network of future tracks through the Amazon Basin. But the network proved fragile and nature stronger. The military engineers had not reckoned with the force of nature: within just a few months, the paths they had cut through the jungle disappeared under mudslides, were washed away or quickly became overgrown. As before, the most reliable way to reach Manaus from the rest of Brazil was by water and later by plane. For this reason, the strategic planners opted to give Manaus a life-blood of its own, declaring it a free trade zone for industrial products and services.

With the sweep of a pen, Manaus was declared a "Zona Franca" in 1967. Any investor who established a trade center

Malaysia, die amerikanischen Militärs schickten die Kautschukzapfer wieder los und sahen in Amazonien ihre eigene strategische Rohstoffreserve. Das gab auch den Brasilianern zu denken – Getulio Varges, Brasiliens Perón, wollte sein Land nicht nur industrialisieren, sondern auch dessen menschenleeren Binnenraum erschließen. »Brasil Grande«, »Groß-Brasilien«, war die Parole. Die Militärs, die 1964 die Macht übernahmen, zogen eine rote Linie, quer durch das Grün, vom Atlantik bis zu den Anden, 5000 Kilometer lang: die Transamazônica. Eine Piste, die Menschen ohne Land in ein Land ohne Menschen bringen sollte.

Lebensraum, Landnahme, Vorstoß zu den letzten Grenzen, in den Köpfen der Militärs mischten sich geostrategische Überlegungen mit gesellschaftlicher Utopie, die Furcht vor dem Eindringen nordamerikanischer Konzerne und Missionare in Amazonien mit der Angst vor sozialen Revolten in den Städten.

Manaus fiel in diesem geostrategischen Projekt eine Schlüsselrolle zu. Es sollte wie eine Spinne im Netz der künftigen Pisten durch das Amazonasbecken liegen. Doch das Netz war brüchig, die Natur war stärker. Die Militäringenieure hatten nicht mit der Gewalt der Natur gerechnet. Binnen weniger Monate verschlammten, verbuschten, verwuschen die Pisten, die sie geschlagen hatten. Manaus blieb, wie bisher, nur auf dem Weg über das Wasser – oder künftig durch die Luft – mit dem Rest von Brasilien verbunden. Gerade deshalb schien es den strategischen Planern angesagt, in Manaus eine eigene Kraftquelle einzurichten: eine Industrie- und Freihandelszone.

or factory along the Rio Negro was able to claim a substantial tax rebate. The free trade zone, the politicians hoped, would give the remote area of Amazonia a considerable economic boost. And they were right.

The total turnover of the companies in the Zona Franca now amounts to 25 billion euros. Televisions, motorcycles, mobile telephones and watches are assembled in Manaus out of numerous individual components, most of which have to be imported. 110,000 workers, most of them women, work on the production lines of some 600 companies with a further 350,000 jobs indirectly associated with the free trade zone. In addition to providing labor and energy, Manaus produces wood wool for packaging. Circuit boards and chassis, screws and coils—millions of individual and prefabricated components are delivered to Manaus for assembly.

The strategy has paid off. With more than two million inhabitants, Manaus is no longer a swampy backwater in the Amazonian "wild west" but the fourth largest industrial city in the country. It is as if its changing fortunes have made it harder and more resilient, just like latex after vulcanization. A 3.5-kilometer-long cable-stayed bridge now spans the dark waters of the Rio Negro, appearing on the horizon like a vast triumphal arch. And a brand new city center with high-rise towers, shopping malls and government buildings has arisen six kilometers outside of the old city, including the city's landmark football stadium, the Arena da Amazônia, which looks like a gigantic wicker basket.

But, just as it was one hundred years ago, Manaus is the primary supply center for the vast labyrinth of rivers in the

Mit einem Federstrich wurde Manaus 1967 zur »Zona Franca« erklärt. Jeder Investor, der am Rio Negro ein Kontor errichten oder eine Fabrik hinstellen würde, sollte mit beträchtlichen Steuernachlässen rechnen können. Die Sonderwirtschaftszone würde dem entlegenen Amazonien einen kräftigen Entwicklungsschub verleihen, meinten die Politiker. Und sie haben recht behalten.

Der Gesamtumsatz aller Unternehmen in der Zona Franca beträgt mittlerweile rund 25 Milliarden Euro im Jahr. Fernsehapparate, Motorräder, Handys und Armbanduhren werden in Manaus aus importierten Einzelteilen montiert. 110.000 zumeist weibliche Arbeitskräfte in insgesamt 600 Unternehmen stehen an den Bändern, rund 350.000 indirekte Jobs hängen darüber hinaus an der Sonderwirtschaftszone. Außer Arbeitskraft und Energie steuert Manaus nur die Holzwolle für die Verpackung bei. Schaltkreise und Chassis, Schrauben und Spulen, Millionen an Einzelteilen und vorfabrizierten Komponenten werden in Manaus angelandet und weiterverarbeitet.

Die Rechnung ist aufgegangen. Manaus mit seinen zwei Millionen Einwohnern ist heute längst nicht mehr ein versumpftes Wildwestnest am süßen Meer, sondern die viertgrößte Industriestadt der Nation. Es ist, als ob die Stadt in ihrer wechselhaften Geschichte immer härter und widerstandsfähiger geworden ist, so wie der Latex durch die Vulkanisierung. Den dunklen Rio Negro überspannt nun eine 3,5 Kilometer lange Schrägseilbrücke; sie wirkt wie ein Triumphbogen. Und ein blendend neues Stadtzentrum mit Wohnhochhäusern, Shoppingmalls, Regierungsgebäuden

Rio is not the only city with a sambadrome: a permanent set of spectator stands specifically for watching the carnival parade.
Nicht nur Rio kann mit einem Sambadrom aufwarten, einer fest installierten Tribünenanlage für das Publikum des Karnevalumzuges.

The Teatro Amazonas is a testimony to the rubber boom some 130 years ago.
Das Teatro Amazonas ist Zeuge des Kautschukbooms vor 130 Jahren.

Amazon. The floating pier is teeming with activity like a full fishing net. Carriers transport goods to the ships from their warehouses. Banana plants and beer crates are stowed away, flustered chickens are packed on board alongside sacks of sugar, bundles of clothes, wooden crates, cardboard boxes, baskets, and barrels. The double-deckers boats, the so-called "gaiolas" ("birdcages") bob up and down at the quayside, their passengers hauling seemingly endless streams of luggage over the slippery gangplanks on board, gesticulating wildly to shoo off the hawkers that swarm around like mosquitos hoping for a last-minute deal.

Farewell Manaus! The ship slips its moorings and sets sail, ridding itself of the ice cream sellers and petty thieves like a dog shaking off its fleas. The bustle, cries, and car horns subside and the noise of the city gradually gives way to the monotonous whirring bass of the ship's motors. The more the city recedes beyond the river, the quieter the rhythmic hum becomes. As dusk approaches, we pass the point at which the Rio Negro and the Solimões join to become the Amazonas. Coffee-black water from Columbia meets the khaki-brown floods from Peru. Like far off stars, the lanterns of ships pass by in the distance, twinkling like comets before they disappear beyond the horizon.

ist sechs Kilometer abseits der Altstadt entstanden. Dazu gehört natürlich auch das neue Wahrzeichen der Stadt, das Fußballstadion Arena da Amazônia, das einem gigantischen Weidenkorb gleicht.

Doch wie vor 100 Jahren ist Manaus Versorgungsbasis für das Flusslabyrinth des Amazonasbeckens. Auf dem schwimmenden Pier von Manaus wimmelt es wie in einem vollen Fangnetz. Träger schleppen aus den Lagerhäusern Fracht heran. Bananenstauden und Bierkisten werden gebunkert, Hühner gehen gackernd auf die Reise, neben ihnen stapeln sich Zuckersäcke, Kleiderbündel, Kisten, Pappschachteln, Körbe und Fässer. Die »Gaiola«, der »Vogelbauer«, der Doppeldecker auf Kiel, schaukelt am Kai. Die Passagiere zerren Unmengen von Gepäck über die glitschigen Planken, wild gestikulierend, um die fliegenden Händler abzuwehren, die wie Mückenschwärme einfallen und in letzter Minute noch ein Geschäft machen wollen.

Manaus, ade! Das Schiff hat die Eisverkäufer und Taschendiebe abgeschüttelt wie ein Köter seine Flöhe, die Leinen losgemacht und Fahrt aufgenommen. Rufe, Schreie, Autohupen, dann erstirbt der Lärm aus der Stadt. Der monotone Bass der Schiffsmotoren setzt ein. Je tiefer die Stadt im Strom versinkt, desto ruhiger schlägt der Takt. Im Zwielicht durchpflügen wir die Stelle, wo sich Rio Negro und Solimões zum Amazonas vermählen. Kaffeschwarzes Wasser aus Kolumbien trifft auf khakibraune Fluten aus Peru. Fernen Gestirnen gleich wandern die Laternen anderer Schiffe vorüber, blitzen wie Kometen auf und versinken hinter der Erdkrümmung.

Manaus is the geographic and economic center of the Amazon basin. Its settlements are supplied predominantly by boat.

Manaus ist das geografische und wirtschaftliche Zentrum des Amazonasbeckens, dessen Ansiedlungen per Schiff versorgt werden.

Falk Jaeger

Fitzcarraldo Would Have Loved It

The Arena da Amazônia—a Symbol of Promise for the Future of Manaus

Fitzcarraldo hätte seine Freude gehabt

Die Arena da Amazônia ist für Manaus eine Option auf die Zukunft.

For the architects and engineers, despite having previously built stadia all over the world in all kinds of climate zones, the building of the largest public building in the two-million-inhabitant city in the heart of the tropical rainforest was a new and fascinating, but also demanding experience. A change of provincial government in the middle of the planning and construction process was just one of the project's particular challenges.

The task was to construct a building with a simple, flexible and efficient structure that could be built using locally available possibilities under the prevailing conditions and moreover in a city that can only be reached by air or river.

The arena lies on a site adjoining the main traffic route linking the historical city center on the Rio Negro with the airport to the north of the city. The actual site of the arena was previously occupied by the Estádio Vivaldão, an earthwork stadium which was part of a larger sports complex. Like Rio de Janeiro and São Paolo, Manaus also has a sambadrome for the annual carnival parades. The elongated U-shaped row of grandstands adjoins the stadium on one side while to the north of the site lies the enclosed building of the Arena Amadeu Teixeira.

The designers set out by examining the tropical forms and colors of the region. The new stadium should not be a foreign object, like the Opera House was in its day, but have a symbolic connection to its place. The resulting overall form of the building is reminiscent of the traditional low baskets woven out of plant fibers, of snakeskin, and of the leafy canopy of the rainforest. These morphological analogies are intended more

Der Bau des größten öffentlichen Gebäudes in der Zweimillionenstadt inmitten des tropischen Regenwalds – für die Architekten und Ingenieure, die zuvor schon Stadien in aller Welt und in den verschiedensten Klimazonen errichtet hatten, war die Arbeit in Manaus eine neue, faszinierende, aber auch aufreibende Erfahrung. Dass während der Planungs- und Bauzeit die Provinzregierung wechselte, war nur eine der besonderen Herausforderungen.

So galt es, einen Bau mit einfacher und flexibler, effizienter Struktur zu konstruieren, der unter den örtlichen Bedingungen und Möglichkeiten zu realisieren war, in einer Stadt überdies, die nur aus der Luft oder auf dem Wasserweg versorgt werden kann.

Gebaut wurde an einer Hauptverkehrsachse auf halber Strecke zwischen dem historischen Zentrum am Rio Negro und dem Flughafen im Norden der Stadt. An der Stelle des Bauplatzes hatte zuvor das Estádio Vivaldo Lima gestanden, ein Erdwallstadion, Bestandteil eines größeren Sportkomplexes. Wie Rio de Janeiro und São Paulo besitzt auch Manaus ein Sambódromo für die alljährlich abgehaltenen Karnevalsparaden. Die lang gestreckte, U-förmige Tribünenanlage liegt unmittelbar neben dem Stadion. Im Norden schließt sich die geschlossene Arena Amadeu Teixeira an.

Als die Entwerfer die Aufgabe angingen, machten sie sich zunächst mit der tropischen Formen- und Farbenwelt der Region vertraut. Das neue Stadion sollte kein Fremdkörper aus einer anderen Welt sein wie damals das Opernhaus, sondern erkennbar mit seinem Ort verbunden sein.

The concrete stadium bowl was the first part of the stadium to be built; ...
Der Bau begann mit dem Betonbau der Stadionschüssel, ...

...the external latticework framework for the façade and roof was then assembled.
... dann erst wurde die äußere Gitterschalenkonstruktion für Fassade und Dach montiert.

as vague associations than literal *architecture parlante*. A color scheme would then follow later as a further aspect using a palette drawn from the surroundings.

The conspicuous "basketwork" of the stadium actually encloses only the upper tier of the spectator stands and special functions. The lower tiers and the sunken playing field as well as the car parking are all part of the plinth building which is cut into the topography of the slightly inclined site.

As a result, it has been possible to provide same-level access to the lower seating tiers on the spacious level 0 via two concentric pathways around the perimeter. Eighteen sets of stairs provide access to special level +1 with the lounges and fan restaurant as well as from level +2 to the comparatively steep upper tiers of seating. The stadium's simple circulation concept as well as its cost-saving compact form give all visitors a good overview of the stadium and ensure easy orientation.

Within the bowl of the stadium, the gently curving spectator stands encircle a harmonious, visually continuous space, a space defined by the equally harmonious, elegant, and protective enclosure of the roof. The ribs of the roof appear to rise directly out of the ground: there is no eaves or edge to the roof around its perimeter, the walls instead transitioning directly into the roof. This biomorphous skin would seem to be the product of both technical and structural principles and conditions as well as natural, organizational principles.

In technical terms, the visually-coherent "wickerwork" of the roof is a three-dimensional system, a kind of gridshell with a compression ring at its inner edge above the

Für die Großform des Bauwerks boten sich Reminiszenzen an traditionelle Flachkörbe an, die aus vegetabilem Material geflochten werden, an Schlangenhaut oder Blätterdächer. Die morphologischen Analogien sollten jedoch vage Assoziation bleiben und nicht zur vordergründigen *architecture parlante* werden. Später sollte die Farbgebung nach einer zum Ort passenden Farbpalette als weiteres Element hinzukommen.

Die nach außen wirksame Korbform des Stadions umhüllt jedoch nur die Sondernutzungen und den Oberrang. Der Unterrang und das abgesenkte Spielfeld sowie die Stellplätze des Parkhauses sind in den die Topografie des leichten Hanges nutzenden Sockelbau integriert.

So kann der Zugang zum Unterrang auf der großzügigen Ebene 0 mit zwei konzentrischen Umgängen zu ebener Erde erfolgen. 18 Treppenhäuser erschließen die Sonderebene +1 mit den Lounges und dem Fanrestaurant sowie von Ebene +2 aus den verhältnismäßig steilen Oberrang. Das einfache Erschließungssystem, aber auch die der Ökonomie geschuldete Kompaktheit gewährleisten für alle Besucher besten Überblick und gute Orientierung.

Im Inneren der Stadionschüssel formen die sanft ausgerundeten Ränge einen harmonischen, optisch ungestörten Raum. Einen Raum, der durch die ebenso harmonisch-elegant geformte, bergende Geste des Daches geschlossen wird. Dabei wachsen die Rippen des Daches gleichsam aus dem Grund des Gebäudes heraus. Es gibt keinen durchlaufenden Dachrand, keine Traufe, Wand und Dach gehen durch die Rippen ineinander über. Die biomorph wirken-

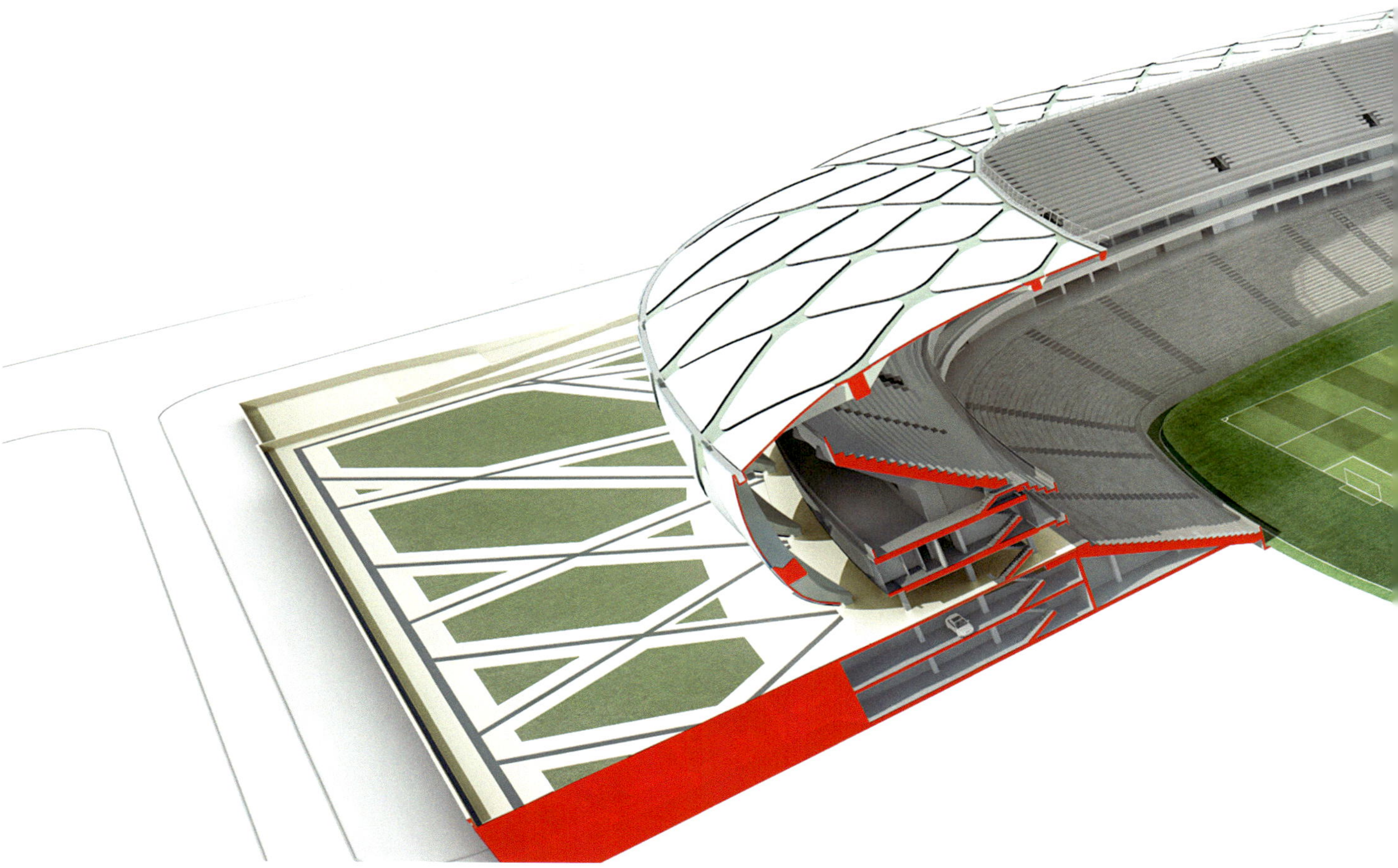

playing field, a tension ring at eaves level and articulated joints where it meets the ground. The grid consists of hollow core girders that were originally designed to curve in two axes with a trapezoidal cross-section that corresponds to the overall geometry of the roof. In a later phase, the sides of the girders were aligned parallel to one another to save costs, with flanges curved in only one axis. The cross-section varies from node to node depending on the load at the respective section which, together with the general simplification of the cross-section, significantly reduced the manufacturing complexity.

The load cases for the spatially complex nodes had to be simulated using elaborate computer-modeled computations in order to correctly calculate all the critical multi-axial tension forces. Careful thought had to be given to the process of construction and the order in which the nodes were welded: the segments of the primary supports, for example, had to be erected with the help of support towers. Likewise, different deformation stresses during the different stages of assembly as well as in the final condition needed to be considered during production in the workshop so that the individual components take up their final position under normal loads after retracting the support towers.

Building near to the equator always involves having to accommodate extreme amounts of rainfall. By extending the flanges (side walls) of the members of the structural framework upwards by twenty-five centimeters, they become gutters able to effectively disperse the large quantities of water from sudden deluges.

de Stadionhülle scheint ihre Ausformung durch technisch-strukturelle Prinzipien und Randbedingungen wie durch natürlich-organische Prinzipien gleichermaßen gefunden zu haben.

Technisch handelt es sich bei dem so schlüssig wirkenden »Flechtwerk« des Daches um ein dreidimensionales System, um eine Art Gitterschale mit Druckring am Innenrand über dem Spielfeld, Zugring in Traufhöhe und Gelenken an den Fußpunkten. Eine Gitterstruktur aus Hohlkastenträgern, die in der ursprünglichen Entwurfsphase der Gesamtgeometrie homogener angepasst, zweiachsig gekrümmt und im Querschnitt trapezförmig sein sollten. Als Ergebnis einer Kostenoptimierungsphase wurden die Stege parallel gestellt und daraus ergaben sich rechteckige Querschnitte mit einachsig gekrümmten Flanschen. Die Querschnitte wurden anschließend gemäß den Belastungen von Knoten zu Knoten schrittweise angepasst, was zusammen mit der Querschnittvereinfachung insgesamt zu einer merklichen Reduktion des Fertigungsaufwandes führte.

Die Lastfälle bei den räumlich komplexen Knoten mussten mit detaillierten Computermodellberechnungen aufwendig simuliert werden, um alle kritischen mehrachsigen Spannungszustände korrekt berechnen zu können. Viel Überlegung erforderte neben der Schweißfolge der Knoten auch der Bauablauf, zum Beispiel die Montage der Primärträgersegmente mit Unterstützung durch Montagetürme. Unterschiedliche Verformungen in unterschiedlichen Montagezuständen und im Endzustand mussten bei der Produktion in der Werkstatt berücksichtigt werden,

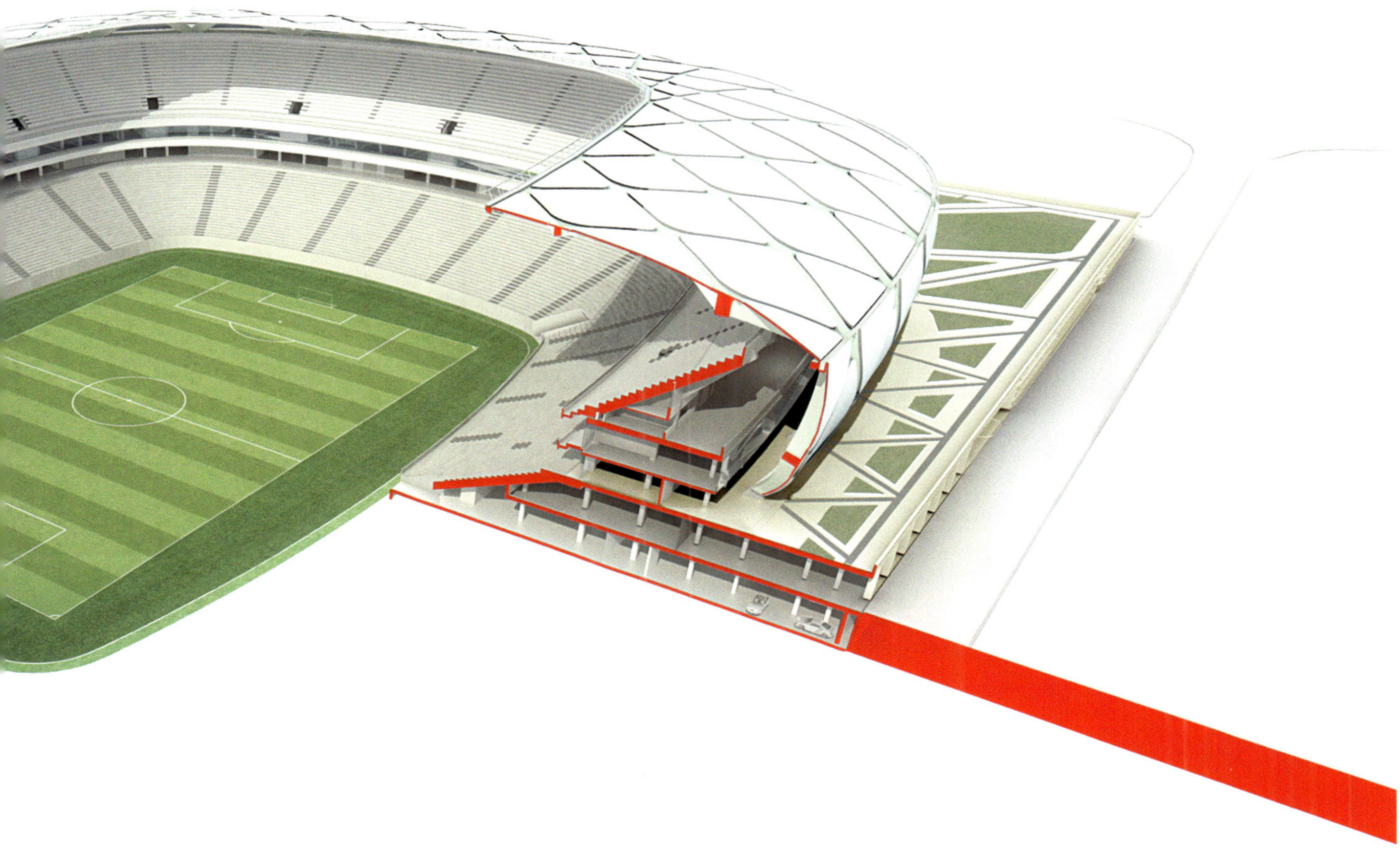

PTFE-coated, translucent fiberglass membranes cover the diamond-shaped openings in the structure, allowing daylight into the interior during the day and lighting up from within at night when the stadium is floodlit. Adjustable lamella at eaves level can be used to control the ventilation of the interior.

The fact that the external appearance and the interior stadium bowl and internal areas of the Arena da Amazônia, such as corridors, lounges, and restaurant, relate to the location even though they are not typically local in their construction, can be attributed in part to the color scheme, which follows an ingenious concept. In their initial studies, the architects undertook studies of colors typical of the region: the lush green tones of the rainforest, the mud-brown floods of the water, the red color of the soil particles as well as the rainbow of colors of the fruit on sale at the markets. These colors reappear in the stadium, for example in the wayfinding signage that denotes the different areas, in the flooring and wall panels, and as color accentuation in the changing rooms and VIP areas. As with many of their earlier stadia, the architects developed a pixelated pattern for the seats within the stadium, creating a shimmering, up-beat pattern that enlivens the interior, especially when the stadium is not full. The colors vary from blood-orange, orange, papaya and mango in the lower seating tiers transitioning gradually to lighter and brighter colors such as melon, pineapple and banana in the upper tiers.

While the interior is dominated by red and yellow colors, the exterior has a light gray-green, creating a color contrast

damit die Bauteile nach Absenken der Montagetürme in Normalbelastung ihre richtige Lage einnehmen konnten.

Bauen in Äquatornähe, das bedeutet immer auch die Bewältigung extremer Niederschlagsmengen. Durch um 25 Zentimeter nach oben verlängerte Flansche (Seitenwände) werden die Stege des Tragwerks zu leistungsfähigen Rinnen, in denen die Sturzbäche abgeführt werden können.

Ausgefacht sind die rautenförmigen Öffnungen des Tragwerks mit PTFE-beschichteten, durchscheinenden Glasfasermembranen, die tagsüber Tageslicht ins Innere lassen und das Bauwerk abends bei Flutlicht von innen heraus zum Leuchten bringen. Drehbare Lamellen im Traufbereich verbessern die Durchlüftung des Innenraums.

Wenn die Amazonasarena in ihrer äußeren Erscheinung, im Inneren der Stadionschüssel und in den Innenräumen, den Fluren, Lounges und Restaurants wenn nicht als ortstypisch, so doch als dem Ort angemessen empfunden wird, so mag das auch an der Farbgebung liegen, der ein ausgeklügeltes Konzept zugrunde liegt. So hatten die Architekten im Vorfeld Studien über die Farben der Region getrieben, die kraftstrotzenden Grüntöne des Regenwalds, die schlammbraunen Wasserfluten und die roten Erden der Bodenkrume, aber auch die leuchtende Farborgie der tropischen Früchte auf den Märkten. Die vorgefundenen Farben tauchen beim Stadion wieder auf, als Leit– und Ordnungsfarben, bei Bodenbelägen und Wandpaneelen. Sie akzentuieren Kabinen und VIP-Bereiche. Wie so oft haben die Architekten auch für die Farbgebung der Sitzschalen im Stadion Manaus' ein Pixelmuster entwickelt, das in

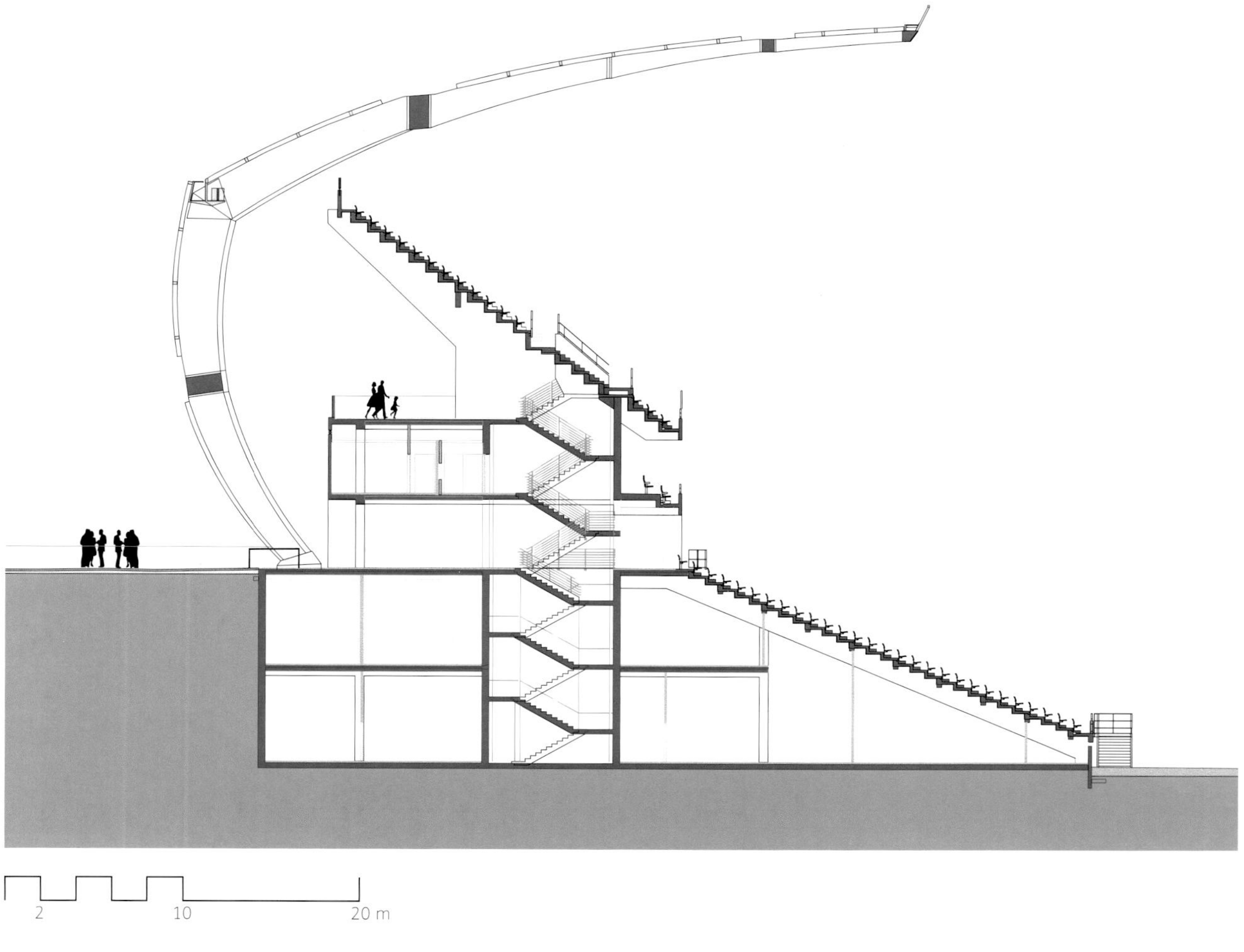

Cross section showing the separate roof construction
Querschnitt mit der eigenständigen Dachkonstruktion

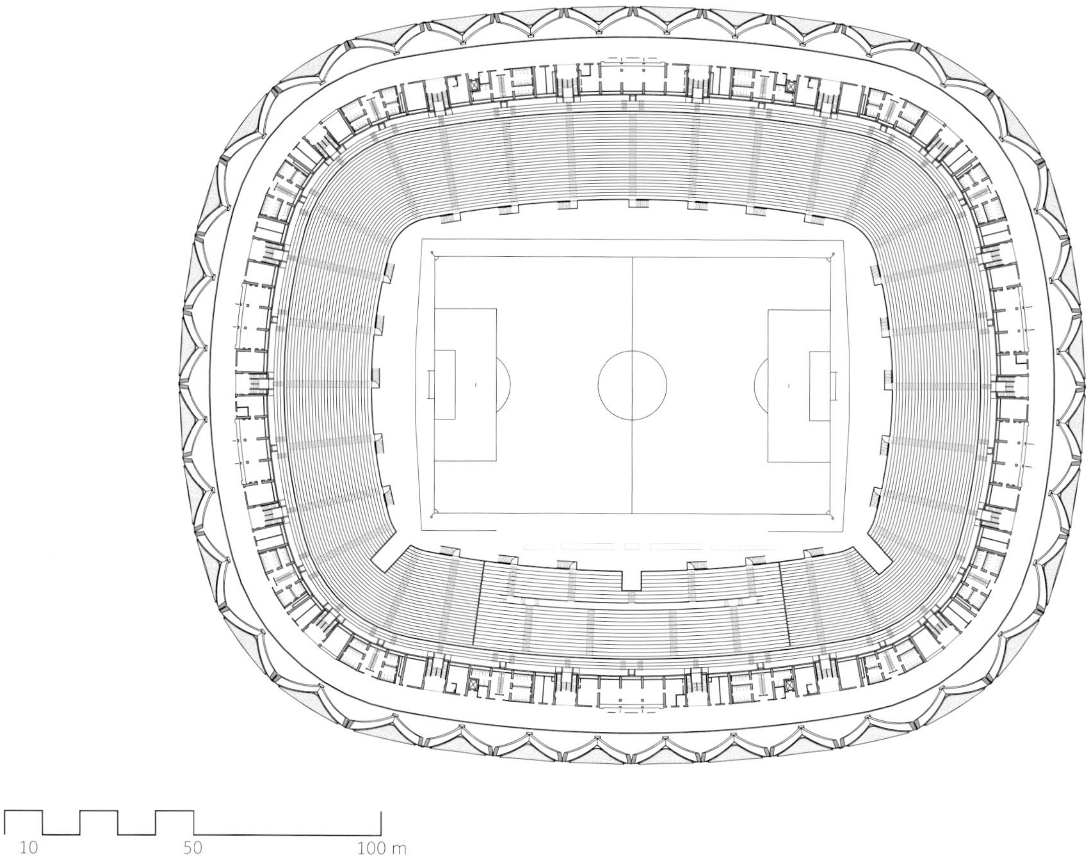

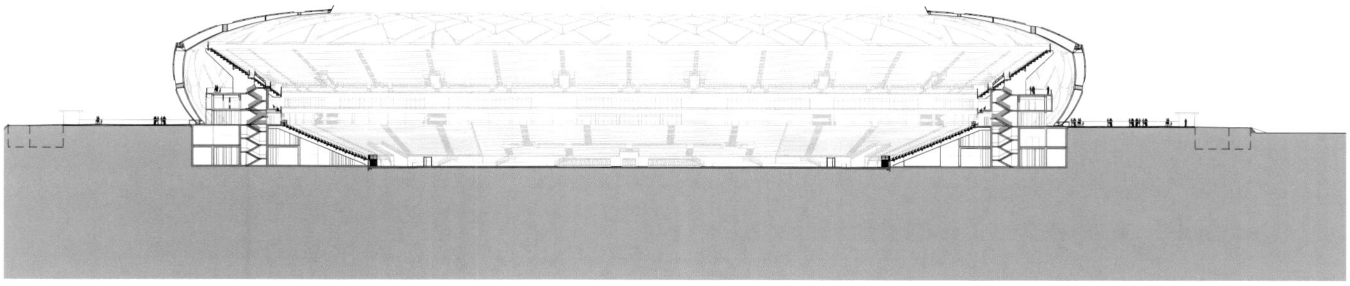

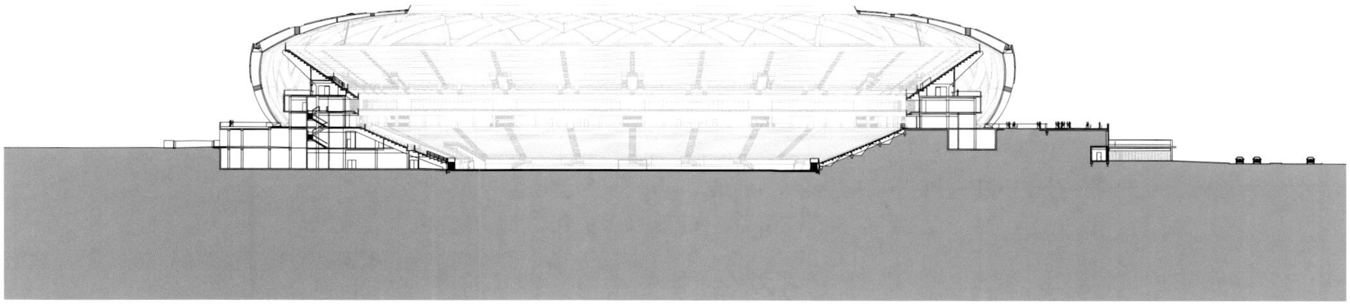

Floor plan just beneath the upper tier, and cross sections

Grundriss unterhalb des Oberrangs sowie Längsschnitt und Querschnitt

GOVERNO DO AMAZO

not unlike that of a pumpkin. The light gray has a metallic, artificial nuance that picks up the colors in the immediate surroundings while differentiating the stadium as an artifact resting on its platform. Paths extend into the surroundings like a visual extension of the ribs of the structural framework, weaving the two together. The Berlin-based architecture office ST raum a. designed the outdoor areas as a symbiosis of architecture and nature and also developed an overall concept for the surrounding sports complex. Unfortunately, the latter has not been realized.

Of all the stadia built for the World Cup in Brazil, the Arena da Amazônia is the most beautiful, most elegant and most characteristic. For many of Manaus' residents, it represents the first emblematic symbol to be built in the otherwise architecturally nondescript city since the great rubber boom. More so than perhaps any of the other World Cup stadia, the Arena da Amazônia represents a signal for hope and confidence in the future economic, sportive and cultural development of the city. Fitzcarraldo would have approved of the radiant arena.

der Gesamtschau ein flirrendes, fast fröhlich wirkendes Bild ergibt – auch und gerade, wenn das Stadion nur wenig besucht ist. Vom Unterrang mit den Farben Blutorange, Orange, Papaya, Mango bis in die höchsten Reihen des Oberrangs mit den Farben Melone, Ananas und Banane werden die Farben heller und lichter.

Innen rot-gelb, außen hell grüngrau, das entspricht vielleicht dem Farbspiel eines Kürbisses, aber das Hellgrau tendiert auch ins Metallische, Künstliche, und so reflektiert das Stadion die Farben der Umgebung und steht als Artefakt auf seiner Plattform. Ein Wegenetz im Umfeld sollte als optische Verlängerung der Tragwerksrippen Gebäude und Umgebung miteinander verwachsen lassen. Die Landschaftsarchitekten des Berliner Büros ST raum a. hatten die Freiräume als Symbiose von Architektur und Natur entworfen und ein Gesamtkonzept für das gesamte Sportzentrum entwickelt. Diese Ideen wurden leider nicht realisiert.

Unter den neuen WM-Stadien in Brasilien ist die Arena da Amazônia eine der schönsten, elegantesten, charakteristischsten. Viele Menschen in Manaus haben seit den Zeiten des großen Kautschukbooms auf ein solches Zeichen in der architektonisch seitdem ziemlich bedeutungslosen Stadt gewartet. Aber kaum eines der neuen WM-Stadien transportiert auch so viel Hoffnung, Zuversicht in die künftige wirtschaftliche, sportliche und kulturelle Entwicklung der Stadt wie die Arena da Amazônia. Der Kautschukbaron Fitzcarraldo hätte an der strahlenden Arena seine Freude gehabt.

Car parking, ancillary functions and plant installations are concealed in the raised plinth on which the stadium is built.
Parkplätze, Nebenfunktionen und Technik sind in der Plattform verborgen, die das Stadion auf eine erhöhte Position hebt.

The arena is also intended to generate employment: it holds future promise for after the football championships. The stadium was conceived from the outset to be usable for a variety of different functions so that it can also be used for other sporting events, for music shows and large-scale religious and political gatherings. Perhaps the fascinating and unusual arena, which perfectly fulfills FIFA standards, will also elevate the level of local football, so that a top-league football club can make the stadium its home and local fans need no longer look further afield to the traditional super clubs in Rio and São Paolo.

Die Arena ist als Jobmotor gedacht, eine Option für die Zukunft, für die Zeit nach dem großen Fußballspektakel. So wird es denn von Bedeutung sein, dass das Stadion bewusst für eine Vielzahl von Nutzungsarten entworfen wurde und neben dem Fußball auch anderen Sportveranstaltungen, Musikshows oder auch religiösen wie politischen Massenveranstaltungen dienen soll. Und vielleicht animiert die faszinierende und ungewohnte FIFA-Perfektion repräsentierende Arena ja doch die örtliche Fußballszene zu größeren Anstrengungen, sodass hier bald auch ein Erstligaverein seine Heimspiele austragen wird und die örtlichen Fans sich nicht mehr den Paradeklubs in Rio und São Paulo verbunden fühlen müssen.

A sturdy skeletal framework supports the roof and façade.
Ein kraftvolles Skelett trägt Fassade und Dach des Stadions.

The tropical colors of the seating contrasts with the gray of the concrete and steel construction.
Das Spiel der Sitze mit tropischen Farben kontrastiert mit den Grautönen von Beton und Stahl.

RECORD

acritica
JLN
AVENIDA

The bays of the construction grid and installation systems define the clear, regular structure of the interiors and circulation areas.

Die die Konstruktions- und Ausbausysteme bestimmende Ordnung des Planrasters prägt auch die ruhigen und übersichtlichen Innenräume und Erschließungswege.

The strong rainfall of the tropics is channeled via deep trough-like gutters in the ribs of the outer façade.

Das Wasser der starken tropischen Regengüsse wird durch die tiefen Rinnen der abgesenkten Tragwerks-rippen abgeführt.

Next page: Sambadrome and footballdrome side by side in Manaus
Nächste Seite: Sambadrom und Fußballdom liegen in Manaus nebeneinander.

Carrefour

Brasília

Jens Glüsing

A Capital City for the Third Century

Brasília—From New Town to Boomtown

Hauptstadt des dritten Jahrtausends

Brasília – der Aufstieg von der Retortenstadt zur Boomtown

Previous page: The emblematic congress and government buildings by Oscar Niemeyer are arranged along the central axis. The stadium in the background is part of the urban concept.

Vorige Seite: Die emblematischen Parlaments- und Regierungsbauten von Oscar Niemeyer sind an der zentralen Achse aufgereiht. Das Stadion im Hintergrund ist Teil dieses städtebaulichen Konzepts.

The bar on the corner is as much a part of Brazil as Caipirinha and Bossa Nova. Behind the bar waits an elderly Portuguese gent, on the cooler stands a penguin made of porcelain, and on the wall hangs a portrait of the Brazilian patron saint *Nossa Senhora Aparecida* next to pennants from the local football club. Rich local delicacies in glass vitrines tempt the guests and the beer is kept "estúpidamente gelada"—incredibly cold—in a refrigerator. Cheap bottles of sugarcane liquor stand on the shelves, while on the ceiling a neon lamp flickers. Leaning against the bar are a few men in shorts and plastic sandals, discussing the last football game.

Such corner bars are to be found everywhere in Brazil, except, that is, in Brasília. Why? Because there are no street corners in Brasília.

Brazil's capital city was built for cars. Pedestrians did not feature in the designs of the urban planners because they interrupt the flow of traffic. Such was the prevailing view over fifty years ago. The roads weave in gentle curves between housing blocks that are raised off the ground on concrete columns. A swathe of green stretches between the ribbon of asphalt and the buildings. There is rarely ever a pavement. My favorite bar in Brasília adjoins a petrol station: beyond the petrol pumps stands a green caravan, in front of it a couple of metal tables surrounded by a handful of plastic chairs. The smell of roasting chicken drumsticks emanates from the open grill. The only normal pub in the vicinity is an outrageously expensive beer bar that recently opened in a nearby slab block. Sometimes

Die Kneipe an der Ecke gehört zu Brasilien wie Caipirinha und Bossa nova. Hinter dem Tresen wacht ein alter Portugiese, auf dem Kühlschrank steht ein Porzellanpinguin, an der Wand hängt Brasiliens Hausheilige Nossa Senhora Aparecida neben dem Wimpel des örtlichen Fußballclubs. In gläsernen Vitrinen locken fettige Köstlichkeiten, das Bier kommt aus der Gefriertruhe und ist »estúpidamente gelada«, irrsinnig kalt. In den Regalen stehen Flaschen mit billigem Zuckerrohrschnaps, an der Decke flackert eine Neonröhre. Am Tresen lehnen Männer in kurzen Hosen und Plastiklatschen und kommentieren das letzte Fußballspiel.

In allen brasilianischen Städten finden sich solche Eckkneipen, nur in der Hauptstadt sucht man sie vergeblich. Hier gibt es keine Straßenecken.

Brasiliens Hauptstadt wurde für Autos gebaut, Fußgänger hatten die Städteplaner nicht vorgesehen, sie behindern den Verkehrsfluss, so sah man das vor über 50 Jahren. Die Straßen schlängeln sich in sanften Kurven zwischen Wohnblöcken, die auf luftigen Betonpfeilern gebaut sind. Zwischen dem Asphaltband und den Gebäuden liegt meist ein breiter Grünstreifen, Bürgersteige sucht man vergeblich. Meine Lieblingskneipe in Brasília liegt neben einer Tankstelle. Der Weg führt zwischen den Zapfsäulen zu einem grün gestrichenen Wohnwagen, davor stehen ein paar Blechtische, die Stühle sind aus Plastik, von dem offenen Grill steigt der Duft von gerösteten Hühnerschlegeln auf. In einem nahen Plattenbau hat jüngst eine sündhaft teure Bierbar eröffnet, die einzige normale Gaststätte weit und

Brasília was planned and built as a car-oriented city.
Die autogerechte Stadt war das Leitbild für die Stadtplanung Brasílias.

I am reminded of the GDR except that it doesn't smell of brown coal.

Brasília is not love at first sight, and still not very endearing on second glance. My first experience of the Brazilian capital was short, dry, and depressing. It was at the beginning of the nineties and the dry season in the Cerrado, the savannah-like bushland in Brazil's interior, was at its peak. The earth was red, hard, and cracked and a yellow-red haze of dust and sun shimmered over the Esplanada dos Ministérios. On arriving at the hotel, the porter welcomed me with a glass of water.

Among the locals, Brasília was regarded as something of a penal colony: to make it more palatable, politicians were given generous allowances and free tickets. The city worked from Tuesday to Thursday, and on Fridays the politicians fled the city and flew back to their local constituencies. Consequently, the city was devoid of people at the weekend.

As a Brasília-beginner, I had planned three days to explore the seat of centralist power. With a stack of books under my arm on the star architect Oscar Niemeyer and Modernism in Brazil, I had prepared myself, made a few appointments with government departments and was looking forward to an extensive stroll about town.

But by the evening of my first day, I was overcome by the Brasília Blues. At the Palácio do Planalto, I got no further than the porter: my contacts at the ministry had already departed for the weekend. My idea of a walkabout also fell flat: in Brasília one travels by car or not at all. Bus trips for tour-

breit. Manchmal fühle ich mich an die DDR erinnert, nur dass es hier nicht nach Braunkohle riecht.

Brasília ist keine Liebe auf den ersten Blick, und auch auf den zweiten fällt die Zuneigung schwer. Meine erste Begegnung mit der brasilianischen Hauptstadt war kurz, trocken und deprimierend. Es war Anfang der neunziger Jahre; die Trockenzeit im Cerrado, dem savannenähnlichen Buschland im Landesinneren, hatte ihren Höhepunkt erreicht. Die Erde war rot, hart und rissig; über der Esplanada dos Ministérios lag ein gelbroter Flimmer aus Staub und Sonnenlicht. Im Hotel reichte der Portier zur Begrüßung ein Glas Wasser.

Brasília galt auch bei Einheimischen als eine Art Strafkolonie, den Politikern wurde der Aufenthalt durch üppige Aufwandsentschädigungen und Gratistickets versüßt. Die Stadt funktionierte von Dienstag bis Donnerstag. Freitags flüchteten die Politiker per Flugzeug in ihre heimischen Wahlkreise, am Wochenende herrschte in der Hauptstadt gähnende Leere.

Drei Tage hatte ich mir als Brasília-Frischling Zeit genommen, um den Sitz der Zentralmacht zu erkunden. Ich war gewappnet mit Büchern über Stararchitekt Oscar Niemeyer und die brasilianische Moderne, ich hatte ein paar Termine bei Regierungsstellen, ich freute mich auf einen ausgiebigen Stadtbummel.

Am Abend des ersten Tages überwältigte mich der Brasília-Blues. Im Palácio do Planalto, dem Regierungspalast, war ich nicht über den Pförtner hinausgekommen. In den Ministerien waren die Gesprächspartner bereits ins Wochenende entflohen. Stadtbummel konnte man ganz ver-

The buildings erected when the city was founded have lost none of their original elegance.

Die Bauten aus der Gründungszeit haben nichts an Eleganz eingebüßt.

The center of the city is marked by the crossover of two traffic axes and a bus station.
Zentraler Punkt der Stadt ist eine Straßenkreuzung mit Busbahnhof.

ists were non-existent. Instead, I hired a taxi but after two hours, I had already seen all the sights.

Today that is no longer possible: despite the car-friendly design of the city, traffic jams are commonplace. The number of cars has tripled in the last ten years and the government has neglected to invest in public transport—only poor people travel by bus, and the majority of the capital's residents are from the upper and middle classes.

Brasília has since developed into an almost normal city, with all its concomitant advantages and problems. The unloved capital, called into life by President Juscelino Kubitschek—or JK as he was known—and built within a space of just four years, has fulfilled its purpose: it helped provide access to the vast, neglected interior of the country.

Brasília is now the gateway to the midwest, to the booming belly of Brazil. Had it not been for the relocation of the capital into Brazil's interior, the vast federal states of Mato Grosso, Goiás, and Tocantins would probably still be isolated and forgotten. Today, soya farmers come by pick-up, or even private airplane, to shop in the elegant shopping centers in Brasília.

The construction of a new capital city had been anchored in the constitution as far back as 1891, and a site on Brazil's upland plateau in the heart of the country was marked out some two years later, far away from the other cities. But Kubitschek, Brazil's erstwhile modernizer, was the first to embark on the project. JK, a descendant of Czech émigrés, was an optimist who captured the spirit of opti-

gessen, in Brasília ist man im Auto unterwegs oder gar nicht. Busrundfahrten gab es nicht, ich heuerte ein Taxi an, nach zwei Stunden hatte ich alle Sehenswürdigkeiten abgeklappert.

Das ist heute nicht mehr möglich: Trotz der autofreundlichen Gestaltung steht man auch in Brasília oft im Stau. Die Anzahl der Autos hat sich in den vergangenen zehn Jahren verdreifacht, den Ausbau der öffentlichen Verkehrsmittel hatte die Regierung vernachlässigt – nur arme Leute fahren mit dem Bus, die meisten Bewohner der Hauptstadt zählen vom Einkommen her zur Ober- und Mittelschicht.

Brasília hat sich zu einer fast normalen Großstadt gemausert, mit allen Vorteilen und Problemen. Die ungeliebte Hauptstadt, die auf Anordnung von Präsident Juscelino Kubitschek, genannt JK, in der Rekordzeit von vier Jahren aus der roten Erde gestampft worden war, hat ihre Bestimmung erfüllt: Sie hat geholfen, das vernachlässigte Innere des Riesenlandes zu erschließen.

Heute ist Brasília das Tor zum Mittleren Westen, dem boomenden Bauch Brasiliens. Die riesigen Bundesstaaten Mato Grosso, Goiás und Tocantins wären ohne die Verlegung der Hauptstadt ins Landesinnere vermutlich immer noch weitgehend vergessen und isoliert. Heute kommen die Sojafarmer mit ihren Pick-ups oder im Privatflugzeug zum Shopping in die eleganten Einkaufszentren von Brasília.

Der Bau einer neuen Hauptstadt war bereits in der Verfassung von 1891 vorgesehen, zwei Jahre später wur-

mism at the end of the fifties. It was the time of Bossa Nova, and the first VW Beetles were leaving the production line in São Paolo. Millions of farm laborers streamed into the cities and the antiquated farmland prepared for its imminent transformation into a modern, urban society. The building of the new capital epitomized the euphoria and the drive to modernize the country at that time.

The cross that Lúcio Costa, the urban designer and architect charged with planning the capital, first marked on the map gradually evolved into the shape of an airplane. At its cockpit he placed the Square of Three Powers around which the Presidential Office, the National Congress and the Federal Supreme Court are gathered, while its fuselage and wings, the Plano Piloto, hold all the important government buildings as well as residential districts. The architect Oscar Niemeyer, then chief architect of the government building authority and a self-confessed communist, was responsible for the design of the architecture. He created buildings of astonishing lightness, such as the bowl housing the Congress and Brasília's famous cathedral. Feminine curves and forms lend his architecture a grace that is also inspired by the gentle undulations of the hills of his home town, Rio.

In terms of its overall concept, however, one cannot deny the influence of the soviet-Stalinist architecture. On his first visit to the city, Poland's former President Lech Wałęsa is reported to have remarked how much Brasília looks like Warsaw. The ministries are housed in uniform blocks arranged in monotonous rows along the Esplanada

de das Gelände auf dem zentralen Hochplateau des Landes abgesteckt, weitab von jeder Großstadt. Aber erst Kubitschek, der Modernisierer Brasiliens, setzte das Vorhaben um. Der optimistische JK, ein Nachfahre tschechischer Auswanderer, verkörperte die Aufbruchstimmung Ende der Fünfzigerjahre. Es war das Zeitalter des Bossa nova, in São Paulo liefen die ersten VW Käfer vom Band. Millionen Landarbeiter strömten in die Städte, das rückständige Agrarland rüstete sich zum großen Wandel in eine moderne, urbane Gesellschaft. Die neue Hauptstadt verkörperte die Euphorie und den Modernisierungswahn jener Jahre.

Stadtplaner und Architekt Lúcio Costa zeichnete ein Kreuz auf die Landkarte, das die Form eines Flugzeugs annahm. Um den Platz der Drei Gewalten in der Kanzel gruppieren sich Präsidentenpalast, Oberstes Bundesgericht und Kongress. Im Plano Piloto aus Rumpf und Flügeln sind alle wichtigen Regierungsgebäude und Wohnviertel konzentriert. Architekt Oscar Niemeyer, damals Chef der staatlichen Baubehörde und bekennender Kommunist, war für die Ausführung verantwortlich. Er schuf Gebäude von bewundernswerter Leichtigkeit, wie die Schüsseln des Kongresses und die berühmte Kathedrale. Weibliche Linien und Formen, die sanft geschwungene feminine Hügellandschaft seiner Heimatstadt Rio, schlagen sich in seinen schönsten Werken nieder.

Aber im Gesamtkonzept der Hauptstadt ist auch der Einfluss sowjetisch-stalinistischer Architektur deutlich zu spüren. »Das sieht hier ja aus wie in Warschau!«, soll Polens damaliger Präsident Lech Wałesa bei seinem ersten

The cathedral and the national congress lie on the Eixo Monumental, the axis that runs down the spine of the city.

Die Kathedrale und der Nationalkongress an der zentralen Achse Eixo Monumental

dos Ministérios. At the end of the axis the tower of the National Congress building dominates the skyline with the elegant bowl of the Chamber of Deputies beside it.

The "Asas", the wings of the city, were divided into sectors which in turn were divided into so-called Superquadras. Postal addresses in Brasília resemble chemical formulae: "SQN 202 Bloco A apto. 208" means "Northern Superquadra 202, Block A, Apartment 208".

A six-lane concrete strip, the so-called Eixo Monumental, is the main axis of the Brazilian capital and separates the hotel sectors to the north and south. The different sectors are grouped on either side of the axis and are divided into districts for housing and offices for government staff, for hotels and for banks. Even the state printing works had a sector of its own. While road signs still give directions for the different districts, the living and working areas are now beginning to intermingle. Over the last twelve years, the city's population has risen by almost a third to nearly 2.4 million inhabitants. The Plano Piloto has expanded in all directions as new housing blocks, hotels and office buildings have been built, and the airplane layout is now barely visible.

For blue-collar workers as well as much of the middle classes, land prices and rents have risen to such an extent that they are barely affordable. In his plan for the city, Lúcio Costa had not foreseen housing for the laborers who built the city, assuming that after completion they would then return to their home towns in the northeast of the country. Most, however, did not, instead settling in

Brasília-Besuch ausgerufen haben. Die Ministerien sind in einförmigen Blöcken untergebracht. Sie reihen sich monoton wie Kasernen entlang der Esplanada dos Ministérios. Am Ende der Straße ragt das Abgeordnetenhochhaus in den Himmel, daneben liegt die elegante Schüssel des Kongresses.

Die »Asas«, die »Flugzeugflügel« der Stadtanlage, wurden in Sektoren unterteilt, die wiederum in sogenannte Superquadras gegliedert sind. Adressen in Brasília gleichen chemischen Formeln: SQN 202 Bloco A apto. 208 steht für »Nördliche Super-Quadra 202, Block A, Wohnung 208«.

Eine sechsspurige Betonpiste, der sogenannte Eixo Monumental, trennt die Hotelsektoren Nord und Süd, er stellt die Hauptachse der brasilianischen Hauptstadt dar. Die verschiedenen Sektoren gruppieren sich zu beiden Seiten dieser Achse. Es gibt Wohnungs- und Arbeitsbereiche für Staatsangestellte, Bezirke für Hotels und Banken, selbst die Staatsdruckerei erhielt einen eigenen Sektor. Schilder weisen den Weg zu den verschiedenen Bezirken, doch mehr und mehr mischen sich Wohn- und Arbeitsbereiche. Die Stadt ist in den vergangenen zwölf Jahren um fast ein Drittel auf etwa 2,4 Millionen Einwohner angewachsen. Neue Wohnblöcke, Hotels und Bürogebäude lassen den »Plano Piloto« in alle Richtungen wachsen, die Flugzeugform ist kaum noch zu erkennen.

Für Arbeiter und auch viele Angehörige der Mittelschicht sind die Grundstückspreise und Mieten in der Hauptstadt kaum noch zu bezahlen. Stadtplaner Costa hatte Unterkünfte für die Arbeiter, die Brasília erbaut hatten,

Small churches serve as Niemeyer-inspired landmarks.

Kleinere Kirchen sind Landmarken nach dem Vorbild Niemeyers.

Designed by Honório Peçanha, the statue of President Juscelino Kubitschek, the founder of modern Brazil, stands on a 28-meter-high pedestal.

Die von Honório Peçanha gestaltete Statue des Präsidenten Juscelino Kubitschek, des Gründers Brasílias, grüßt von einer 28 Meter hohen Säule.

the satellite towns that emerged within a radius of sixty kilometers around the Plano Piloto. More recently an influx of the middle classes has led to frenetic building activity in the satellite towns, among them Sobradinho, Ceilandia and Taguatinga. Dozens of guarded complexes, so-called Condominios, have sprung up, many of them illegal constructions. Millions now live in the mega-settlements that are gradually encroaching on the capital. And with them comes organized crime and drug trafficking, which is beginning to flourish just a few kilometers from the presidential palace.

That is one of the ugly faces of Brasília. The euphoria of the Kubitschek years quickly gave way to disillusionment. The construction of Brasília had been largely financed by excessive inflation that burdened the economy for years to come. Only the military, who were in power from 1964 to the mid-eighties, seemed happy to reside in Brasília, profiting from Brasília's "splendid isolation", thousands of kilometers from the vibrant metropolises of Rio and São Paolo. The generals were able to prevail undisturbed in the comparative isolation of the Planalto, Brazil's upland plateau.

After the end of the military dictatorship, the civil government likewise discovered the advantages of the capital's isolated position: far removed from the electorate they were able to wheel and deal without inhibition, and corruption and nepotism flourished.

Until June 2013, that is: vast demonstrations protesting against corruption and mismanagement began in São Paolo and quickly spread to the capital and mass protests

gar nicht erst vorgesehen. Nach vollendetem Werk sollten sie gefälligst in ihre Heimatorte im fernen Nordosten des Landes zurückkehren. Doch sie dachten nicht daran. Die meisten ließen sich in Satellitenstädten nieder, die sich in einem Umkreis von etwa 60 Kilometern um den Plano Piloto erstrecken. Heute ziehen auch immer mehr Mittelschichtangehörige in diese Vorstädte. In Sobradinho, Ceilandia und Taguatinga, den größten dieser Satellitensiedlungen, sind in den vergangenen Jahren Dutzende bewachte Wohnanlagen, sogenannte Condominios, aus dem Boden geschossen, viele wurden illegal errichtet. Millionen leben in diesen Megasiedlungen, sie rücken immer näher an die Hauptstadt heran. Wenige Kilometer vom Präsidentenpalast blühen Kriminalität und Drogenhandel.

Das ist eine der hässlichen Seiten Brasílias. Tatsächlich war auf die euphorischen Kubitschek-Jahre rasch Ernüchterung gefolgt. Der Bau Brasílias wurde mit einer überbordenden Inflation finanziert, die den Haushalt auf Jahre belastete. Nur die Militärs, die von 1964 bis Mitte der Achtzigerjahre regierten, lernten Brasília rasch schätzen. Sie genossen die Splendid Isolation, tausende Kilometer entfernt von den unruhigen Metropolen Rio und São Paulo. In der Einsamkeit des Planalto, der zentralbrasilianischen Hochebene, konnten die Generäle ungestört walten.

Nach dem Ende der Militärherrschaft entdeckten auch die zivilen Regierungen die Vorzüge einer isolierten Hauptstadt: Weit entfernt vom Wähler ließ es sich ungestört mauscheln und kungeln, Korruption und Vetternwirtschaft blühten.

engulfed the city for the first time. Militant protestors attempted to set fire to the delicate structure of the foreign office, the Palácio do Itamaraty, and they climbed the vast bowl of the congress building. These images have become imprinted in the nation's collective memory.

Despite its many embassies and international organizations, the capital city remains somewhat provincial. Taxi drivers and waiters only occasionally speak English and youths pass the time with *esquibunda*—sliding down the steep grassy slopes between the ministries on boards. The aroma of dried meat and roast white cheese, the favorite dish of the immigrants from the northeast, lies in the air. Dusty paths have been trodden into the endless stretches of green between the blocks of houses and passers-by hold umbrellas to protect themselves against the heat of the sun—Brazilian pragmatism compensating for the shortcomings of the urban design.

Today the city is booming. In no other city in Brazil is the per capita income as high as it is in Brasília. Most of the government staff earn a good wage and the politicians have ensured that public services in the capital function better than in the rest of the country. The residents of Brasília enjoy a comparatively high standard of living and the structure of the Plano Piloto now resembles that of American city suburbs. Each evening, an army of domestic workers returns to the surrounding satellite towns. The politicians' working week has adapted accordingly: its is now possible to make appointments for Friday and Monday. There are bars and restaurants with live

Jedenfalls bis zum Juni 2013: Die riesigen Demonstrationen gegen Korruption und Misswirtschaft, die in São Paulo begonnen hatten, sprangen rasch auf die Hauptstadt über. Erstmals erlebte Brasília Massenproteste. Militante Demonstranten versuchten, den filigranen Bau des Außenministeriums, den Palácio Itamaraty in Brand zu stecken, eine Ikone von Brasília; sie erklommen die Schüssel des Kongresses. Diese Bilder haben sich ins kollektive Bewusstsein gebrannt.

Trotz der vielen Botschaften und internationalen Organisationen wirkt die Hauptstadt immer noch provinziell. Taxifahrer und Kellner sprechen kaum Englisch, auf der steilen Wiese zwischen den Ministerien vergnügen sich Jungen beim *esquibunda* – sie rutschen auf Brettern die Abhänge hinunter. Der Duft von Trockenfleisch und geröstetem weißem Käse, der Lieblingsspeise der Zuwanderer aus dem Nordosten, hängt in der Luft. Staubige Trampelpfade führen über die endlosen weiten Flächen zwischen den Häuserblöcken, Passanten schützen sich mit Regenschirmen gegen die pralle Sonne. Der Pragmatismus der Brasilianer hat über die Städteplaner gesiegt.

Heute boomt die Stadt, nirgendwo in Brasilien ist das Pro-Kopf-Einkommen höher. Die meisten Staatsangestellten verdienen gut; die Politiker haben dafür gesorgt, dass alle Dienstleistungen in der Hauptstadt besser funktionieren als im Rest des Landes. Ihre Bewohner schätzen Brasília wegen der hohen Lebensqualität, im Plano Piloto geht es zu wie in einer amerikanischen Vorstadt. Das Heer der Hausangestellten kehrt abends in die Satellitenstädte zu-

music and the city is no longer as desolate as it once was at the weekends.

The designers of Brasília, however, did not relocate to the capital city. Lúcio Costa died in 1998, alone and bitter in a tiny apartment in Rio. The much-celebrated Oscar Niemeyer also lived in Rio. The *Jornal do Brasil* once asked him why he never took up residence in one of his buildings in Brasília. In reply he mumbled that he felt most at home in Rio.

rück. Auch der Arbeitsrhythmus der Politiker hat sich angepasst: Man kann heute Termine am Montag oder Freitag machen. Es gibt Kneipen und Restaurants mit Live-Musik, am Wochenende wirkt die Stadt nicht mehr ganz so öde wie früher.

Die Erbauer Brasílias haben ihren Wohnsitz nie in die Hauptstadt verlegt. Lúcio Costa starb 1998 einsam und verbittert in einem winzigen Apartment in Rio. Auch der gefeierte Niemeyer lebte in Rio. Warum er nie ein von ihm entworfenes Gebäude in Brasília bewohnt habe, wollte einmal die Zeitung *Jornal do Brasil* von ihm wissen.

Am wohlsten fühle er sich in Rio, grummelte der Meister.

Dubbed by Brazilians as the largest flag mast in the world, the Pantheon of the Fatherland and Freedom and the dovecote tower flank the expansive Praça dos Três Poderes (Square of Three Powers).
Der nach brasilianischer Lesart größte Flaggenmast der Welt, das Pantheon des Vaterlands und der Freiheit sowie der Taubenturm flankieren den weiten Praça dos Três Poderes (Platz der drei Gewalten).

Even the new television tower in the distance echoes the elegant forms for which Niemeyer is famous.
Selbst der neue Fernsehturm in der Ferne zeigt die eleganten Formen, für die Niemeyer berühmt ist.

Falk Jaeger

A New Landmark for the Capital

The Estádio Nacional Mané Garrincha in Brasília

Ein neues Wahrzeichen für die Hauptstadt

Das Estádio Nacional Mané Garrincha in Brasília

The capital city of Brazil is listed by the UNESCO as a world heritage site, while for architects it is the "holy ground" of modernism. The chance to realize not only a building but also to contribute another monument to this city is a special privilege—at least, that is how the architects and engineers saw it.

Lúcio Costa's newly-built capital city did already possess a stadium: named after Brazil's second most famous national footballer and twice World Cup winner, the Estádio Mané Garrincha was built between 1972 and 1974 to a design by Icaro de Castro Mello. The multi-purpose arena with a capacity of 53,000 spectators was located as per Costa's plan to one side of the north edge of the Eixo Monumental, the main central axis of the capital city. Now, thirty-six years later, the World Cup presented the fitting occasion to create a new, contemporary venue for modern football, and to erect a new national stadium on the same site, to be planned by the original architect's son, Eduardo Castro Mello.

Work began on the project in 2010 with the demolition of the existing building. Only the main grandstands were left standing for incorporation into the new building. But, as is often the case with such politically, architecturally, and structurally complex projects, developments transpired to put an end to the idea, with the result that nothing remains of the original building as it proved too complex to strengthen structurally and too constraining for a coherent redesign. Instead, a new stadium bowl has been constructed with a different geometrical arrangement and an internal arrangement more conducive to current requirements regarding

Zum Weltkulturerbe ist die brasilianische Hauptstadt von der UNESCO erklärt worden, für Architekten ist Brasília »heiliger Boden« der Moderne. Hier bauen zu dürfen, ein weiteres Monument zumal, ist ein besonderes Privileg. So empfanden es jedenfalls die Architekten und Ingenieure.

Ein Stadion hatte es in Lúcio Costas Hauptstadt aus der Retorte durchaus schon gegeben. Es war nach dem zweitberühmtesten Fußballnationalspieler Brasiliens und zweifachen Weltmeister benannt, das 1972–74 von Icaro de Castro Mello erbaute Estádio Mané Garrincha. Eine Mehrzweckarena mit einem Fassungsvermögen von gut 53.000 Zuschauern, die nach Costas Plan für Brasília seitlich am Nordrand der Eixo Monumental, der großen Zentralachse der Hauptstadt ihren Platz fand. Nun, nach 36 Jahren, war Zeit und Anlass, neue, zeitgemäße Bedingungen für den Fußball moderner Prägung zu schaffen und an selber Stelle Platz zu machen für ein neues Nationalstadion, das der Sohn des Erbauers, Eduardo Castro Mello, planen sollte.

2010 begannen die Arbeiten mit dem Abriss des Bestandsbaus. Lediglich die Haupttribüne sollte stehen bleiben und in den Neubau integriert werden. Doch wie so oft in derlei Fällen gewann das architektonisch, bautechnisch und politisch hochkomplexe Bauvorhaben eine Eigendynamik, die unter anderem dazu führte, dass vom Bestandsbau am Ende nichts mehr erhalten blieb, weil die Ertüchtigung sich doch als zu aufwendig erwies und die Relikte einer schlüssigen Neuplanung im Weg waren.

The Estádio Mané Garrincha, built in 1974, was originally intended to be kept and converted.

Das 1974 erbaute Estádio Mané Garrincha sollte ursprünglich im Rahmen eines Umbaus weitgehend erhalten bleiben.

The stadium bowl and the ring-shaped hallway with the roof are in principle two separate construction sites that are only connected via gangway-like bridges.
Die Stadionschüssel und die Ringhalle mit Dach waren faktisch zwei getrennte Baustellen, die nur über die Zugangsbrücken miteinander in Verbindung standen.

infrastructure, cloakroom arrangements, and football practice, as well as restaurants and lounges.

These developments were, however, the product of a long and complicated process and it turned out to be fortuitous that the architects at gmp and the engineers from schlaich bergermann und partner were able to work on their part of the project from a distance and to develop their design largely independently of the inner stadium bowl.

Their task was to construct a roof covering the stadium bowl and to organize access to the spectators' seating areas. In effect there were two different building sites, an inner site for the stadium core for which Castro Mello arquitetos was responsible and an external site for the "esplanade" with stairs, ramps and the roof covering the stadium.

Of all the Brazilian World Cup stadia, the Estádio in Brasília is more of a freestanding object than any of the other national stadia in Brazil. It is visible from all directions and it can still be seen in its entirety from far away. As such, it cannot help but stand alongside the phalanx of Oscar Niemeyer's other radiant landmarks with their characteristic silhouettes, and must assert its position alongside them. And, as the largest and most public of the city's buildings, a certain monumentality is not amiss. Its appearance from afar was therefore an important aspect for the designers in their consideration of the scale of the exterior articulation of the arena, as well as how motorists see it as they drive past.

Stattdessen entstand eine neue Tribünenschüssel mit veränderter Geometrie und mit einem nach aktuellen Bedürfnissen geplanten Innenleben für Infrastruktur, Garderoben und Übungsbereiche sowie Gastronomie und Lounges.

Diese Entwicklung des Projekts war jedoch ein längerer, komplizierter Prozess, und so erwies es sich als günstiger Umstand, dass die Architekten von gmp · von Gerkan, Marg und Partner und die Ingenieure von schlaich bergermann und partner bei ihrem Part an dem Projekt von Anbeginn auf räumlichen Abstand gegangen waren und weitgehend abgekoppelt vom inneren Stadion planen konnten.

Ihnen oblag es, die Tribünenschüssel mit einem Dach zu überfangen und die Ränge zu erschließen, das heißt, die Zugänge rings um die Tribünenschüssel zu organisieren. Es gab faktisch zwei Baustellen, eine innere des Kernstadions unter der alleinigen Verantwortung von Castro Mello arquitetos und eine äußere der Esplanade mit Treppenanlagen, Rampen und dem alles überdeckenden Dach.

Kaum eines der brasilianischen WM-Stadien steht so frei wie das Nationalstadion in Brasília. Von allen Seiten und zum Teil aus größerer Entfernung ist es in seiner Gänze wahrzunehmen. Es reiht sich damit zwangsläufig ein in die Phalanx der strahlenden Solitäre Oscar Niemeyers, die der Hauptstadt ihr weltbekanntes Gepräge geben – und muss sich in dieser Gesellschaft behaupten. Immerhin ist es das größte und öffentlichste Gebäude der Stadt und durfte durchaus eine gewisse Monumentalität ver-

The symbolic presence of the stadium therefore plays a greater role here than in most of the other stadium projects. Likewise, it was more important here than in the other projects not only to find a suitably coherent, logical, and appropriate form and architectonic articulation but also to design a powerful landmark that can hold its own alongside Niemeyer's significant buildings. The intention was neither to create a piece of retro-architecture nor to employ a totally new visual language, i. e. to use a similar repertoire of forms and materials.

As such, it is not surprising that the designers, like the Modernist masters before them, elected to employ concrete and to cast the structural members under compression in the material that since the days of Niemeyer has been used most commonly in Brazil.

The flat concrete ring of the roof construction of the stadium encircles the stadium like one of Saturn's rings. Unlike many other stadia, which have an oval shape to stay as close as possible to the playing field as possible, its form describes a perfect circle, the most efficient form for a compression ring for a cable-net roof.

This vast modern-day Tholos, with an impressive diameter of 309 meters, recalls the round temple of Hercules in ancient Rome, except that instead of being borne by 20 columns it is supported by 288 columns arranged in three con-

körpern. So war die Fernwirkung für die Gestalter ein wichtiger Aspekt bei der Planung der Maßstäblichkeit der äußeren Erscheinung der Arena, aber auch die Erlebbarkeit aus den die umgebenden Straßen befahrenden Autos heraus.

Mehr noch als bei den anderen Stadien spielte die Zeichenhaftigkeit eine Rolle. Mehr noch als bei den anderen ging es nicht nur darum, für das gewaltige Tragwerk gemeinsam mit den Ingenieuren eine schlüssige und logische, angemessene Form zu finden und diese architektonisch zu bewältigen, sondern auch ein kraftvolles Zeichen zu setzen, das mit Niemeyers signifikanten Bauten mitreden kann. Und das nicht als Retroarchitektur, aber auch nicht in einer gänzlich neuen Sprache, sondern mit einem verwandten formalen und materiellen Repertoire.

So lag es nahe, wie der Altmeister der Moderne den Beton sprechen zu lassen, die tragenden und die druckbeanspruchten Glieder des Tragwerks aus dem in Brasilien seit Niemeyer allgegenwärtigen Material zu gießen.

Wie ein Saturnring umkreist der flache Betonring der Dachkonstruktion das Stadion, nicht wie bei anderen Stadien dem Spielfeld angenähert und Platz sparend oval, sondern ausgreifend kreisrund, als effizienteste Form des Druckrings für ein von Seilen getragenes Dach.

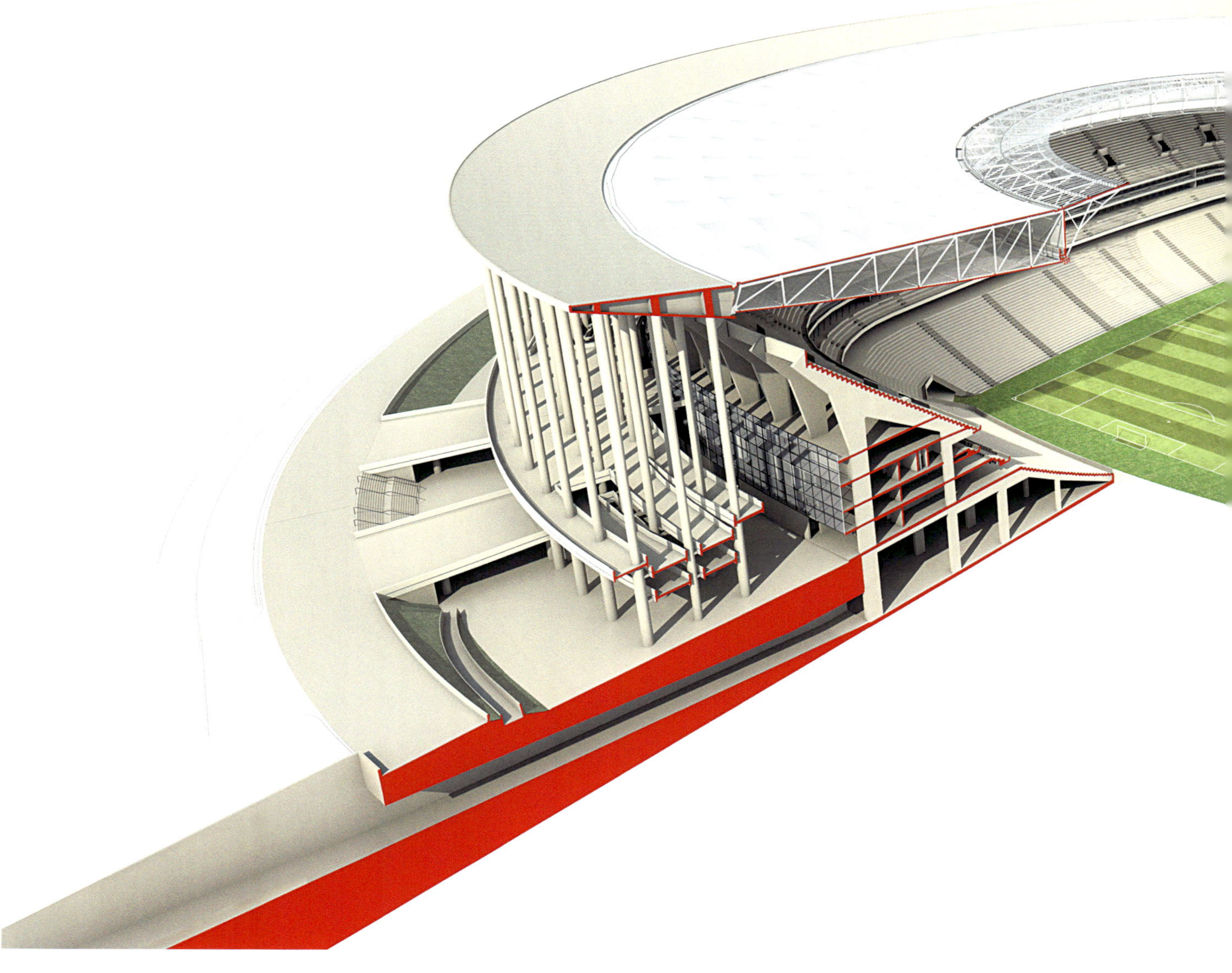

centric rings. From nearby it looks as if a forest of columns holds up the broad ring of the roof because seen from the ground the circular columns appear to stand randomly, although their actual layout is perfectly concentric and radial. The further away one moves from the building, the clearer the arrangement becomes, the better one appreciates it as a whole, and the more monumental and statuary it looks. Individuals walking around on the platform between the house-high columns then look like miniature figures in a scene by Piranesi.

This structure is designed to accommodate large numbers of visitors, who can either pass beneath the roof from outside straight to the middle level or who ascend the long ramps that rise around the perimeter until they reach bridges that lead to the mouths of the openings on the upper tier of the spectator stands. As elsewhere in Brasília, the ramps are generally wide and extend for long distances, but this makes them safer in the event of an emergency. The ramps ascend in one direction towards their destination, making it almost impossible to lose one's orientation. The different geometries of the circular esplanade and the oval stadium bowl produce attractive half-moon-shaped spaces between them.

The stadium bowl with its lower and upper tiers and two lounge levels sandwiched between them hugs the shape of

Eindrucksvolle 309 Meter Durchmesser hat diese gewaltige Tholos der Neuzeit, die an den Rundtempel des Herkules im antiken Rom erinnerte, hätte sie wie dieser 20 Säulen und nicht derer 288, angeordnet in drei konzentrischen Ringen. Ein ganzer Säulenwald trägt den breiten Dachring, so scheint es aus der Nähe, denn das Auge sieht die Rundstützen wie Bäume locker gruppiert, nicht in ihrer geometrisch tadellosen konzentrischen und radialen Ordnung. Je weiter sich der Betrachter allerdings entfernt, desto klarer wird die Ordnung, desto überschaubarer wird der Bau, desto statuarischer, monumentaler wirkt er. Einzelne Menschen, die sich auf der Plattform zwischen den haushohen Stützen aufhalten, wirken wie die schemenhaften Figuren in einer Szenerie von Piranesi.

Doch das Bauwerk ist für Besucherströme gebaut, die unter dem Dach zu ebener Erde auf Höhe des Mittelrangs das Stadion erreichen oder die langen Rampen zur oberen, das Stadion umrundenden Esplanade emporgehen und über Brücken zu den Mundlöchern des Oberrangs streben. Breite Rampen, wie sie in Brasilien bevorzugt werden, weil sie zwar lange Wege bedeuten, aber im Panikfall als sicherer gelten. Die Rampen mit einer Wendung führen in klaren Wegen zum Ziel. Niemand wird hier die Orientierung verlieren. Durch die unterschiedlichen Geo-

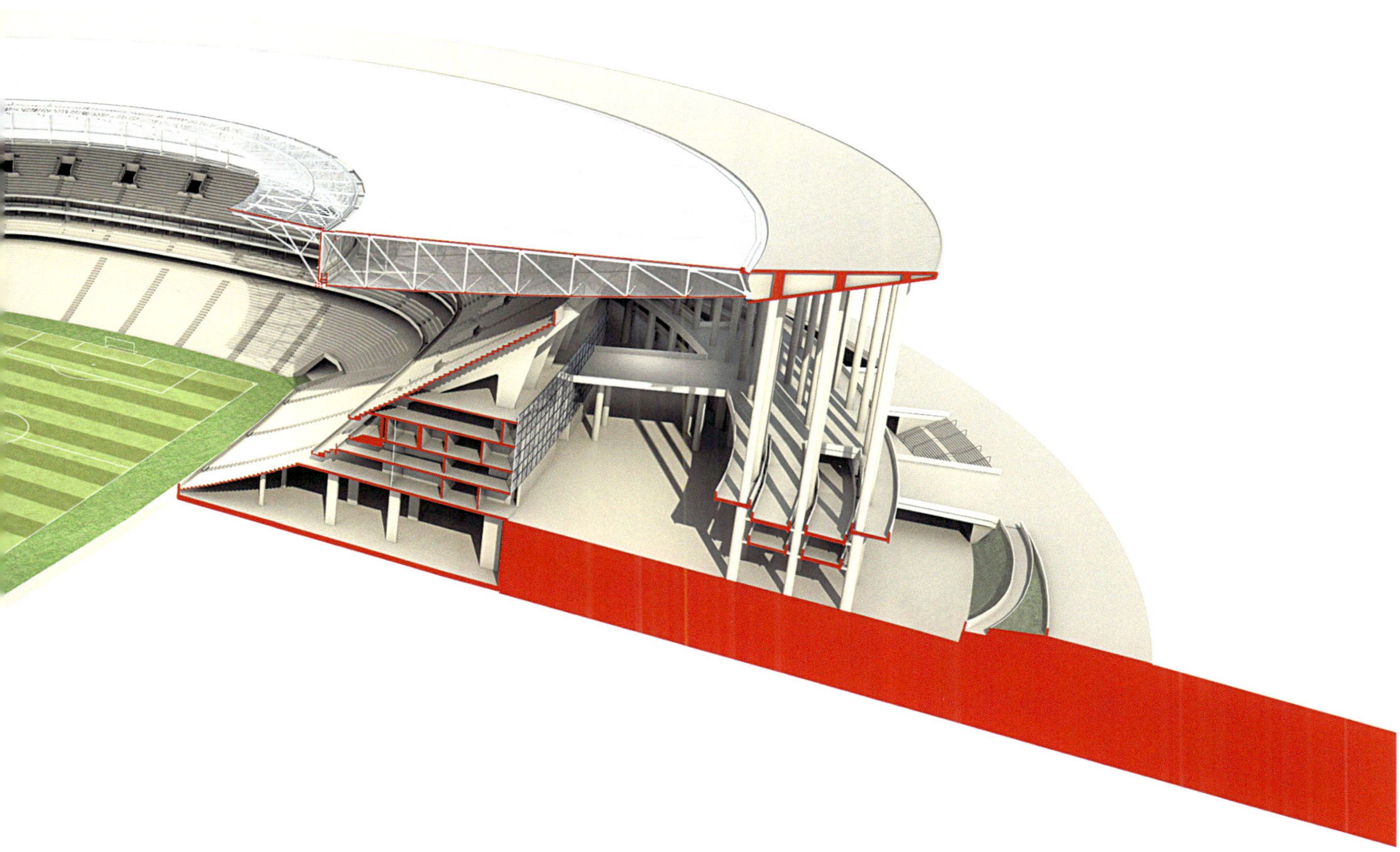

Mercure
CULLINAN
EXECUTIVE OFFICE TOWER

the playing field in an oval-rectangular shape. The hole open to the sky in the center over the playing field is circular like the entire roof construction around it, which appears to levitate over stadium, an effect heightened by the lack of a connection between the top of the stadium bowl and the roof.

The extremely delicate-looking cable-net roof is anchored to the concrete compression ring, while the columns that hold up the concrete circle look impossibly slender—36 meters high and 1.20 meters in diameter—and are rigidly anchored both to the upper concrete ring and to the ramps below so that together they can dissipate all the horizontal loads, thus obviating the need for unsightly diagonal braces or stiffening wall planes which the architects and engineers were anxious to avoid.

The compression ring is a hollow-section box-beam in cross-section, twenty-two meters wide and five meters high at its inner face, tapering to a thin line at its outer edge. What looks simple from the outside has a complex internal structure subdivided by radial and tangential dividing walls over each of the axes of the columns. The radial cables of the cable-net structure are anchored to every second dividing wall, which contain pre-stressing tensioning elements that transfer the high tension forces from the cable-net roof to the outer perimeter of the concrete ring, creating a compressive stress that is needed for concrete elements.

The supporting cables span radially inwards to the tension ring over the center of the stadium. On each of the radial cables stand masts and diagonals that carry a top chord, which, together with the cable as tensioning element, form

metrien der ovalen Stadionschüssel und der kreisrunden Esplanade entstehen attraktive halbmondförmige Zwischenräume.

Die Stadionschüssel mit Unter- und Oberrang sowie zwei dazwischengeschobenen Lounge-Etagen rückt an allen vier Seiten unmittelbar an das Spielfeld heran und bildet ein dem Rechteck angenähertes Oval. Das Himmelsauge über dem grünen Rasen hingegen ist kreisrund wie die gesamte Dachkonstruktion, die wegen des offenen Abstands oberhalb des Tribünenrands über dem Stadion zu schweben scheint.

Getragen wird das ungemein leicht wirkende Seilnetzdach vom Betondruckring. Die den flachen Betonreifen spielerisch in die Höhe hebenden Betonstützen, über der Esplanade 36 Meter hoch und mit einem Durchmesser von 1,20 Meter sehr schlank wirkend, sind oben in den Druckring und unten in die Rampen eingespannt, damit sie alle gemeinsam die Horizontallasten übertragen können, denn die Ingenieure und Architekten wollten bei der Säulenhalle diagonale Streben und Wandscheiben zur Aussteifung unbedingt vermeiden.

Der Druckring ist ein im Querschnitt dreieckiger Hohlkastenträger, 22 Meter breit, am Außenrand spitz auslaufend und am inneren Rand 5 Meter hoch. Der von außen simpel erscheinende Hohlkasten hat allerdings ein kompliziertes Innenleben. Dort ist er jeweils über den Stützenachsen von radialen und tangentialen Schottwänden unterteilt. An jeder zweiten Schottwand sind die Radialseile des Seiltragwerks angeschlossen. In diesen Schott-

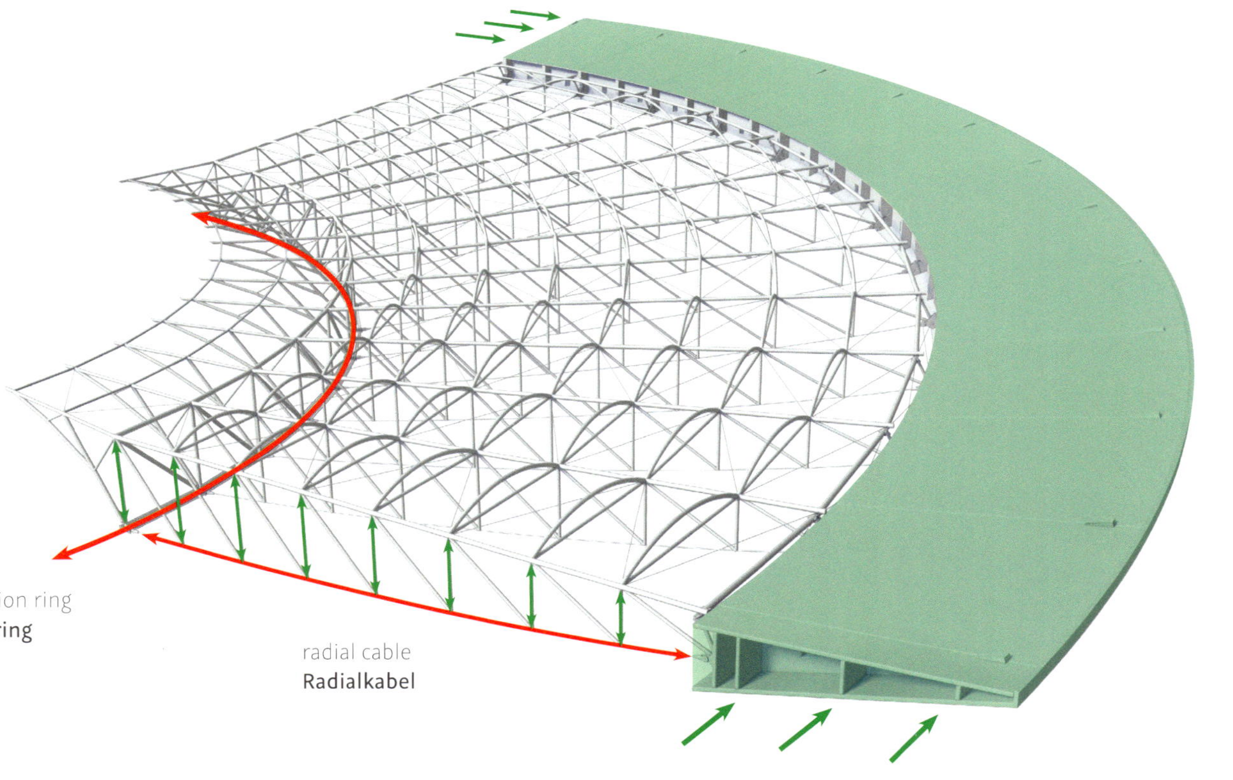

The construction of the roof with the wide compression ring (green), the tension ring (red) and the cable construction in-between with the vertical struts (green) that stand on the radial cables (red)
Das Tragwerk des Daches mit dem breiten Druckring (grün), dem Zugring (rot) und der Seilkonstruktion dazwischen mit auf den Radialseilen (rot) stehenden Pfosten (grün)

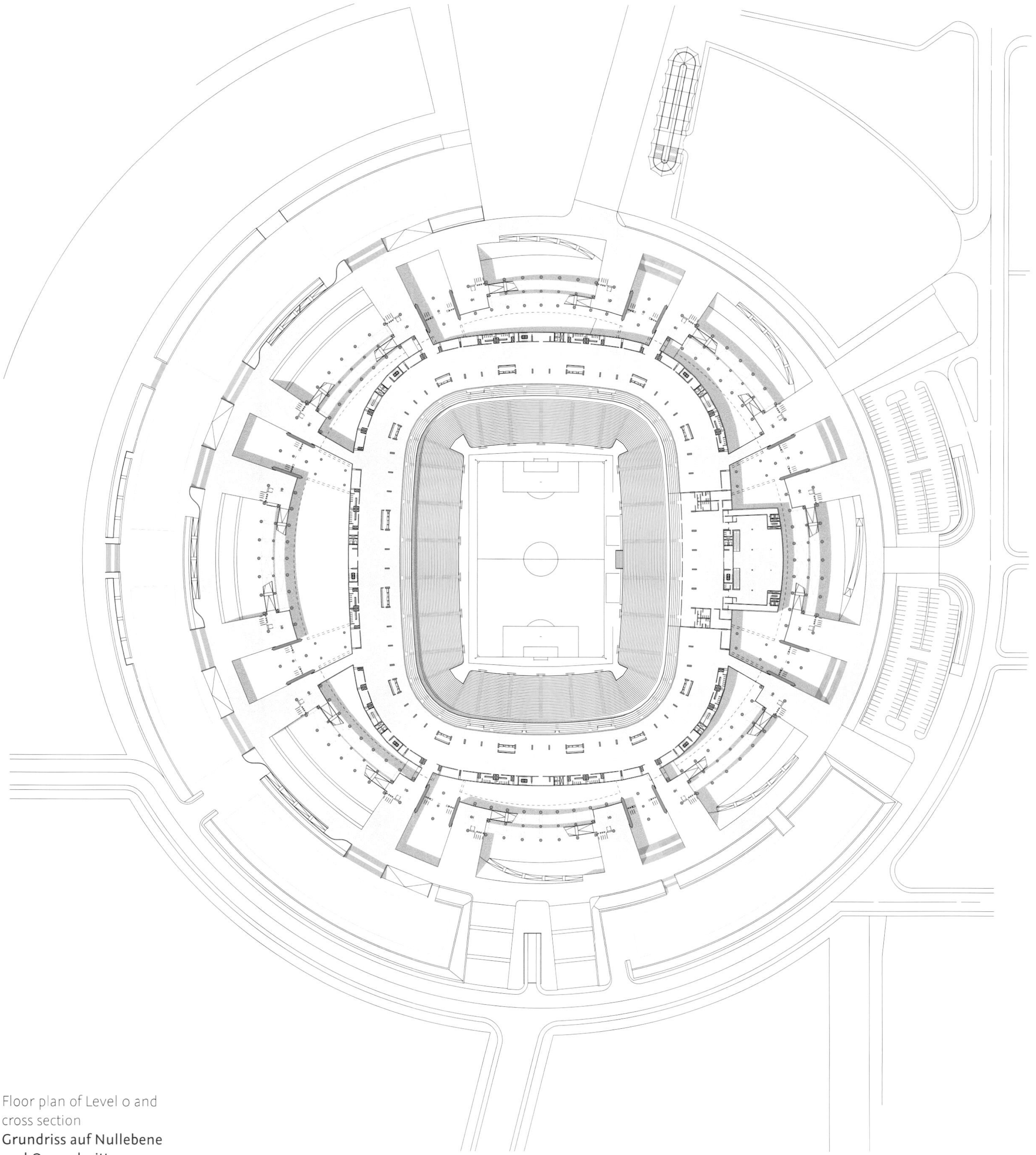

Floor plan of Level 0 and cross section

Grundriss auf Nullebene und Querschnitt

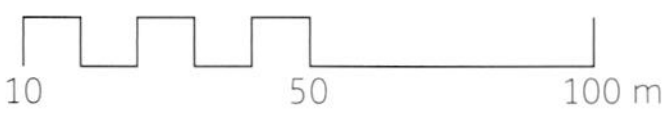

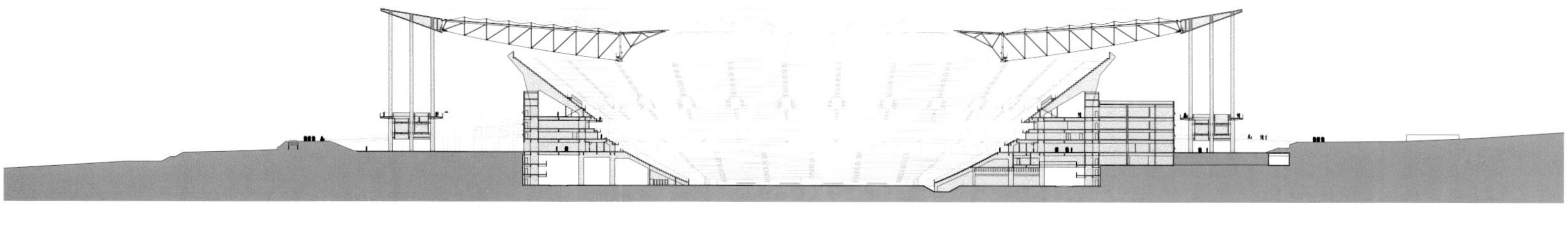

a truss. Distributed evenly around the circle of the stadium, these forty-eight slender trusses are connected by shallow arching purlins over which the translucent membrane of the roof has been spanned so that it flexes in two axes. The underside of the trusses is likewise transparent and porous allowing light and noise to pass through it, giving the roof a diaphanous solidity with the delicate roof construction just visible within it. All the necessary roof installations, such as drainage systems, floodlighting and sound systems, can therefore be concealed cleanly within the roof and, with the exception of two video walls suspended from the roof, the underside of the roof is smooth and uninterrupted.

Additional trussed beams hung from the inner tension ring extend a further 17.5 meters towards the center and hold the innermost ring of roof covering, which is made of solid polycarbonate panels that ensure the pitch is sufficiently illuminated.

The upper surface of the roof, which can be seen from the television tower nearby, has been prepared for equipping with photovoltaic collectors around the compression ring so that it fulfills LEED certification as recommended by FIFA.

Through the combination of spoke-wheel principle and suspended cable roof, it has been possible to produce a roof with a surface area of 47,000 square meters and roof cantilevers of over 81 meters using a lightweight construction method that requires just 2,200 tons of steel. The regular, visible construction and order of the roof and its almost demonstrative lightness gives the interior a sense of calm grandeur without appearing monumental.

wänden verlaufen Spannglieder, die die Verankerung der hohen Zugkräfte aus dem Seildach am äußeren Rand des Druckrings gewährleisten und so im ganzen Ring eine Druckspannung erzeugen, wie es für Beton materialgerecht ist.

Die Tragseile laufen radial nach innen bis zum über dem Stadioninneren schwebenden Zugring. Auf den Radialseilen stehen Pfosten und Diagonalen, die einen Obergurt aus Stahlrohr tragen und insgesamt mit dem Seil als Zugglied einen Fachwerkträger bilden. Die 48 sehr schlanken Fachwerkträger des Stadionrunds sind durch flachbogige Pfetten verbunden, über die die transluzente Membrandachhaut zweiachsig gekrümmt gespannt ist. Auch die Unterspannung des Dachraums ist transluzent und offenporig, um Tageslicht und Schall passieren zu lassen. So wirkt der Dachkörper räumlich und die filigrane Dachkonstruktion ist schemenhaft zu erkennen. Alle Installationen für Dachentwässerung, Licht und Beschallung sowie der Catwalk für die Wartung sind innerhalb des Dachkörpers auf ästhetisch problemlose Weise untergebracht. Die Dachuntersicht ist bis auf zwei abgehängte Videowände glatt und ungestört.

Vorn an den Zugring angehängt kragen zusätzliche leichte Fachwerkträger 17,50 Meter weit aus und tragen den innersten Ring der Dachhaut, der aus glasklaren, massiven Polycarbonatplatten besteht und die ausreichende Belichtung des Rasens ermöglicht.

Die Dachfläche, immerhin vom nahen Fernsehturm aus zu sehen, ist im Bereich des Druckrings für die Bestü-

The distinctive concrete structure with its flat "ring of Saturn" resting on a three concentric rings of columns lends the outward appearance of the building the requisite strength and stature to exist in its own right alongside the fascinating ensemble of monumental buildings in Brasília. Its imposing presence is a factor of its dimensions and prominent urban disposition, but also of its simple but significant and unmistakable form and typology, which is unique in its kind around the world. Alongside the President's Palace and Congress, the cathedral and the museum, the national stadium, which bears the name of the still-legendary footballer Mané Garrincha, will in the future also represent a monumental national landmark of the Brazilian capital.

ckung mit Fotovoltaikkollektoren vorgesehen, um die von der FIFA empfohlene LEED-Zertifizierung zu erreichen.

Durch die Kombination aus Speichenradprinzip und Seilhängedach wird die Auskragung von mehr als 81 Metern und einer Fläche von 47.000 Quadratmetern mit einem eleganten, ressourcenschonenden Leichtbauprinzip und einem Stahleinsatz von lediglich 2200 Tonnen bewältigt. Der Innenraum des Stadions gewinnt durch die regelhafte, erlebbare konstruktive Ordnung und die fast demonstrative Leichtigkeit an Ruhe und Erhabenheit, ohne monumental zu wirken.

Die das äußere Erscheinungsbild prägende Betonkonstruktion mit dem flachen »Saturnring« auf seinem dreifachen Stützenkranz wiederum verleiht dem repräsentativen Bauwerk die notwendige Kraft und Erhabenheit, um im faszinierenden Ensemble der Monumentalbauten Brasílias bestehen zu können. Seine enorme Präsenz erwächst dem Stadion aus seiner Dimension und seiner herausgehobenen städtebaulichen Position, aber auch aus der einfachen, aber signifikanten, unverwechselbaren Form und Typologie, die zudem weltweit ohne Beispiel ist. Neben Präsidentenpalast und Parlament, Kathedrale und Museum repräsentiert künftig auch das Nationalstadion, das noch immer den berühmten Namen des Mané Garrincha trägt, als Monument und Wahrzeichen die Hauptstadt Brasiliens.

Previous page: The tension ring is comprised of individual cables, while the inner, transparent part of the roof is borne by supporting cantilevered trusses.
Vorige Seite: Der Zugring besteht aus einzelnen Seilen. Der innere, transparente Teil des Daches ruht auf unterstützten Kragträgern.

The radial structural framework is just about visible between the upper and lower membranes of the roof.
Zwischen unterer und oberer Membran wird die radiale Tragkonstruktion schemenhaft sichtbar.

196 | 197
Brasília

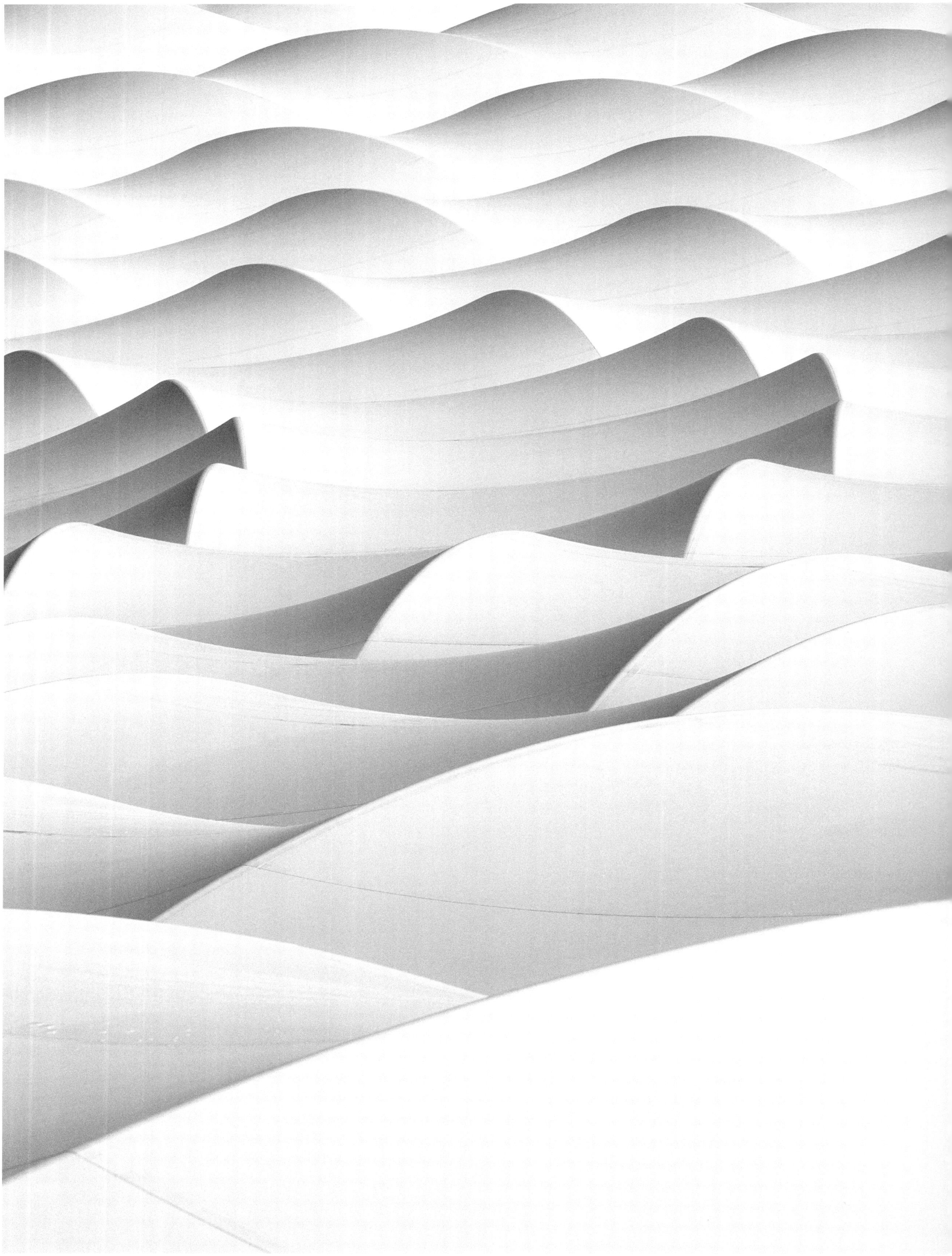

Tobias Käufer

Sport, Politics or Religion?

The Role of Football in Brazilian Society

Sport, Politik oder Religion?

Der Fußball in der Gesellschaft Brasiliens

To understand what football means to Brazil, one need only consider Sócrates Brasileiro Sampaio de Souza Vieira de Oliveira (1954–2011). With a name that itself sounds like an intricate eight-part ballplay maneuver, it is no surprise that he was known to his fans simply as "Dr. Socrates" because he also held a doctorate in medicine. Although he never actually won a World Cup title, he is still one of the most popular Brazilian footballers of all time. During the military dictatorship in the nineteen-eighties, "Dr. Socrates" used his popularity to demonstrate civil courage and set about establishing democratic structures at his football club, the São Paolo Corinthians. "Democracia Corinthiana" was not, however, just about giving the players more say; it was also about more freedom for the oppressed people of Brazil. Walking onto the pitch wearing t-shirts emblazoned with the slogan "Democracy now" was a direct affront to the military rulers and a dangerous balancing act for the players. But by then "Dr. Socrates" had become a national institution and his arrest would have provoked an uprising. His courage earned him great respect among the people, despite failing to bring the World Cup back home from Spain in 1982 after playing a series of outstanding games. Brazil can point to a string of world-class players—Pelé, Ronaldo or Ronaldinho to mention just a few—but the Seleção of the nineteen-eighties is still regarded as one of the strongest national football teams that Brazil ever had.

In Brazil, football is more than just a sport. It is also religion and politics, and it holds the promise of public recognition and economic success. In a documentary entitled *Pelada—Futebol na Favela*, made in the run-up to the 2014 World

Schon der volle Name klingt wie ein gelungener Spielzug über acht Stationen: Wer Brasiliens Fußball verstehen will, kommt an Sócrates Brasileiro Sampaio de Souza Vieira de Oliveira (1954–2011) nicht vorbei. »Dr. Socrates«, wie ihn seine Fans wegen des absolvierten Medizinstudiums nannten, hat nie einen WM-Titel gewonnen. Und doch gehört der Spielmacher zu den populärsten brasilianischen Fußballern aller Zeiten. »Dr. Socrates« zeigte während der brasilianischen Militärdiktatur in den Achtzigerjahren Zivilcourage und nutzte seine Popularität für die Umsetzung basisdemokratischer Strukturen bei seinem Klub Corinthians São Paulo. Doch hinter der sogenannten Democracia Corinthiana stand mehr als nur der Ruf nach mehr Freiräumen für die Spieler, es ging um mehr Freiheit für ein ganzes unterdrücktes Volk. Für den Nationalspieler war das alles ein gefährlicher Drahtseilakt. Die Corinthians liefen mit einem Schriftzug »Demokratie jetzt« auf das Spielfeld. Für die herrschenden Militärs ein Affront, doch »Dr. Socrates« war längst eine Institution, die zu verhaften einen Aufstand provoziert hätte. Diesen Mut haben ihm die Brasilianer stets hoch angerechnet. Und sie verziehen ihm, dass »Dr. Socrates« trotz überragender Leistungen bei der WM 1982 in Spanien ohne Titel nach Hause kam. Bis heute gilt die Seleção der Achtzigerjahre, auch wenn sie ohne einen Pelé, Ronaldo oder Ronaldinho auskommen musste, als die spielstärkste, die Brasilien je hatte.

Fußball ist in Brasilien nicht nur Sport, er ist auch Religion, Politik und eine Chance zu gesellschaftlicher Anerkennung und wirtschaftlichem Aufstieg. Filmemacher Alex Miranda hat vor der WM 2014 der gesellschaftlichen

The Maracanã: hallowed ground for all kickers on Copacabana beach
Das große Ziel aller Kicker am Strand von Copacabana: das Maracanã

Just married in Manaus and already football-bound
Auch das Hochzeitspaar in Manaus zieht es zum Fußball.

Cup, the film director Alex Miranda examines the social importance of football and attempts to uncover why Brazilian football is so successful. Brazil, the largest country in South America, has won the World Cup five times and is the most successful football nation in the world. "The DNA of Brazilian football has its roots in these bare, grassless patches of ground. What the players learn here in this special environment shapes their whole lives as footballers," says Miranda of the world of the favelas, where new talent seems to surface almost every day. Because the hard playing grounds of the favelas are so far removed from the glamour of international football and their vast, costly arenas, this is, according to Miranda, "probably the purest and most honest form of the game." In his film, Miranda invites many stars to recall their childhood memories. Neymar, Brazil's superstar of the digital age, recalls: "When I was young, I played on pitches where the only grass left was at the sides of the pitch."

This is why so many children and youngsters identify with the professional player who now plays internationally for FC Barcelona: like him, they know—or rather he, like them, knows—what football means to someone who has had to work their way up from the bottom. Every year more than 700 footballers leave Brazil to play in professional leagues around the world. Not everyone's dream of becoming an international footballer can be as glamorous as Neymar's—some end up playing in the Czech Republic's third league. Football in Brazil also has less savory sides: corrupt association and club functionaries on the one hand and unscrupulous agents on the other make a fast buck selling

Bedeutung in seinem Dokumentarstreifen *Pelada – Futebol na Favela* Rechnung getragen und versucht, den Erfolg des brasilianischen Fußballs zu ergründen. Mit fünf WM-Titeln ist das größte südamerikanische Land die erfolgreichste Fußballnation der Welt. »Die DNA des brasilianischen Fußballs stammt von diesen nackten Plätzen, ohne Rasen. Hier erhalten die Spieler eine ganz besondere Ausbildung, die ihr weiteres fußballerisches Leben prägt«, sagt Miranda über die Welt der Favelas, in der nahezu täglich neue Talente geboren werden. Gerade weil das Spiel auf den harten Plätzen der Favelas so gar nichts mit dem Glanz des internationalen Fußballs, den riesigen, millionenschweren Arenen zu tun habe: »Es ist die wahrscheinlich ehrlichste und einfachste Form des Spiels.« Miranda lässt in seinem Streifen viele Stars über ihre Kindheitserinnerungen berichten. »Als ich jung war, musste ich auf einem Platz spielen, der nur Rasen an den Seitenflächen hatte«, erinnert sich Neymar, Brasiliens Superstar des digitalen Zeitalters, in Mirandas Film.

Genau deswegen identifizieren sich so viele Kinder und Jugendliche mit dem Profi des FC Barcelona, weil sie wie er – nein, weil er wie sie den Fußball aus der Perspektive des Überlebenskünstlers kennt. Rund 700 Fußballer exportiert Brasilien jedes Jahr in alle Profiligen dieser Welt. Längst nicht alle Träume von der internationalen Karriere gehen so auf wie die von Neymar. Einige enden auch in der dritten tschechischen Liga. Der Fußball hat in Brasilien auch seine hässlichen Seiten. Korrupte Verbands- und Vereinsfunktionäre gehören ebenso dazu wie skrupellose Spielervermittler, die des schnellen Geldes wegen junge Talente auf dem Profimarkt

In bars, restaurants and public areas in Brazil, TV screens are a constant reminder of the all-pervasive presence of football.
Kneipen, Restaurants, öffentliche Treffpunkte, überall hängen Bildschirme mit der Omnipräsenz des Fußballs.

off young talent cheap to the professional market. And, of course, violence has also cast a dark shadow over the sport. Clashes between fans are an unpleasant side to the game in most countries, but in Rio de Janeiro and São Paolo, it can regularly be a matter of life and death, and not just during a local derby. In some areas, wearing the wrong football shirt in the wrong part of town is tantamount to a death sentence as the favelas are in the hands of *Ultras* who are not shy to use violence.

Violence has also contributed to a dramatic decline in spectator numbers in the Brazilian championships, with an average of just 15,000 people attending home matches. Intimidated by an increase in brutal hooliganism in recent years, people are also staying away from normal league matches. Even local derby fixtures between traditional clubs such as Fluminese and Flamengo in the freshly renovated Maracanã in Rio de Janeiro are not sold out. A further reason is also the high price of tickets, not to mention the late kick-off time, which is dictated by television programming. The stupendous viewing figures of the *telenovelas*, the television soaps, mean that football must wait until they are over before kick-off can begin. Brazilian league games are also not as attractive as the European Championships, in which the majority of the national players now plays. Instead, the "Cariocas" in Rio prefer to meet for a beer at their local bar. Football fever has shifted from the stadia to the bars where it is both safer to watch and more sociable. The stadia are only full when the Seleção play at home, but the opportunities to see the national stars play live in the flesh are few

verscherbeln. Natürlich ist da auch die Gewalt, die sich wie ein dunkler Schatten über den Fußball legt. Fanausschreitungen sind auch in anderen Ländern unschöne Begleitumstände, in Rio de Janeiro oder São Paulo geht es jedoch auch abseits der Derbys regelmäßig um Leben und Tod. Das falsche Trikot im falschen Stadtteil kann das Todesurteil bedeuten. Favelas sind fest in der Hand von gewaltbereiten Ultras.

Die Gewalt ist es auch, die dafür sorgt, dass der Zuschauerschnitt bei den Heimspielen der brasilianischen Meisterschaft bei zuletzt gerade einmal 15.000 Besuchern lag. In den letzten Jahren nahm die Zahl brutaler Ausschreitungen am Rande ganz normaler Ligaspiele zu. Selbst die Lokalderbys im frisch renovierten Maracanã von Rio de Janeiro von Traditionsklubs wie Fluminese und Flamengo sind nicht ausverkauft. Das liegt zwar auch an den gestiegenen Eintrittspreisen, vor allem aber an den späten Anstoßzeiten. TV-Fußball findet in Brasilien meist nach den Telenovelas statt, die wegen der traumhaften Einschaltquoten sogar das runde Leder in der Programmfolge nach hinten schieben. Zudem ist die brasilianische Liga nicht so attraktiv wie die europäische Champions League, in der nahezu alle brasilianischen Nationalspieler aktiv sind. Stattdessen treffen sich die Cariocas in Rio lieber zum gemeinsamen Bier in der Stammkneipe nebenan. Die Fußballbegeisterung hat sich von den Stadien in die Bars verlagert. Hier ist es spätabends sicherer und geselliger. Nur die Heimspiele der Seleção haben die Strahlkraft, für ausverkaufte Stadien zu sorgen. Die in Europa tätigen Stars einmal live und hautnah in Farbe zu sehen, ist allerdings ein seltenes Erlebnis in Brasilien, denn

and far between in Brazil: many of the players are in Europe for much of the year, and a marketing agency ensures that the national team often plays in the USA, Asia or in Europe. The hope is that the new world-class stadia built for the 2014 World Cup in Brazil will provide more opportunities for the national team to play at home more frequently.

In no other country can one hear such tragic tales of the rise and subsequent downfall of celebrated national heroes, for example that of Mané Garrincha, who died young and penniless—just forty-nine years old—as a consequence of his extravagant lifestyle. Twice a winner of the World Cup, playing alongside footballer of the century Pelé, his inimitable running style earned him the nickname of a Brazilian jungle bird. In Brazil, he is still regarded as the second-best player of all time and the football stadium in Brasília, which will host some of the World Cup matches, is named after him. Garrincha's life story, from his ascent to become an icon of Brazil to his bitter end in poverty and sickness, captivated the people and was made into a film. The only other country to harbor such melancholy tales of triumph and downfall is Argentina. Such extremes are typical of Brazil. In Brazil, winning the World Cup is not categorical proof of outstanding ability: only when it is achieved with "Jogo Bonito"—with beautiful playing—is it truly worthy. For this reason, many see the World Cup title in 1994 as a blemish in the history of Brazilian football because it was won by a side employing using unusually defensive tactics.

This criticism, however, cannot be leveled at Edson Arantes do Nascimento, more popularly known in Brazil, and in-

eine Vermarktungsagentur lässt die Nationalmannschaft oft in den USA, Asien oder Europa auflaufen. Die neue Stadionwelt, die Brasilien nach der WM 2014 zur Verfügung steht, könnte zumindest die Zahl der tatsächlichen Heimspiele der Nationalmannschaft deutlich erhöhen.

Kein anderes Land bietet so tragische Geschichten von Helden, die nach ihrem umjubelten Triumph so tief stürzten. Wie die von Mané Garrincha, der viel zu früh und bettelarm – im Alter von 49 Jahren – an den Folgen seines ausschweifenden Lebensstils starb. Zweimal gewann Garrincha an der Seite von Jahrhundertfußballer Pelé den WM-Pokal. Sein unnachahmlicher Laufstil brachte ihm den Spitznamen eines brasilianischen Urwaldvogels ein. Er gilt bis heute in Brasilien als zweitbester Spieler aller Zeiten. In der Hauptstadt Brasília werden in dem nach ihm benannten Stadion einige WM-Spiele ausgetragen. Das Leben Garrinchas, vom Aufstieg zu einer brasilianischen Ikone bis zum eher bitteren Ende, gezeichnet von Krankheit und Armut, fand den Weg auf die Kinoleinwände. Diese melancholische Verbindung von Triumph und Niedergang gibt es ansonsten nur noch in Argentinien. Der Brasilianer mag es extrem, deswegen gilt auch ein gewonnener WM-Titel nicht als Ausweis ausgewiesener Klasse. Der Triumph muss auch noch mit dem »Jogo bonito«, dem schönen Spiel, errungen werden. Bis heute gilt deswegen der WM-Titel von 1994, errungen von einer erstaunlich defensiv ausgerichteten Mannschaft, als Makel der brasilianischen Fußballgeschichte.

Auf Edson Arantes do Nascimento, den sie in Brasilien und überall auf der Welt nur Pelé rufen, trifft dieser Vor-

deed all over the world, as Pelé. The list of honors that the "man who scored over 1,000 goals" has received is as long as his successes. Pérola Negra (Black Pearl), O Rei do Futebol (The King of Football), O Rei Pelé (King Pelé) or simply O Rei (The King) are just some of the nicknames he has been given. His exceptional skill has earned him the title of FIFA World Player of the 20th Century and the IOC elected him Athlete of the Century. "Football says a lot about the soul of a nation," Pelé once remarked while describing the style of Brazilian football, "and our soul wants to dance." More than anyone else, Pelé and the three World Cup titles he won, has contributed to Brazil's advancement to a football super power.

Today the incredible power of football is palpable all over Brazil. No news program is complete without an extensive report on the match of the day. There are numerous talk shows devoted to the topic of football every day, and several sports newspapers vie with each other to provide the most comprehensive reports on Brazil's number one favorite sport.

Several footballers have also been successful in the political arena. The former world champions Bebeto and Romário are now both members of parliament, having used their popularity to secure them a political career.

Ex world champion Bebeto is part of the 2014 World Cup organizational committee and firmly believes that it represents a great opportunity for his country. "It's not just about the wonderful new stadia that Brazil will get but also the infrastructure projects, the new forms of mobility which will encourage further investment," says Bebeto. "The World Cup will generate growth. Brazil will be a better country after the

wurf ganz bestimmt nicht zu. Die Reihe an Ehrenbezeugungen für den »Mann der über 1000 Tore« ist genauso lang wie seine Liste an Erfolgen. »Pérola Negra« (»Schwarze Perle«), »O Rei do Futebol« (»König des Fußballs«), »O Rei Pelé« (»König Pelé«) oder ganz einfach »O Rei« (»Der König«) sind nur ein kleiner Auszug der Spitznamen des von der FIFA zum Weltfußballer des 20. Jahrhunderts und vom IOC zum Sportler des Jahrhunderts gekürten Ausnahmekickers. »Fußball sagt viel über die Seele eines Volkes aus. Und unsere Seele will tanzen«, sagte Pelé einmal, um den Stil des brasilianischen Fußballs zu erklären. Wie kein anderer hat Pelé mit seinen drei WM-Titeln für den Aufstieg Brasiliens zur Fußball-Supermacht gesorgt.

Heute ist die ungeheure Macht des Fußballs in Brasilien überall greifbar. Keine Nachrichtensendung kommt ohne eine ausführliche Berichterstattung über das runde Leder aus. Unzählige Fußball-Talkshows widmen sich täglich dem Thema. Mehrere Sport-Tageszeitungen kämpfen an den Kiosken mit einer ausführlichen Berichterstattung über den Lieblingssport Nummer eins der Brasilianer um ihre Leserschaft.

Nicht wenige Fußballer haben den Sprung auf die politische Bühne geschafft. Auch die ehemaligen Weltmeister Bebeto und Romário sitzen mittlerweile im Parlament. Sie nutzen ihre Popularität für politische Karrieren.

Ex-Weltmeister Bebeto ist in das Organisationskomitee der WM 2014 eingebunden und glaubt fest an eine große Chance für sein Land: »Es geht ja nicht nur um die wunderschönen neuen Stadien, die Brasilien bekommen wird,

World Cup." But not all Brazilians share his opinion and have taken to the streets repeatedly in protest. In Brazil, football has the capacity to mobilize both the masses and millions. And this in turn has led to public debate of a kind that is only possible in Brazil. During the Confederation Cup in Summer 2013, members of the Brazilian national team spoke out in favor of the demands of the demonstrators for more transparency and more democracy in the distribution of investments for the World Cup. At the same time, the demonstrators were careful not criticize the national team or football itself. Afterwards, Brazil's national manager Luiz Felipe Scolari made a point of praising "how his players stood behind the nation". This solidarity between the national team and the demonstrators produced a very special atmosphere over the course of the tournament.

The immense influence of football in Brazil cannot be measured purely in terms of viewing ratings, revenue, and transfers. It reaches deep into the Brazilian soul. It is no coincidence that the Maracanã Stadium in Rio de Janeiro is known to this day as the Stadium of the People. It is not only a stage on which football dreams come true but also one that unites people from different social backgrounds in the joy and elation of enjoying the game together. Brazil will most certainly change as a result of the 2014 World Cup and the power of football. In which direction we do not yet know.

sondern auch die Infrastrukturprojekte, die neue Mobilität, die die Investitionen mit sich bringen«, sagt Bebeto. »Die Weltmeisterschaft wird Wachstum generieren. Das Land Brasilien wird nach der WM ein besseres sein.« Nicht alle Brasilianer glauben das und gehen deshalb immer wieder auf die Straße. Der Fußball bewegt in Brasilien Massen und Milliarden. Das führt zu Diskussionen und auch zu einer Eigendynamik, wie sie wohl nur in Brasilien möglich ist. Die Nationalspieler Brasiliens stellten sich während des Confed Cup 2013 im Sommer hinter die Forderungen der demonstrierenden Brasilianer nach mehr Transparenz und mehr Demokratie im Rahmen der WM-Investitionen. Aber die Demonstranten stellten zugleich klar, es geht nicht gegen die Nationalmannschaft oder den Fußball. Brasiliens Nationaltrainer Luiz Felipe Scolari lobte anschließend ausdrücklich das »Auftreten meiner Spieler vor der ganzen Nation«. Der Schulterschluss zwischen Nationalmannschaft und Demonstranten entwickelte eine ganz besondere Atmosphäre bei diesem Turnier.

Nicht nur in Einschaltquoten, Umsätzen und Transfers ist der ungeheure Einfluss des Fußballs zu messen. Er reicht bis tief in die brasilianische Seele. Nicht umsonst gilt das Maracanã-Stadion in Rio de Janeiro bis heute als das Stadion des Volkes. Die Bühne, auf der nicht nur sportliche Träume wahr werden, sondern auch Menschen unterschiedlicher sozialer Herkunft vereint in der Freude und der Begeisterung das Spiel gemeinsam zusammen genießen. Brasilien wird sich durch die WM 2014 und die Macht des Fußballs verändern, nur in welche Richtung, ist im Moment noch nicht absehbar.

The Magic Word is Tropicalization

Falk Jaeger in Conversation with Miriam Sayeg and Knut Stockhusen (schlaich bergermann und partner) and Ralf Amann and Martin Glass (gmp · von Gerkan, Marg and Partners) about their Work in Brazil

Tropikalisieren, das Zauberwort

Falk Jaeger im Gespräch mit Miriam Sayeg und Knut Stockhusen (schlaich bergermann und partner) sowie Ralf Amann und Martin Glass (gmp · von Gerkan, Marg und Partner) über ihre Arbeit in Brasilien

FALK JAEGER
How did these commissions come about? Were they the result of architecture competitions like they would be in Germany?

RALF AMANN
Of the twelve World Cup stadia in Brazil, only one competition was organized for the stadium in Salvador da Bahia. Our stadia came about as a result of initial simple conceptual studies that we were commissioned to produce. Of course, we weren't the only competitors: some concepts had been drawn up previously and other offices were also asked to produce competing studies. But our concepts won through and the cities then used these as part of their applications to host World Cup matches. After the cities qualified for inclusion, we were then commissioned to undertake the subsequent planning stages.

MIRIAM SAYEG
In Maracanã, we had a most fortunate experience. One day, the director of one of the contractors called me and invited us to be part of the design team. He simply said: "we need the best engineers in the world". There was no competition and that point marked the beginning of a relationship of mutual trust.

FALK JAEGER
How would you describe the climate at the time when you started on the projects?

FALK JAEGER
Wie kam es zu den Beauftragungen? Wurden Wettbewerbe ausgeschrieben, wie man das in Deutschland kennt?

RALF AMANN
Es gab bei den zwölf WM-Stadien nur einen Wettbewerb, und zwar in Salvador da Bahia. Bei unseren Stadien haben wir mit einfachen Konzeptstudien begonnen, mit denen wir direkt beauftragt wurden. Aber wir waren natürlich nicht die einzigen Bewerber. Es hatte zuvor schon Konzepte gegeben und es gab parallel konkurrierende Konzeptstudien. Unsere Vorschläge haben sich dann durchgesetzt und bildeten die Grundlage für die Bewerbungsunterlagen der Städte als Spielorte der WM. Die Städte haben sich qualifiziert. Daraus resultierte dann die Beauftragung für weitere Planungsphasen.

MIRIAM SAYEG
Beim Maracanã machten wir eine ganz besondere Erfahrung. Ich erinnere mich gut an den Tag, als der Direktor eines der Bauunternehmen anrief und uns in das Entwurfsteam einlud. Er sagte: »Wir brauchen die besten Ingenieure der Welt« – also kein Wettbewerb, sondern vom ersten Augenblick an eine Beziehung gegenseitigen Vertrauens.

FALK JAEGER
Wie könnte man das Klima beschreiben, das Sie vorgefunden haben?

Knut Stockhusen
schlaich bergermann und partner

Miriam Sayeg
schlaich bergermann und partner

Ralf Amann
gmp · Architekten

Miriam Sayeg

We were very lucky that the projects began at a time when people were very motivated and positive in Brazil. The country was very enthusiastic about the possibility of hosting two of the most prestigious sporting events in the world, the FIFA World Cup in 2014 and the Rio Olympics in 2016. We were given a free hand to develop our own design, and our clients were very positive about our technical proposals, which allowed us to develop the project in a very supportive atmosphere.

Martin Glass

The clients were extremely trusting of us, especially when we pitched our concepts and designs to them. Our designs, which we had developed to be archetypical of their respective location, were received with great appreciation and even gratitude. That was unusually positive, even in our own experience.

Knut Stockhusen

The Brazilian contractors nevertheless had to get used to us supervising them so intensively during the construction period, something they were not used to from Brazilian engineers. We fought hard to be able to take on this role, and it was also necessary in order to ensure that the construction would be built as planned. The incredible effort of the planning and construction phases is to thank for the final success of the project.

Miriam Sayeg

Wir hatten großes Glück, dass die Anfangsphase der Projekte in Brasilien in eine Zeit fiel, die von positiver Aufbruchsstimmung geprägt war. Die Möglichkeit, Gastgeber für die beiden wichtigsten Sportereignisse der Welt sein zu können, die FIFA WM und danach die Olympischen Spiele 2016, hatte das Land in einen Begeisterungstaumel versetzt. Wir hatten beim Entwerfen fast völlig freie Hand. Unsere technischen Ideen wurden von unseren Auftraggebern stets sehr positiv aufgenommen, sodass das Projekt in sehr kooperativer Atmosphäre entwickelt werden konnte.

Martin Glass

Die Auftraggeber haben uns ein enormes Vertrauen entgegengebracht, insbesondere als es darum ging, die Entwürfe und die Konzepte zu lancieren. Die Lösungen, welche wir archetypisch für die einzelnen Orte entwickelt hatten, wurden mit sehr großer Dankbarkeit entgegengenommen. Das ist nach unserer sonstigen Erfahrung eher ungewöhnlich.

Knut Stockhusen

Die brasilianischen Generalunternehmer mussten sich dennoch erst daran gewöhnen, in der Ausführungszeit so intensiv von uns betreut zu werden. Das sind sie von brasilianischen Ingenieuren nicht gewöhnt. Erstens haben wir uns das erkämpft, und zweitens musste das ja erfolgen, damit die Ausführung so geschah, wie es von uns geplant wurde. Doch der unglaublich große planungs- und baubegleitende Aufwand hat dann eben auch zum Erfolg geführt.

FALK JAEGER
That means that Brazilian contractors usually hire an engineer to undertake the structural planning, then send them home and finish off the rest themselves?

RALF AMANN
Yes. In Brazil, general contractors have a special standing: they undertake much of the work independently and are free to realize the construction largely on their own, especially when it comes to economizing.

FALK JAEGER
Would you say that the political system had a large influence on the projects? For example, did a local governor stand up and say "No, the stadium has to be green not red"?

MARTIN GLASS
World Cup stadia are, of course, inherently very political projects. But in this case we had the feeling that politics did not overly meddle in the projects—and certainly not where the architectural design was concerned.

FALK JAEGER
Could this be because the clients were not so well informed about world-class stadia and what they look like?

FALK JAEGER
Das heißt, die brasilianischen Unternehmer bestellen normalerweise die Ingenieurplanung, schicken den Ingenieur dann nach Hause und bauen es selbst fertig?

RALF AMANN
Ja, die Generalunternehmer haben eine sehr exponierte Stellung in Brasilien. Sie arbeiten ziemlich autark und realisieren die Projekte weitestgehend selbst, vor allem im Hinblick auf die wirtschaftliche Optimierung.

FALK JAEGER
Kann man sagen, dass das politische System viel Einfluss genommen hat? Gab es zum Beispiel einen Gouverneur, der gesagt hat: »Nein – das Stadion muss grün und nicht rot werden«?

MARTIN GLASS
Natürlich sind WM-Stadien immer sehr politische Projekte. Trotzdem hatten wir das Gefühl, dass die Einflussnahme der Politik auf diese Projekte – insbesondere auf die Gestaltung des Architekturentwurfes – sehr moderat war.

FALK JAEGER
Hat das auch damit zu tun, dass es sich nicht um wohlinformierte Auftraggeber handelte, die wissen, wie weltweit Spitzenstadien aussehen?

Martin Glass
gmp · Architekten

Falk Jaeger

Ralf Amann
On the contrary, they were very well informed, both at a governmental level as well as among the contractors. They were very familiar with our stadia projects in South Africa, and that probably helped earn us the commissions. A further motivation—as is often the case in Brazil—was the express wish to be seen as being world-class. That's why they commissioned stadia of this size and wanted them to have a distinctive design.

Martin Glass
Interestingly, our stadia projects in South Africa were much more influential than those in Germany. Perhaps also because they are more recent.

Ralf Amann
And also because status symbols in general are very important in Brazil. That applies not only to fashion and music, but also to architecture and engineering. Leading international examples are therefore often favorable points of reference.

Knut Stockhusen
In the case of Maracanã, we were not aware of any direct political influence. Because we work exclusively for general contractors in Brazil, they often serve as the client although they are actually the client's representative. Consequently there is a long period of intensive collaboration between the planners and the consortium. In Rio, we were also particularly aware of the active involvement of the historic preservation authorities on maintaining the cultural legacy of Maracanã.

Falk Jaeger
What role do architects play in this entire process? Is this comparable to their position in Germany, or something else entirely?

Ralf Amann
One has to earn one's position as an architect. In Germany, architects play a much more central role. In Brazil, architects are commonly regarded as interior designers or decorators. In fact, about 90 percent of architects in Brazil do work like that. There are, of course, architecture offices like gmp but not on the same scale or with the same depth of planning involvement. In Brazil, architecture offices usually undertake the design planning up to planning permission and only rarely do the extensive detailed planning and working drawings that architects undertake in Germany. The person "wearing the trousers" is usually tne engineer, especially the engineer supervising work on site. While that person knows they need to have an architect, they do not give them much say in the matter.

Martin Glass
That was a learning process—both with the specialist planners as well as with the clients—as they were not used to architects contributing so intensively to the details and the

Ralf Amann
Sie waren sehr gut informiert, sowohl auf Regierungsebene als auch auf Unternehmerebene, und kannten natürlich auch unsere südafrikanischen Stadien sehr gut, was uns sicher für unsere Beauftragung qualifiziert hat. Außerdem war es sogar der ausdrückliche Wunsch – wie so oft in Brasilien –, jetzt zur ersten Garde gehören zu wollen. Deshalb der Auftrag, Stadien in dieser Größenordnung und mit starker Ausdruckskraft zu liefern.

Martin Glass
Interessanterweise waren unsere Stadien in Südafrika in deutlich stärkerem Maße Referenz als jene in Deutschland. Auch natürlich, weil sie aktueller sind.

Ralf Amann
Das liegt aber auch daran, dass man sich in Brasilien gerne an Statussymbolen orientiert. Das betrifft Mode, Musik, aber auch Architektur, Ingenieurbau usw. Was international gerade das Aktuellste ist, wird oft als Vorbild genommen.

Knut Stockhusen
Beim Maracanã haben wir keine wirkliche politische Einflussnahme mitbekommen. Da wir aber in Brasilien ausschließlich für Generalunternehmer arbeiten, diese dann in die Rolle des Bauherren schlüpfen, obwohl sie ja nur Bauherrenvertreter sind, gibt es eine ganz intensive und lang anhaltende Zusammenarbeit zwischen den Planern und den Konsortien. In Rio war es zudem besonders auffällig, wie stark sich der Denkmalschutz eingebracht hat, um das Kulturerbe Maracanã zu bewahren.

Falk Jaeger
Wie ist die Stellung des Architekten in diesem ganzen Verfahren? Ist die mit der Position in Deutschland vergleichbar, oder ist sie ganz anders?

Ralf Amann
Die Position als Architekt muss man sich erkämpfen. In Deutschland spielt der Architekt eine wesentlich zentralere Rolle. Das Bild, das die brasilianische Bevölkerung von einem Architekten hat, ist eher das eines Innenarchitekten/Dekorateurs. Auf diesem Niveau arbeiten auch 90 Prozent der Architekten in Brasilien. Architekturbüros wie gmp gibt es natürlich auch, aber nicht in der Größe und auch nicht mit der Planungstiefe. In Brasilien ist es meistens üblich, dass Projekte vergleichbar bis zur Leistungsphase 3 und 4 abgewickelt werden, aber die Detailtiefe und umfangreiche Planung wie in Deutschland ist in Brasilien nicht üblich. Derjenige, der »die Hosen an hat«, ist der Ingenieur, vor allem der Bauingenieur auf der Baustelle. Der weiß zwar, dass er einen Architekten braucht, aber der soll möglichst nicht viel mitreden.

Martin Glass
Das war ein Lernprozess – sowohl mit den Fachplanern als auch mit den Bauherren –, wie stark wir Architekten uns

technical plans of the specialists, to the work of the construction firms, and indeed how much we involved ourselves in the process in general.

Knut Stockhusen
Because construction firms and planners work together so closely, the primary interest—especially when it comes to tendering—is in cost-intensive measures and technical facts: things that the engineer provides and which dictate material usage and the extent of construction work necessary, and in turn affect the cost and success of the project as a whole.

Ralf Amann
The construction firms ultimately determine what will be built and how. And they are not shy about altering the design or how it is realized, even when there is a detailed specification.

The degree of interpretation allowed in a specification is very broad. If the spec says "a house with a roof", the end result could have a pitched roof, a shed roof, or a flat roof. Any old roof as long as it's a roof.

And consequently they find it unsettling when an architect comes along and starts raising objections. This is a side effect of the fact that Brazilians like to bring in renowned partners from abroad: while they respect their input and expertise, they are not always aware of what that entails.

Falk Jaeger
Was it beneficial that the design is a collaboration between German architects and German engineers?

Knut Stockhusen
It is, of course, simpler for both our offices when we collaborate together on a project, but in the case of the Rio project, where we undertook the project on our own, it was an intensive struggle to ensure that everything was realized as we had planned it. At Maracanã the general contractor was sufficiently convinced that they would be able to realize a particular technical solution for the project in collaboration with ourselves, and that there was no need for further "players". That's why we were commissioned to realize the solution for the roof on our own. The Brazilian architect Fernandez was responsible for the stadium bowl: his commission ended with the upper tier of the stadium, while ours started with the roof.

Miriam Sayeg
In that case, we were therefore responsible for both the architecture and the engineering.

Falk Jaeger
What impact does the difference in mentality have?

Ralf Amann
In Brazil it is indispensable to have a presence in the country as near to the clients as possible. The relationship can be described almost like a marriage over a period of a few

in die Details und die technische Ausarbeitung durch die Fachingenieure, aber auch die Baufirma einbringen und in wie viele Dinge wir uns einmischen.

Knut Stockhusen
Dadurch, dass es so eine enge Zusammenarbeit zwischen der ausführenden Firma und den Planern gibt, sind hauptsächlich – gerade zum Zeitpunkt der Auftragserteilung – kostenträchtige Maßnahmen und technische Fakten von Interesse, die eben der Ingenieur liefert, und somit geht es um Materialeinsatz und Produktionsaufwand und damit um Geld und um den Erfolg des Unternehmens.

Ralf Amann
Die Baufirmen bestimmen letztendlich, was und wie gebaut wird. Sie ändern auch schon mal den Entwurf eigenmächtig ab und natürlich auch dessen Umsetzung, selbst wenn es eine Ausschreibung gab.

Der Interpretationsspielraum einer Ausschreibungsplanung wird sehr weit gefasst. Wenn da zum Beispiel steht: »Ein Haus mit Dach«, dann kann das später ein Satteldach, ein Pultdach oder ein Flachdach sein, Hauptsache Dach.

Und darum ist es für sie häufig unverständlich, warum der Architekt den Finger hebt. Hier kommt wieder der Effekt zum Tragen, dass sich Brasilianer gerne Renommee aus dem Ausland holen, die Expertise auch schätzen, sich aber nicht immer der Konsequenzen bewusst sind.

Falk Jaeger
War die Zusammenarbeit zwischen deutschen Architekten und deutschen Ingenieuren von Vorteil?

Knut Stockhusen
Für unsere beiden Büros ist es natürlich einfacher, wenn wir Projekte gemeinsam bearbeiten, aber auch in Rio, wo wir das Projekt allein gemacht haben, mussten wir uns massiv dafür einsetzen, dass alles auch so ausgeführt wird, wie es geplant wurde. Beim Maracanã war der Generalunternehmer schon so weit überzeugt, das Projekt auf eine gewisse technische Art mit uns lösen zu können, dass es keinen Platz für weitere »Mitspieler« gab. Deshalb sollten wir die Aufgabe der Überdachung allein lösen. Der brasilianische Architekt Fernandez hat sich um die Tribünenschüssel gekümmert – sein Auftrag endete quasi mit dem oberen Umgang des Stadions – und die Schnittstelle war das Dach.

Miriam Sayeg
Also lieferten wir sowohl das architektonisch-gestalterische als auch das ingenieurtechnische Konzept.

Falk Jaeger
Wie wirkten sich die Mentalitätsunterschiede aus?

Ralf Amann
In Brasilien ist es unumgänglich, dass man vor Ort und möglichst ganz nah bei den Bauherren sitzt. Das ist dann wie eine Ehe über Jahre hinweg, in der man gemeinsam

years in which both parties go "through thick and thin" together and the relationship has to be very close to ensure the success of the project. It is well nigh impossible to do that from afar. That's a mistake that many foreign companies and offices make, when trying to realize projects remotely from home. One has to have an office in Brazil and be available at any time.

Miriam Sayeg
During the planning and construction processes, Brazilian clients and contractors expect responses to their requests on a continuous basis, i.e. at any time of the day. One of my tasks is to be available around the clock for their calls, and it is not uncommon for calls to come at weekends or late in the evening. For them it is absolutely fundamental to know that there is someone they can speak to in Brazil, a Portuguese speaker, who can relay their invariably urgent requests to the German team.

Knut Stockhusen
By way of example: let's say we send an experienced German project director to Brazil to run a project, someone who has been able to "push through" projects all over the globe. If this person does not adjust to the mentality of this country, he or she will likely come up against problems regardless of his or her technical and personal abilities. If you cannot demonstrate to your partner that you respect and value them, you might as well go home.

Falk Jaeger
Is construction and building in Brazil primarily the domain of men, perhaps more than in other countries? Was that an advantage or a disadvantage for you as a woman working in this realm?

Miriam Sayeg
I am a positive person and always see an advantage in being a feminine presence in a predominantly male world. First of all, I am always very supportive to the client and they know they can count on me to get a quick response from the German team. We built up a friendly relationship, and as a woman the client never treated me aggressively or disrespectfully. As a bridge between the client and the German team, I think I manage to filter and adapt the messages to the different German and Brazilian ways of communicating and therefore to maintain a harmonious relationship between the respective parties.

Knut Stockhusen
Aside from the technical aspects of the job that Miriam, myself, and the colleagues in Germany do, it was also important to absorb the sometimes significant emotional tensions and hiccups in the project and to communicate these in a normal manner back to Germany. You have to adapt to the country you are working in. If you approach things as a planning team only from a structured, German point of view, you will fail. To succeed, you need to become a bit "tropicalized". As such, it is important to signalize a degree of normal-

»durch dick und dünn geht« und das Verhältnis so eng wie möglich gestalten muss, um das Projekt zum Erfolg zu bringen. Das alles aus der Ferne zu steuern, ist de facto unmöglich. Ein Fehler, den viele ausländische Firmen und Büros machen, die versuchen, Projekte von zu Hause aus zu realisieren. Man muss vor Ort sitzen und jederzeit abrufbar sein.

Miriam Sayeg
Für brasilianische Auftraggeber und Vertragspartner ist es ganz normal, während der Planungs- und Bauprozesse durchgehend Rückmeldung auf Anfragen zu erwarten – 24 Stunden am Tag. Es gehörte zu meinen Aufgaben, immer für sie erreichbar zu sein; oft kamen Anrufe am Wochenende oder am späten Abend. Es ist für sie von höchster Bedeutung, dass sie einen Ansprechpartner in Brasilien haben, jemanden, der Portugiesisch spricht und ihre – immer dringenden – Anliegen an das deutsche Team weiterleiten kann.

Knut Stockhusen
Sagen wir einmal, man nimmt einen erfahrenen deutschen Projektleiter, der schon Projekte überall auf der Weltkugel gemanagt hat, und schickt den nach Brasilien, um dort so ein Stadion »durchzupeitschen«, dann könnte er trotz seiner technischen und seiner menschlichen Qualifikation an Grenze stoßen, wenn er sich nicht auf dieses Land einlässt und mitspielt. Wenn du deinem Partner nicht zeigst, dass er dir etwas bedeutet und dass du ihn wertschätzt, dann kannst du wahrscheinlich wieder nach Hause fahren.

Falk Jaeger
Ist denn Brasilien in dem Zusammenhang nicht noch viel mehr eine Männerwelt – das Bauen, Konstruieren etc.? War das ein Vorteil oder ein Nachteil für Sie, als Frau hier zu agieren?

Miriam Sayeg
Ich habe eine positive Grundeinstellung und finde, es ist ein Vorteil, in einer männerdominierten Welt als Frau wahrgenommen zu werden. Zunächst habe ich die Auftraggeber stets spüren lassen, dass ich sie voll unterstütze und dass sie auf mich zählen können. Unsere Beziehung war freundschaftlich und ich habe als Frau nie Aggressivität oder Respektlosigkeit von ihrer Seite erfahren. Ich glaube, es ist mir als Vermittlerin zwischen Auftraggeber und deutschem Team gelungen, die zu vermittelnden Botschaften herauszufiltern und jeweils den deutschen und brasilianischen Kommunikationsscodes anzupassen, sodass immer eine harmonische Beziehung zwischen den Parteien bestand.

Knut Stockhusen
Neben dem technischen Job, den Miriam, unsere Kollegen in Deutschland und ich machten, war es andererseits wichtig, die wirklich großen emotionalen Spannungen und Wellen in den Projekten auszugleichen und Themen normalisiert nach Deutschland zu kommunizieren. Denn na-

ity back to Germany because otherwise the teams at home would quickly grow nervous when constantly confronted with bad news.

Martin Glass
Projects in Brazil are inherently something of an emotional rollercoaster. They can shift from phases of total desperation to unbridled enthusiasm and back on a daily basis. Seen against this background, "tropicalization" is a kind of survival strategy.

Falk Jaeger
So, what is "tropicalization"?

Martin Glass
In Brazil, the term "tropicalization" is commonly used to denote a kind of cultural filter between Germany and Brazil. On the one hand, for example, this can be applied to technical aspects: the adjustment—or "tropicalization"—of German planning methods so that they can be built by a Brazilian firm; and on the other hand to the emotional level of personal interactions, i.e. to avoid "German thoroughness" from coming across as arrogance and to prevent one from overreacting to Brazilian emotional volatility.

türlich muss man sich auf das Land einlassen. Wenn man als Planungsteam, das absolut deutsch denkt und strukturiert ist, auftritt, scheitert man. Also muss man ein bisschen »tropikalisiert« sein, um es zu schaffen. Insofern ist es wichtig, nach Deutschland Normalität zu signalisieren, weil sonst die Teams zu Hause total nervös werden, wenn sie regelmäßig irgendwelche Hiobsbotschaften erhalten.

Martin Glass
Projekte in Brasilien sind per se immer eine emotionale Achterbahn. Sie bewegen sich im Tagesrhythmus von totaler Verzweiflung bis hin zu überschwänglicher Freude und wieder zurück. In diesem Kontext ist »Tropikalisieren« eine Art Überlebensstrategie.

Falk Jaeger
Was heißt »Tropikalisieren«?

Martin Glass
Der im Brasilianischen gängige Begriff des »Tropikalisierens« beschreibt einen Kulturfilter zwischen Deutschland und Brasilien. Einerseits zum Beispiel auf der technischen Ebene, um eine deutsche Planung so anzupassen, also zu »tropikalisieren«, dass eine brasilianische Firma diese bauen kann, aber auch auf der emotionalen, menschlichen Ebene, damit »deutsche Gründlichkeit« nicht als Arroganz und brasilianische emotionale Schwankungen nicht als Überreaktion verstanden werden.

Falk Jaeger
What have you learned as a result?

Martin Glass
We have become calmer and less easily perturbed.

Knut Stockhusen
We have also learned a lot about how to realize and transport large and technically complex projects, which are developed mostly in fantastic teams in Germany, across great geographical and cultural distances, to "tropicalize" them and yet to maintain the same high quality of design and technical standards. And that is something that is very useful when working in other countries around the world.

Miriam Sayeg
The most positive aspect of my experience over the last few years is to see that my country now has first class, first world stadia made using state-of-the-art technologies and materials.

Brazilian architects, engineers and contractors are now much more technically experienced and better prepared to work with international and multidisciplinary teams. In Brazil, this has opened doors and minds for the new—for me, this has been the greatest achievement of the World Cup experience.

Falk Jaeger
Was haben Sie gelernt?

Martin Glass
Wir sind gelassener geworden.

Knut Stockhusen
Wir haben viel dazugelernt, technisch sehr komplexe Projekte, die maßgeblich in Deutschland in großartigen Teams entwickelt wurden, über große geografische und kulturelle Distanzen zu transportieren, zu tropikalisieren und letztlich dennoch mit unseren hohen technischen und gestalterischen Anforderungen umzusetzen. Und das kann man sehr gut mitnehmen, auch für weitere Ziele auf der Welt.

Miriam Sayeg
Die positivste Erfahrung für mich aus der Arbeit in den letzten Jahren war die Erkenntnis, dass mein Land nun erstklassige »Erste Welt«-Stadien besitzt, in denen die allerneuesten Techniken und Materialien zur Anwendung kamen.

Brasilianische Architekten, Ingenieure und Bauunternehmer haben technisch enorm an Erfahrung gewonnen und sind besser auf die Arbeit mit internationalen und multidisziplinären Teams vorbereitet. Brasilien hat seine Türen und seine Köpfe dem Neuen geöffnet – für mich war das die größte Leistung dieser Weltmeisterschafts-Erfahrung.

Facts and Figures **Zahlen Daten Fakten**

Roof **Überdachung**
Estádio do Maracanã (Estádio Jornalista Mário Filho), Rio de Janeiro

Coordinates **Koordinaten** –22,912 –43,23
Client **Bauherr** EMOP, Rio de Janeiro
Concept and planning of stadium roof **Idee und Planung Überdachung** schlaich bergermann und partner – Knut Göppert with **mit** Knut Stockhusen, Thomas Moschner, Miriam Sayeg
Staff (in alphabetical order) **Mitarbeiter (alphabetisch)** Andreas Bader, Markus Balz, Tiago Carvalho, Arnaud Deillon, Uli Dillmann, Stefan Dziewas, Alberto Goosen, Stefan Hinrich, Jana Pavlovic, Bernd Ruhnke, Christiane Sander Fernando Sima, Augusto Tiezzi, Chih-Bin Tseng, Gerhard Weinrebe, Markus Wöhrbach
Lighting concept, roof **Lichtkonzept Dach** schlaich bergermann und partner
Planning of photovoltaic system **Planung Photovoltaik** schlaich bergermann und partner
Structural analysis, roof **Prüfstatik Dach** Nelson Szilard
Wind tunnel testing **Windkanaluntersuchungen** Wacker Ingenieure
Technical services, roof **Haustechnik Dach** WSDG, Cobrae, Lumens, Mingrone
Construction planning, stadium bowl **Planung Stadionschüssel** Daniel Fernandes Arquitetos, São Paulo
Structural design, stadium bowl **Tragwerksplanung Stadionschüssel** Cobrae, Casagrande Engenharia
Building contractors **Bauunternehmer** Consórcio Maracanã (Construtora Norberto Odebrecht / Construtora Andrade Gutierrez)
Seating **Sitzplätze** 73 531
Covered surface **Überdachte Fläche** 45 500 m²
Dimensions **Abmessungen** 260 × 298 m
Construction duration **Bauzeit** 2009–2013

Estádio Mineirão (Estádio Governador Magalhães Pinto), Belo Horizonte

Coordinates **Koordinaten** –19,866 –43,971
Concept and design **Konzept und Entwurfsplanung** Gustavo Penna Arquiteto e Associados with consulting by **mit Consulting durch** gmp · von Gerkan, Marg und Partner and **und** schlaich bergermann und partner
Construction planning **Ausführungsplanung** Architektur BCMF Arquitetos, Belo Horizonte
Construction planning of structure **Ausführungsplanung Tragwerk** Engserj, Belo Horizonte
Design **Entwurf** Volkwin Marg and **und** Hubert Nienhoff with **mit** Martin Glass, 2008
Project management **Projektleitung** Martin Glass, Lena Brögger, Maike Carlsen
Project management, Brazil **Projektleitung Brasilien** Robert Hormes
Director of **Direktor** gmp do Brasil Ralf Amann
Staff (in alphabetical order) **Mitarbeiter (alphabetisch)** Sophie-Charlotte Altrock, Martina Maurer-Brusius, Silke Flaßnöcker, Ruth Gould, Claudio Aceituno Husch, Juliana Kleba-Rizental, Jochen Köhn, Martin Krebes, Helge Lezius, Veit Lieneweg, Lucia Martinez Rodriguez, Tobias Mäscher, Adel Motamedi, Dirk Peissl, Lisa Pfisterer, Ivanka Perkovic, Camila Preve, Florian Schwarthoff, Katerine Witte
Partnership with **Arbeitsgemeinschaft mit** schlaich bergermann und partner, Stuttgart; Gustavo Penna Arquiteto e Associados, Belo Horizonte, Engserj, Belo Horizonte
Structural design and planning, roof **Tragwerksentwurf und -planung Dach** schlaich bergermann und partner – Knut Göppert with **mit** Knut Stockhusen and **und** Miriam Sayeg
Staff (in alphabetical order) **Mitarbeiter (alphabetisch)** Birgit Dephoff, Uli Dillmann, Stefan Dziewas, Frauke Fluhr, Hansmartin Fritz, Sebastian Grotz, Roman Kemmler, Bernd Ruhnke, Tilman Schober, Augusto Tiezzi
Structural design, stadium bowl **Tragwerksplanung Stadionschüssel** Engserj, Belo Horizonte
Technical services (concept and design) **Haustechnik (Konzept und Entwurfsplanung)** b. i. g. Bechtold Ingenieurgesellschaft mbH; Lumens, Belo Horizonte; STE, Belo Horizonte
Landscape design and podium (concept and design) **Freiraumplanung und Podium (Konzept und Entwurfsplanung)** Gustavo Penna Arquiteto a Associados, Belo Horizonte
Seating **Sitzplätze** ca. 66 000
Dimensions **Abmessungen** 280 × 220 m
Height of the stadium **Höhe des Stadions** ca. 23.60 m
Construction duration **Bauzeit** 2010–2012
The LEED certification process is currently underway. **Bewerbung um LEED Zertifikat läuft**

Facts and Figures **Zahlen Daten Fakten**

Arena da Amazônia, Manaus

Coordinates **Koordinaten** –3,0833 –60,028
Concept and design **Konzept und Entwurfsplanung** gmp · von Gerkan, Marg und Partner and **und** schlaich bergermann und partner with **mit** stadia, São Paulo
Construction planning **Ausführungsplanung** gmp · von Gerkan, Marg und Partner and **und** schlaich bergermann und partner
Design **Entwurf** Volkwin Marg and **und** Hubert Nienhoff with **mit** Martin Glass, 2008
Project management **Projektleitung** Martin Glass, Maike Carlsen
Project management, Brazil **Projektleitung Brasilien** Burkhard Pick, Sander-Christiaan Troost
Director of **Direktor** gmp do Brasil Ralf Amann
Staff (in alphabetical order) **Mitarbeiter (alphabetisch)** Sophie-Charlotte Altrock, Felipe Bellani, Lena Brögger, Claudia Chiappini, Lieselotte Decker, Barbara Düring, Stephanie Eichelmann, Konstanze Erbe, Silke Flaßnöcker, Priscila Lima da Silva Giersdorf, Elke Glass, Ruth Gould, Jacqueline Gregorius, Claudio Aceituno Husch, Fabian Kirchner, Juliana Kleba-Rizental, Jochen Köhn, Martin Krebes, Helge Lezius, Veit Lieneweg, Ausias Lobatón Ortega, Guilherme Maia, Rodrigo Mathias Duro Teixeira, Lucia Martinez Rodriguez, Adel Motamedi, Dirk Müller, Dirk Peissl, Ivanka Percovic, Camila Preve, Nicolai Reich, Stefan Saß, Florian Schwarthoff, Fariborz Rahimi, Sara Taberner Bonastre, Sonia Taborda, Anguelica Larocca Troost, Katerine Witte
Partnership with **Arbeitsgemeinschaft mit** schlaich bergermann und partner; stadia, São Paulo
Structural design and planning **Tragwerksentwurf und -planung** schlaich bergermann und partner – Knut Göppert with **mit** Knut Stockhusen and **und** Miriam Sayeg
Staff (in alphabetical order) **Mitarbeiter (alphabetisch)** Tiago Carvalho, Uli Dillmann, Andreas Eisele, Florian Geiger, Alberto Goosen, Sebastian Grotz, Jochen Gugeler, Achim Holl, Roman Kemmler, Hubert Kunz, Sandra Küstner, Walter Paganucci, Jana Pavlovic, Bernd Ruhnke, Guilherme Sayeg, Tilman Schober, Alexander Stäblein, Alfred Strasdeit, Kai Zweigart
Structural design, concrete and masonry works **Tragwerksplanung Massivbau** in conjunction with **in Zusammenarbeit mit** EGT, São Paulo; Ruy Bentes, São Paulo
Technical services **Haustechnik** b. i. g. Bechtold Ingenieurgesellschaft mbH (design phase **Entwurfsphase**); mha, São Paulo; Teknika Projetos e Consultoria ltda, São Paulo; Soeng Construção hidroelétrica ltda, São Paulo; Bosco & Associados ltda, São Paulo; Loudness Sonorização Ltda, São Paulo
Design, external areas **Freiraumplanung** ST raum a., Berlin (design phase **Entwurfsphase**); Interact, São Paulo
Seating **Sitzplätze** ca. 44 400
Length of stadium **Länge des Stadions** ca. 240 m
Width of stadium **Breite des Stadions** ca. 200 m
Construction duration **Bauzeit** 2010–2014
The LEED certification process is currently underway.
Bewerbung um LEED Zertifikat bzw. LEED Silver läuft

Estádio Nacional Mané Garrincha, Brasília

Coordinates **Koordinaten** –15,7835 –47,899
Concept and design of roof and esplanade and construction planning of esplanade **Konzept und Entwurfsplanung Dach und Esplanade sowie Ausführungsplanung Esplanade** Castro Mello arquitetos with consulting by **mit Consulting durch** gmp · von Gerkan, Marg und Partner and **und** schlaich bergermann und partner
Construction planning, roof **Ausführungsplanung Dach** gmp · von Gerkan, Marg und Partner and **und** schlaich bergermann und partner
Design, stadium bowl **Planung Stadionschüssel** Castro Mello arquitetos, São Paulo
Design **Entwurf** Volkwin Marg and **und** Hubert Nienhoff with **mit** Knut Göppert, 2008
Project management **Projektleitung** Martin Glass
Project management, Brazil **Projektleitung Brasilien** Robert Hormes
Director of **Direktor** gmp do Brasil Ralf Amann
Staff (in alphabetical order) **Mitarbeiter (alphabetisch)** Ante Bagaric, Holger Betz, Rebecca Bornhauser, Carsten Borucki, Lena Brögger, Martina Maurer-Brusius, Kacarzyna Ciruk, Laura Cruz Lima da Silva, Stefanie Eichelmann, Ruth Gould, Florian Illenberger, Jochen Köhn, Martin Krebes, Helge Lezius, Tobias Mäscher, Adel Motamedi, Burkhard Pick, Jutta Rentsch Serpa, Lucia Martinez Rodriguez, Maryna Samolyuk, Florian Schwarthoff, Sara Taberner Bonastre
Partnership with **Arbeitsgemeinschaft mit** schlaich bergermann und partner; Castro Mello arquitetos, São Paulo
Structural design and planning, roof and esplanade **Tragwerksentwurf und -planung Dach und Esplanade** schlaich bergermann und partner – Knut Göppert with **mit** Knut Stockhusen and **und** Miriam Sayeg
Staff (in alphabetical order) **Mitarbeiter (alphabetisch)** Andreas Bader, Tiago Carvalho, Arnaud Deillon, Uli Dillmann, Stefan Dziewas, Hansmartin Fritz, Alberto Goosen, Hartmut Grauer, Jochen Gugeler, Andreas Hahn, Achim Holl, Hubert Kunz, Christoph Paech, Jana Pavlovic, Bernd Ruhnke, Tilman Schober, Klaus Straub, Cornelia Striegan, Peter Szerzo, Hiroki Tamai, Augusto Tiezzi, Feridun Tomalak, Chih-Bin Tseng, Gerhard Weinrebe, Rüdiger Weitzmann, Andrzej Winkler, Markus Wöhrbach, Kai Zweigart
Structural design, stadium bowl **Tragwerksplanung Stadionschüssel** Etalp, São Paulo
Technical services, roof (concept and design) **Haustechnik Dach (Konzept-, Entwurfsplanung)** b. i. g. Bechtold Ingenieurgesellschaft mbH; mha, São Paulo
Lighting design, roof (concept and design) **Lichtkonzept Dach (Konzept-, Entwurfsplanung)** Conceptlicht GmbH, Traunreut; Peter Gaspar, São Paulo; mha, São Paulo
Seating **Sitzplätze** ca. 72 800
Dimensions (diameter) **Abmessungen (Durchmesser)** 309 m
Construction duration **Bauzeit** 2010–2013
The LEED certification process is currently underway. **Bewerbung um Zertifikat LEED Platinum läuft**

Practices Büros

gmp
Architekten von Gerkan, Marg und Partner

The gmp architectural partnership was founded in 1965 by Meinhard von Gerkan and Volkwin Marg. It has now expanded to include four further partners, a partner for China and eleven associate partners. With over 500 staff in thirteen locations, gmp · von Gerkan, Marg und Partner works within Germany and abroad. Their range of projects covers detached houses, hotels, museums, theaters and concert halls, office buildings, commercial centers, and hospitals, extending to include research, sports, and educational establishments as well as transport and industrial buildings and master plans. Their very first project, the Berlin-Tegel airport made gmp · von Gerkan, Marg und Partner famous. Further airport terminals followed, including those in Hamburg, Stuttgart and Frankfurt am Main as well as the new "Willy Brandt" Berlin-Brandenburg airport for the capital city. Their work also focuses on larger trade fair and exhibition halls in Leipzig, Rimini in Italy, as well as in Nanning and Shenzhen in China. Along with commitments in numerous European countries, Brazil, India, and Vietnam, China is the center of the practice's work abroad. In China, gmp · von Gerkan, Marg und Partner have created or are creating residential and commercial buildings, conference centers, cultural buildings, and museums, including the National Museum of China in Beijing. They have drawn up a master plan for the new city of Lingang for a population of 1.3 million. More recently gmp · von Gerkan, Marg und Partner has established itself worldwide as a specialist for stadia and arenas. Buildings in Berlin, Cologne and Frankfurt were followed by stadia projects including those in Capetown, Durban and Port Elizabeth, New Delhi, Foshan, Shenzhen and Shanghai, Warsaw, Kiev, and Bucharest. In addition to the stadia for the World Cup championships in Brazil, gmp · von Gerkan, Marg und Partner is also planning sports facilities for the Olympic Games in 2016 in Rio de Janeiro. gmp · von Gerkan, Marg und Partner has had an office in Rio de Janeiro since 2009 with a view of Guanabara Bay and Sugarloaf Mountain.

gmp
Architekten von Gerkan, Marg und Partner

Die Architektensozietät gmp wurde 1965 von Meinhard von Gerkan und Volkwin Marg gegründet. Mittlerweile sind vier weitere Partner, ein Partner für China und elf assoziierte Partner hinzugekommen. Mit über 500 Mitarbeitern an 13 Standorten ist gmp im In- und Ausland aktiv. Die Projekte reichen von Einfamilienhäusern, Hotels, Museen, Theatern und Konzerthallen, Bürogebäuden, Handelszentren und Krankenhäusern bis hin zu Forschungs-, Sport- und Bildungseinrichtungen sowie Verkehrsbauten, Gewerbebauten und Masterplanungen. Bekannt wurde gmp bereits mit dem ersten Projekt 1975, dem Flughafen Berlin-Tegel, dem weitere Flughafenterminals unter anderem in Hamburg, Stuttgart und Frankfurt am Main sowie der neue Hauptstadtflughafen Berlin Brandenburg »Willy Brandt« folgten. Einen weiteren Schwerpunkt bilden große Messeanlagen wie in Leipzig, in Rimini in Italien sowie Nanning und Shenzhen in China. China bildet neben Engagements in zahlreichen europäischen Staaten, in Brasilien, Indien und Vietnam den Schwerpunkt der Auslandsaktivitäten. Dort entstanden oder sind im Bau Wohn- und Geschäftshäuser, Kongresszentren, Kulturbauten und Museen, darunter das Chinesische Nationalmuseum in Peking. Ein Masterplan entstand für die neue Stadt Lingang für 1,3 Millionen Einwohner. In jüngerer Zeit hat sich gmp weltweit als Spezialist für Stadien und Arenen etabliert. Auf Bauten in Berlin, Köln und Frankfurt folgten Stadionprojekte unter anderem in Kapstadt, Durban, Port Elizabeth, Neu Delhi, Foshan, Shenzhen und Shanghai, Warschau, Kiew und Bukarest. In Planung ist unter anderen der grundlegende Umbau des Bernabeu Stadions in Madrid. Neben den WM-Stadien in Brasilien planen gmp Sportanlagen für die Olympischen Spiele 2016 in Rio de Janeiro. Seit 2009 unterhält gmp in Rio de Janeiro ein Büro mit Blick auf die Bucht und den Zuckerhut.

schlaich bergermann und partner
Structural consulting engineers

In 1980, structural engineers Jörg Schlaich and Rudolf Bergermann founded their own practice in Stuttgart, having worked together before as engineers responsible for the roofscape of the Olympic sports facilities in Munich. Today the practice has 125 staff and is managed by Knut Göppert, Andreas Keil, Sven Plieninger and Mike Schlaich. In Stuttgart, Berlin, New York, São Paolo, and Shanghai, employees are working on bridges, railway stations, widespan roofs, high-rise buildings, and solar power plants. Their best-known projects in Germany include the new main railway station and the Olympic Stadium in Berlin, the airport terminals in Stuttgart and Leipzig, as well as numerous road, rail, and pedestrian bridges. Internationally, the practice has made a name for itself with large cable-stayed bridges in Calcutta, Hong Kong, and New Delhi and involvement in the planning of the new World Trade Center in Manhattan, as well as working on many implemented solar thermal power generation projects in Spain. Their extensive series of stadium designs began with the 1993 design of the roof for what was then the Neckarstadion in Stuttgart. Their oeuvre includes some fifty executed stadia projects on four continents, among them all the stadia that have hosted a final of the last few World Cup and European football championships (in Berlin, Johannesburg and Kiev). The final of the 2014 World Cup in Rio de Janeiro will also take place under a roof designed by schlaich bergermann und partner. Through their branch office in São Paolo, the engineers are also working on projects for the Olympic Games in 2016, as well as on many other projects that require special structural solutions.

schlaich bergermann und partner
Beratende Ingenieure im Bauwesen

Die Bauingenieure Jörg Schlaich und Rudolf Bergermann gründeten 1980 in Stuttgart ihr eigenes Büro, nachdem sie schon zuvor als verantwortliche Ingenieure für die Dachlandschaft der olympischen Sportanlagen in München zusammengearbeitet hatten. Inzwischen hat das Büro über 100 Mitarbeiter und wird von Knut Göppert, Andreas Keil, Sven Plieninger und Mike Schlaich geleitet. In Stuttgart, Berlin, New York, São Paulo und Shanghai arbeiten Mitarbeiter an Brücken, Bahnhöfen, weit gespannten Dächern, Hochhäusern und Solarkraftwerken. Zu den bekanntesten Projekten in Deutschland zählen in Berlin der neue Hauptbahnhof und das Olympiastadion, die Flughäfen in Stuttgart und Leipzig sowie eine Vielzahl spektakulärer Straßen-, Eisenbahn- und Fußgängerbrücken. International hat sich das Büro mit großen Schrägseilbrücken in Kalkutta, Hongkong und New Delhi und der Beteiligung an der Planung des neuen World Trade Center in Manhattan sowie der Mitwirkung an vielen ausgeführten Projekten der thermischen Solarstromerzeugung einen Namen gemacht. Mit dem Entwurf des Dachtragwerks über das damalige Neckarstadion in Stuttgart begann 1993 die lange Reihe der Stadionplanungen, die mit inzwischen fast 50 realisierten Projekten in vier Kontinenten zu Buche schlägt, darunter alle Stadien der letzen Endspiele von Fußballwelt- und Europameisterschaften (in Berlin, Johannesburg, Kiew); auch das Finale in Rio de Janeiro wird wieder unter einem Dach von schlaich bergermann und partner stattfinden. Mit der Präsenz in São Paulo arbeitet das Büro auch in Brasilien erfolgreich an Projekten für die Olympischen Sommerspiele 2016 und an vielen anderen Projekten, die besondere Tragwerkslösungen erfordern.

Authors **Autoren**

Ralf Amann
Dipl.-Ing. architect, born in 1966 in Tettnang am Bodensee, studied architecture and urban design at the Berlage Institute in Amsterdam, Düsseldorf Academy of Art and the University of Stuttgart where he obtained his diploma. In 1996 he worked with Gigantes Zenghelis Architects in Athens, before moving to Rio de Janeiro in 1997 where he set up his own office. He began working with gmp · von Gerkan, Marg und Partner in 2007 and became director of gmp do Brasil in Rio de Janeiro in 2009 where he manages the office's operations in Latin America.

Ralf Amann
Dipl.-Ing. Architekt, geboren 1966 in Tettnang am Bodensee, studierte Architektur und Stadtplanung am Berlage Institut Amsterdam, an der Kunstakademie Düsseldorf und an der Universität Stuttgart, wo er sein Diplom ablegte. 1996 arbeitete er mit Gigantes Zenghelis Architects in Athen. Seit 1997 lebt er in Rio de Janeiro, wo er zunächst sein eigenes Büro führte. 2007 begann seine Zusammenarbeit mit gmp. Seit 2009 ist er Direktor bei gmp do Brasil in Rio de Janeiro und für die Betreuung des lateinamerikanischen Marktes verantwortlich.

Marcus Bredt
Born in Göttingen in 1968, trained as a photographer from 1992 to 1994 at the Lette-Verein in Berlin. From the very beginning of his freelance career, he concentrated on architecture photography. In 1995 he founded the partnership Bitter Bredt Photography together with Jan Bitter which continued until 2001. After his international work with Daniel Libeskind and Sauerbruch Hutton, he began working closely with gmp · von Gerkan, Marg und Partner in 2004 and has since photographed numerous buildings throughout the world including in China, Vietnam, and South America. Marcus Bredt lives in Berlin.

Marcus Bredt
geboren 1968 in Göttingen, wurde von 1992 bis 1994 am Lette-Verein Berlin zum Fotografen ausgebildet. Gleich zu Anfang seiner selbstständigen Tätigkeit konzentrierte er sich auf die Architekturfotografie. 1995 gründete er zusammen mit Jan Bitter die Fotografengemeinschaft Bitter Bredt Fotografie, die bis 2001 bestand. Nach internationalen Arbeiten für Daniel Libeskind und Sauerbruch Hutton begann 2004 eine engere Zusammenarbeit mit gmp, für die er zahlreiche Bauten u. a. in China, Vietnam und Südafrika dokumentierte. Marcus Bredt lebt in Berlin.

Martin Glass
Dipl.-Ing. architect, born in 1969 in Pforzheim, studied architecture at Kaiserslautern University of Applied Arts. He joined the Berlin office of von Gerkan, Marg und Partner in 1999 where he worked predominantly on stadium, airport and urban design projects. His special field is the design of wide-span membrane constructions and roofs. Since 2009, he coordinates, together with Ralf Amann at gmp do Brasil, the office's projects in Latin America.

Martin Glass
Dipl.-Ing. Architekt, geboren 1969 in Pforzheim, studierte Architektur an der Fachhochschule Kaiserslautern. Seit 1999 ist er im Büro von Gerkan, Marg und Partner in Berlin hauptsächlich für Stadien, Flughäfen und Städtebauprojekte verantwortlich. Einen Schwerpunkt bilden weit spannende Membrankonstruktionen und Dächer. Seit 2009 ist er bei gmp do Brasil gemeinsam mit Ralf Amann für die Betreuung des latein-amerikanischen Marktes verantwortlich.

Jens Glüsing
Born in 1960 in Hamburg, he studied political science (diploma) and Spanish at Hamburg University. After attending the Henri-Nannen School of Journalism (Grüner + Jahr/DIE ZEIT) he joined *Der Spiegel* in 1990 as an editor responsible for Latin America. Since 1991, he lives and works in Rio de Janeiro as a Latin American correspondent for *Der Spiegel*. In 2005 he was awarded the premiere Brazilian award for journalism, the "Premio Embratel", in the "foreign correspondent" category. He is the author of two books on Brazil: *Das Guayana-Projekt* (2008) and *Brasilien – Ein Länderporträt* (2013), both of which are published by the Christoph Links Verlag Berlin.

Jens Glüsing
geboren 1960 in Hamburg, studierte Politikwissenschaft (Diplom) und Spanisch an der Universität Hamburg. Nach dem Besuch der Henri-Nannen-Journalistenschule (Gruner + Jahr/DIE ZEIT) ging er 1990 als Redakteur für Lateinamerika zum *Spiegel*. Seit 1991 lebt und arbeitet er als Lateinamerika-Korrespondent des *Spiegel* in Rio de Janeiro. Im Jahr 2005 wurde er mit dem wichtigsten brasilianischen Journalistenpreis »Premio Embratel« in der Kategorie »Auslandskorrespondent« ausgezeichnet. Er ist Autor zweier Bücher über Brasilien: *Das Guayana-Projekt* (2008) und *Brasilien – Ein Länderporträt* (2013), beide erschienen im Christoph Links Verlag, Berlin.

Knut Göppert
Dipl. Ing., born in Triberg in 1961, studied structural engineering at the universities of Stuttgart, Karlsruhe, and Calgary. In 1989, he joined the Stuttgart office of schlaich bergermann und partner – structural consulting engineers, and has been a partner since 1998. Since 2002, he has been one of the CEOs of the firm which has branches in Berlin, New York, São Paulo, and Shanghai. Due to his roofings for numerous stadiums, including Frankfurt, Johannesburg, Cape Town, Warsaw, Brasilia, and Rio he is regarded as a leading engineer in the field.

Knut Göppert
Dipl.-Ing., geboren 1961 in Triberg, studierte Bauingenieurwesen an den Universitäten Stuttgart, Calgary und Karlsruhe. 1989 trat er in das Stuttgarter Büro schlaich bergermann und partner – Beratende Ingenieure im Bauwesen ein und ist seit 1998 Partner. Seit 2002 ist er einer der vier Geschäftsführer des Büros mit weiteren Niederlassungen in Berlin, New York, São Paulo und Shanghai. Mit seinen Überdachungen für zahlreiche Stadien, unter anderem in Frankfurt, Johannesburg, Kapstadt, Warschau, Brasilia und Rio, gilt er heute als führender Ingenieur auf diesem Gebiet.

Carl D. Goerdeler
Born in 1944 in Leipzig, he came as part of the diplomatic corps (Tokyo, Brasília) to his second home Brazil. As a travel writer and correspondent for numerous German newspapers, he has lived in Rio de Janeiro for 30 years, together with his wife and two children. *Kulturschock Brasilien* ("Brazil, Cultural Shock") and *Die Luftschlösser von Rio: Geschichten aus Brasilien* ("Rio's Castles in the Air: Stories from Brazil") are two of his books.

Carl D. Goerdeler
geboren 1944 in Leipzig, kam über den diplomatischen Dienst (Tokio, Brasília) in seine zweite Heimat Brasilien. Der Reisebuchautor und Korrespondent zahlreicher deutschsprachiger Zeitungen lebt seit 30 Jahren mit Frau und zwei Kindern in Rio de Janeiro. *KulturSchock Brasilien* und *Die Luftschlösser von Rio: Geschichten aus Brasilien* sind die Titel zweier seiner Bücher.

Falk Jaeger
Prof. Dr.-Ing. (arch.), born in Ottweiler/Saar in 1950, studied architecture and art history in Brunswick, Stuttgart and Tübingen and was awarded his doctorate by the TU Hanover. Since 1976, he has worked as an independent architectural critic. From 1983 to '88, he was an academic assistant at the Institute of Building History and Surveying at the TU Berlin; he has held lecturing posts at various universities and colleges, and was professor of architectural theory at the TU Dresden from 1993 to 2000. Falk Jaeger lives and works in Berlin as a freelance publicist, lecturer, curator, and journalist for radio, daily press, and professional journals.

Falk Jaeger
Prof. Dr.-Ing. (arch.), geboren 1950 in Ottweiler/Saar, studierte in Braunschweig, Stuttgart und Tübingen Architektur und Kunstgeschichte und wurde an der TU Hannover promoviert. Seit 1976 arbeitet er als freier Architekturkritiker. 1983–88 war er Assistent am Institut für Baugeschichte und Bauaufnahme der TU Berlin, übernahm Lehraufträge an verschiedenen Hochschulen und hatte 1993 bis 2000 den Lehrstuhl für Architekturtheorie an der TU Dresden inne. Er lebt als freier Publizist, Dozent, Kurator und Fachjournalist für Rundfunk, Tages- und Fachpresse in Berlin.

Tobias Käufer
Born in 1967 in Korschenbroich, he trained with Kurier-Verlag in Neuss before joining the Sport-Informations-Dienst (SID) and later the communications agency PRINT in Düsseldorf. In 2007, he became Latin American correspondent with offices in Bogotá, Columbia, and Rio de Janeiro, Brazil, reporting on sport in South America for the *Frankfurter Allgemeine Zeitung* with special focus on the 2014 World Cup in Brazil and the 2016 Olympic Games in Rio de Janeiro.. He also writes for the Deutscher Fußball-Bund (German Football Association), the *Neue Zürcher Zeitung*, and *Die Welt*, and represents the Catholic News Agency with special focus on human rights, politics, and society. He has also produced television documentaries for the Deutsche Welle.

Tobias Käufer
geboren 1967 in Korschenbroich, absolvierte sein Volontariat beim Kurier Verlag in Neuss. Danach Wechsel zum Sport-Informations-Dienst (SID) und später zur Kommunikationsagentur PRINT in Düsseldorf. Seit 2007 ist er als Lateinamerika-Korrespondent mit eigenen Büros in Bogota/Kolumbien und Rio de Janeiro/Brasilien tätig. Er berichtet für die *Frankfurter Allgemeine Zeitung* über den Sport in Südamerika und speziell über die WM 2014 in Brasilien und die Olympischen Spiele 2016 in Rio de Janeiro. Darüber hinaus schreibt er als Autor für den Deutschen Fußball-Bund, die *Neue Zürcher Zeitung* und *Die Welt* und vertritt die Katholische Nachrichtenagentur (Schwerpunkt Menschenrechte, Politik, Soziales). Für die Deutsche Welle hat er TV-Dokumentationen in Peru und Kolumbien produziert.

Volkwin Marg
Prof. Dr.-Ing. h.c. Dipl.-Ing. architect, was born in Königsberg/East Prussia in 1936 and grew up in Gdánsk. He studied at the TH Braunschweig (Brunswick). In 1965, together with Meinhard von Gerkan, he founded the office gmp · von Gerkan, Marg und Partner in Hamburg. From 1986 to 2001 he was professor of urban district planning and planning practice in Aachen. He was appointed to the Free Academy of Arts in Hamburg in 1972 and to the German Academy of Urban Development and Regional Planning in 1974. In 1975, he became vice-president of the Association of German Architects (BDA), and later president from 1979 to 1983. Since 2007, he has been principal of the Academy for Architectural Culture (aac) in Hamburg. In 2009 he was awarded the Federal Cross of Merit of the Federal Republic of Germany.

Volkwin Marg
Prof. Dr.-Ing. h.c. Dipl.-Ing. Architekt, geboren 1936 in Königsberg/Ostpreußen und aufgewachsen in Danzig, studierte an der TH Braunschweig. 1965 gründete er mit Meinhard von Gerkan in Hamburg das Büro von Gerkan Marg und Partner. 1986 bis 2001 hatte er den Lehrstuhl für Stadtbereichsplanung und Werklehre inne. 1972 wurde er an die Freie Akademie der Künste in Hamburg und 1974 an die Deutsche Akademie für Städtebau und Landesplanung berufen. 1975 wurde er Vizepräsident, 1979–83 war er Präsident des Bundes Deutscher Architekten (BDA). Seit 2007 ist er Prinzipal der Academy for Architectural Culture (aac) in Hamburg. 2009 wurde er mit dem Bundesverdienstkreuz 1. Klasse ausgezeichnet.

Michaela Metz
Born in 1967 in Munich, she spent a year living in Brazil. After an apprenticeship as a publishing manager, she studied romance philology with special focus on Latin America, history and communication studies. For a while she conceived and researched exhibitions, language and internet projects for the Goethe Institute in Munich and in Kiev. In 2006–2007 she took part in an aid project for children living on the streets in Rio de Janeiro. Since 2003, she has worked as an author, primarily for the *Süddeutsche Zeitung*, most recently writing a column in 2013 entitled "Literaturland Brasilien".

Michaela Metz
geboren 1967 in München, hat ein Jahr in Brasilien gelebt. Sie absolvierte zunächst eine Ausbildung als Verlagskauffrau und studierte anschließend romanische Philologie mit Schwerpunkt Lateinamerika, Geschichte und Kommunikationswissenschaften. Zwischenzeitlich recherchierte und konzipierte sie in Projekten der Goethe-Institute München und Kiew Ausstellungen, Sprach- und Internetprojekte. 2006/2007 beteiligte sie sich in Rio de Janeiro an einem Hilfsprojekt für Straßenkinder. Sie arbeitet seit 2003 als Autorin, vorwiegend für die *Süddeutsche Zeitung*, 2013 mit der Kolumne »Literaturland Brasilien«.

Thomas Moschner
Dipl.-Ing.. (arch.), born in 1963 in Reutlingen, studied civil engineering at the University of Stuttgart. From 1991 to 1999 he worked for schlaich bergermann und partner. After a period (2000–03) working in the field of finite elements as a partner of Nolasoft, he returned to work for schlaich bergermann und partner in 2003, where he is largely responsible for the design of stadium roof structures all over the world.

Thomas Moschner
Dipl.-Ing. (arch.), geboren 1963 in Reutlingen, studierte Bauingenieurwesen an der Universität Stuttgart. Von 1991 bis 1999 arbeitete er im Ingenieurbüro schlaich bergermann und partner. Nach einem Exkurs (2000–03) in die Welt der finiten Elemente als Gesellschafter bei Nolasoft, kehrte er 2003 zu schlaich bergermann und partner zurück. Seitdem beschäftigt er sich hauptsächlich mit der Planung von Stadiondächern in aller Welt.

Hubert Nienhoff
Dipl.-Ing.. architect, born in Kirchhellen/Westphalia in 1959, studied architecture at the RWTH in Aachen. From 1985 to 1987 he worked in the office of Christoph Mäckler in Frankfurt am Main, before spending a period in the USA undertaking urban studies. From 1988 to 1991, he was an assistant under Prof. Volkwin Marg at the department of urban district planning and planning practice at the RWTH Aachen. In 1988, he joined the office gmp · von Gerkan, Marg und Partner and has been a partner since 1993. He is responsible for leading the design and construction of numerous stadia on four continents, as well as trade fair and airport projects.

Hubert Nienhoff
Dipl.-Ing. Architekt, geboren 1959 in Kirchhellen/Westfalen, studierte Architektur an der RWTH Aachen. 1985–87 arbeitete er im Büro für Architektur und Stadtbereichsplanung Christoph Mäckler in Frankfurt am Main. Es folgte ein Aufenthalt in den USA für städtebauliche Studien. 1988–1991 war er Assistent bei Prof. Volkwin Marg am Lehrstuhl für Stadtbereichsplanung und Werklehre an der RWTH Aachen. 1988 trat er in das Büro von Gerkan Marg und Partner ein und ist seit 1993 Partner. Unter seiner Leitung wurden zahlreiche Stadien in vier Kontinenten, aber auch Messe- und Flughafenprojekte geplant und realisiert.

Miriam Haddad Sayeg
Born in 1960 in São Paulo, Brazil, she studied architecture and urban design at the University of São Paulo. For ten years she worked as a design coordinator at Zanettini, one of the leading design offices in Brazil. In 2007, she joined schlaich bergermann und partner and helped co-found the Brazilian subsidiary, sbp do Brasil, in 2008. Since then she co-manages the company's operations in Brazil and Latin America, including stadia, Olympic venues, glass roofs, bridges, infrastructure, and institutional projects.

Miriam Haddad Sayeg
Geboren 1960 in São Paulo, Brasilien, studierte Architektur und Stadtplanung an der Universität von São Paulo. Arbeitete zehn Jahre lang als Design Coordinator bei Zanettini, einem der führenden Designbüros in Brasilien. 2007 trat sie schlaich bergermann und partner bei und unterstützte bei der Gründung der brasilianischen Niederlassung sbp do Brasil in 2008. Seitdem leitet sie gemeinsam mit Knut Stockhusen die Projekte in Brasilien und Lateinamerika. Dazu zählen Stadien, olympische Sportstätten, Glasdächer, Brücken, Infrastruktur und öffentliche Bauten.

Knut Stockhusen
Dipl.-Ing., born in 1974 in Stuttgart, studied civil engineering at the University of Stuttgart. In 2000 he became a partner of the Stuttgart office of schlaich bergermann und partner and since 2008 has been responsible as part of the extended management team for the development, organization, and implementation of international projects, and of sports facilities in particular. In 2008, he was responsible for the founding of the Brazilian subsidiary, sbp do Brasil in São Paulo, which he co-manages together with Miriam Sayeg.

Knut Stockhusen
Dipl.-Ing., geboren 1974 in Stuttgart, studierte Bauingenieurwesen an der Universität Stuttgart. 2000 trat er in das Stuttgarter Büro schlaich bergermann und partner ein und ist seit 2008 in der erweiterten Geschäftsleitung für Entwicklung, Organisation und Abwicklung internationaler Projekte, vorrangig Sportbauten, zuständig. 2008 verantwortete er die Gründung der brasilianischen Niederlassung sbp do brasil in São Paulo und leitet diese seither gemeinsam mit Miriam Sayeg.

Photo Credits **Bildnachweis**

Angular Fotos Aéreas / João Luiz dos Anjos 21 27
Marcus Bredt 9 10 11 13 14 15 16 17 19 23 30 (left/links) 31 33 35 38/39 41 42 43 44 45 46 47 48 49 51 56 57 58/59 60/61 62/63 64/65 66/67 68/69 70/71 72/73 74/75 77 78 79 80 81 82 83 84 85 87 89 92 94/95 97 98/99 100/101 102/103 104/105 106/107 109 110 111 112 113 114 115 116 117 118 119 120 121 123 130/131 132 133 134/135 136 137 138 139 140/141 142/143 144/145 146/147 148/149 150/151 152/153 154/155 157 158 159 160 161 162 163 164 165 166 167 169 174/175 178/179 180 181 182 183 184 185 186/187 188/189 192/193 194/195 196/197 198/199 200/201 203 204 205 206 207 208 209 210 211 213 214 215 216 221 222 223 224 225
Michael Elkan 24 (right/rechts)
Kristyan Geyr 229 (3)
gmp 90/91 93 126/127 128 129 172/173 177
gmp-Archiv 88 170 228 (1)
gmp / Burkhard Pick 125
Anette Koroll 228 (3)
Katrin Lütge 228 (2)
Thomas Milz 228 (4)
Jose Zamith de Oliveira Filho 124
privat 229 (2) 229 (4) 230 (2)
sbp 28 29 30 (right/rechts) 53 54 55 171 176 231 (2)
sbp / Knut Göppert 190/191
sbp / Christoph Paech 24 (left/links)
sbp / Knut Stockhusen 25 26 52
sbp / Michael Zimmermann 229 (1) 230 (3) 231 (3)
Timmo Schreiber Photography 231 (1)
Seggelke / Ute Karen 230 (1)

Every effort has been made to identify all rights holders before publication. We would ask any rights holders we did not manage to contact to get in touch with the editor.
Trotz intensiver Recherche ist es nicht gelungen, sämtliche Rechteinhaber ausfindig zu machen. Zur Klärung bitten wir, sich mit dem Herausgeber in Verbindung zu setzen.

Cover photos **Umschlagfotos** Marcus Bredt

Translation **Übersetzung** Julian Reisenberger, Weimar
Design and setting **Gestaltung und Satz** Phillip Hofmeister, Berlin
Lithography **Lithografie** Bild1Druck, Berlin
Printing and binding **Druck und Bindung** Grafisches Centrum Cuno, Calbe
Printed in **gedruckt im** Ultra HD Print®

Bibliographic information published by the Deutsche Nationalbibliothek
The Deutsche Nationalbibliothek lists this publication in the Deutsche Nationalbibliografie; detailed bibliographic data are available on the Internet at http://dnb.d-nb.de

Bibliografische Information der Deutschen Nationalbibliothek
Die Deutsche Nationalbibliothek verzeichnet diese Publikation in der Deutschen Nationalbibliografie; detaillierte bibliografische Daten sind im Internet über http://dnb.d-nb.de abrufbar.

jovis Verlag GmbH
Kurfürstenstraße 15/16
10785 Berlin
www.jovis.de

ISBN 978-3-86859-326-6